Perils: NAMED
and UNNAMED

Perils: NAMED
and UNNAMED

The Story of the Insurance

Company of North America

by WILLIAM H. A. CARR

McGRAW-HILL BOOK COMPANY
New York Toronto London Sydney

Contents

[vii]

Contents

1: 'Adventures and Perils'

DURING World War II an Army major in uniform and a civilian arrived in Philadelphia and went to the home office of the Insurance Company of North America, where they asked for Herbert P. Stellwagen, executive vice president of the company's casualty affiliate.

When they were ushered into his office, they introduced themselves, and the major said:

"We're from the Manhattan District."

"I see," said Stellwagen; "you're from New York."

"Oh, no," the major said. "We're from the Manhattan District."

"What's that?"

"Well, it's—it's a government war project."

The two men told Stellwagen they wanted to arrange an insurance program to cover thirty men.

"What do these men do?" the insurance executive inquired.

"I can't tell you," the major said.

"Are they subject to common hazard?"

"Maybe; maybe not."

"Do they work with their hands? Are they mechanics?"

"Yes and no. They may do some work with their hands, but not necessarily. You couldn't describe them as mechanics."

Frustrated, Stellwagen finally asked:

"Who are these men?"

"We can't tell you," the major said. "We'd like you to insure them, but instead of giving you names, we'll number the men—one, two, three, and so on, up to thirty. If number three, say, is hurt, we will notify you, and you will pay."

It was possibly the strangest proposal ever advanced to an insurance company. The company was to issue policies protecting men without knowing their names, their ages, their occupations, their location, the work they were doing, the hazards to which they might be exposed, the safety measures, if any, taken to guard them against injury, their skill in doing whatever work it was that occupied them—in short, all of the essential facts upon which an underwriter determines whether he should insure a risk and at what premium.

Pleading for time to consider the problem, Stellwagen wished the two men a pleasant journey back to Washington and then talked the matter over with the company's president, John A. Diemand, who agreed with him that patriotism required the company to issue the insurance if at all possible. With the approval of the board of directors, Stellwagen reviewed the rates for various occupations and ages. Then he "pulled a rate out of the air," hoping that it was realistic, and the policy was written.

After the first atomic bomb was dropped on Japan, Stellwagen discovered that the insurance, on which there was never a claim, had covered the top scientists, many of them Nobel Prize winners, who were developing that awesome weapon. Unwittingly, INA, as the company is usually referred to today, had played a part in the most epochal event of modern times.

When the subject of insurance for the scientists arose, several of them had suggested INA, recalling that the company insured university cyclotrons used in nuclear research before the war. The Army officers responded to the suggestion immediately, for they, too, were well acquainted with the company, which had often been called upon for insurance by many branches of the government, including the military services. For example, INA travel accident insurance protected civilians and military personnel throughout the world while they flew as passengers on airplanes operated by the Army Air Transport Command and the Naval Air Transport Service in support of the war.

Moreover, INA was famous for its philosophy that "any risk can be underwritten for a price."

It was this philosophy that gave INA the reputation of being "the American Lloyd's."

Certainly all manner of things have been insured by INA. Every time Telstar whirled around the earth in space, the satellite was a reminder of the reach of INA's underwriters. At a lower altitude, Edmund Hillary and Tenzing Norkey, in an expedition insured by INA, scaled Mount Everest. Still closer to the surface, two airliners collided over New York City in 1960, and INA wrote it down as a loss.

Under an INA policy covering United Nations officials, the company paid a claim for the death of Count Folke Bernadotte after the UN Mediator for Palestine was ambushed in Jerusalem in 1948. Two decades later the Middle East was still in ferment, and a *Time* magazine correspondent, Paul Schutzer, insured by INA, was shot dead during an Israeli-Arab battle.

Part of the loss in the sinking of the supposedly unsinkable liner *Andrea Doria* in 1956 was borne by INA, which lost money a half-century earlier when the also unsinkable *Titanic* went to the bottom. Having lost ships in innumerable wars, the company unexpectedly paid a war risk claim in 1954, one of those rare years of peace, when a bomb was dropped down the stack of the M/S *Springfjord* during a brief civil war in Guatemala.

In 1935 INA insured the Boy Scouts for $300,000 against the possibility of having to call off their first national jamboree; at the last moment, a polio outbreak forced cancellation of the event, and the company paid. Even in the 1960's, in the era of miracle drugs, a medical problem proved expensive to INA—the tragedy of the so-called "Thalidomide babies," born deformed; an INA products liability policy covered the manufacturer of the drug which was at the center of the controversy.

Like Lloyd's, INA will insure almost anything. Nevertheless, despite the range and diversity of its customers and coverages, the American company is altogether different from the British organization, with which it has competed amiably but earnestly since the eighteenth century.

After all, Lloyd's is not a company but an association of about 5,500 underwriting members in some 300 syndicates, while INA is a corporation owned by stockholders—a remarkably successful company. As the Alfred M. Best Company, authoritative observer of the American insurance industry, said in 1967, "The company, the oldest capital stock insurance carrier in the United States, enjoys an enviable reputation."

Its stature may be gauged by the fact that 350 of the 500 biggest corporations in the United States have insurance with INA.

Its assets of close to $2,000,000,000 made it the richest multiple-line insurance company in the nation. Its wholly owned subsidiary, the Life Insurance Company of North

America, had nearly $2,250,000,000 of insurance in force. The market value of INA's investments was more than twice the amount that INA paid for the securities.

Of the approximately 3,000 insurance companies in the United States, INA ranked first among independent marine insurers, first among independent aviation underwriters, third in policyholders' surplus, fourth as a writer of property and casualty coverages, and seventh in annual premium volume. Its reinsurance department, which competed almost entirely against companies engaged only in reinsurance, was in third place among American reinsurance companies and fifth place worldwide.

One of the few worldwide American insurance companies, INA counted cash receipts of $2,800,000 on a typical day in March 1967, from forty-seven service offices in the United States, five in Canada, and agencies in more than thirty other countries on six continents. The company had balances in some sixty-five foreign currencies around the world.

Claims payments of more than $1,000,000 were not at all uncommon, but the biggest check ever signed by the secretary-treasurer, Geoffrey Stengel, in the amount of $37,000,000, was not a claim payment but part of a transaction in government bonds.

A number of the 22,440 stockholders were descendants of the founders of the company. C. Jared Ingersoll, who was a director from 1949 to 1966, was directly descended from Jared Ingersoll, the company's first legal counsel. Edward Hopkinson, Jr., a director from 1936 until his death on April 6, 1966, was the latest of a series of members of his family who had been directors or officers of the company since its first decade.

With such roots in the community, it is apparent why so many Philadelphians simply say "the insurance company" when they are talking about INA, which has, after all, been around since 1792. Even relative newcomers soon acquire the attitude. One day late in the 1940's an Italian immigrant walked into INA's home office and announced that he wanted to buy some life insurance, one form of protection which INA did not offer between 1817 and 1957.

"I'm sorry," the man was told. "You'd better see an agent who can arrange a policy for you. But not with us. We don't sell life insurance."

"No!" the man exclaimed heatedly. "Here! I get it here! My friends, they tell me, 'Go to the insurance company.' So I come here. *This* the insurance company!"

It took some effort to persuade him that there were other insurance companies in Philadelphia.

As a matter of fact, although Hartford and New York City outrank Philadelphia on the basis of city comparisons, a comparison of the states gives a different picture, according to the Insurance Information Institute. With 384, Pennsylvania ranks first among the states in the number of property-liability company home offices. It is followed, in order, by Illinois, Wisconsin, and New York State, with Connecticut far down the list.

There is a prestige to insurance in Philadelphia that is usually not found elsewhere.

"Insurance is older in Philadelphia," wrote social historian Nathaniel Burt in *The Perennial Philadelphians*; "[it] has a longer and more elegant tradition, is surrounded by more of an aura, and even has a halo of beneficence and altruism about it."

As the "largest and oldest and most Philadelphian" of these companies, INA thinks well of itself, but also sets higher standards for itself than it might expect of others. Many old Philadelphians have almost "a feeling of reverence," as Stengel put it; "a feeling that the company does do things a little bit differently—in a way a lot of commercial corporations perhaps wouldn't do."

Old the company certainly is. It had already been in business four years when we became involved in an undeclared naval war with France, out of which grew claims which INA is still pressing against the United States government.

Barbary pirates were cause for anxiety in the early days, a fear reflected in the words still used today in the standard marine insurance policy covering hulls:

"Touching the adventures and perils which we, the said underwriters, are contented to bear and take upon us, they are of the seas, men-of-war, fire, lightning, earthquake, enemies, pirates, rovers, assailing thieves, jettisons, letters of mart and counter-mart, surprisals, takings at sea, arrests, restraints and detainments of all kings, princes, and peoples of what nation, condition, or quality soever. Barratry of the master and mariners and of all other perils, losses, and misfortunes that have or shall come to the hurt, detriment, or damage of said vessel. . . ."

When the War of 1812 broke out, the company was already twenty years old and beginning its expansion across the country, having founded the American Agency System by appointing an independent agent in Lexington, Kentucky, in 1807. One hundred and sixty years later the company had 15,000 agents, many of whom had been associated with the company for several generations. The six oldest agencies in 1967 were Cunningham and Kerr in Massachusetts, which became an INA agency in 1849; Thompson, Puff, and Boyden in Massachusetts, 1852; Root and Boyd in Connecticut, 1853; W. H. Squire in Connecticut, 1857; Chancellor in West Virginia, 1862; and Ruhl and Ruhl in Nebraska, 1862.

During the Civil War, the company consolidated its leading position in the North and West, and by 1871 it was in a position to handle its losses in the Chicago fire when other companies failed.

Then came the time of trial, the San Francisco earthquake and fire, when INA was one of the relatively few companies to pay their obligations to policyholders, though the losses reduced INA's assets by twenty-five per cent.

After that, even the German submarine attacks and the destruction of American munitions plants by enemy sabotage in World War I couldn't faze the company. Nor the frenzied finance of the Roaring Twenties nor the bleak Depression days of the Thirties.

Through the long pageant of the company's, and the country's, history moved successive generations of INA men (and, in later years, women), some courageous, others fearful; many magnanimous, a few petty; most gallant, a handful boorish; but almost all of them touched by the pride of the living thing that was the company and all of them convinced of the social importance of their work, remembering the words of the United States Supreme Court in 1944:

"The modern insurance business holds a commanding position in the trade and commerce of our nation. . . . Perhaps no modern commercial enterprise directly affects so many persons in all walks of life as does the insurance business. Insurance touches the home, the family, and the occupation or business of almost every person in the United States."

No hyperbole, that. From the time an American or Canadian or, to a lesser extent, a citizen of almost any other non-Communist country, rises in the morning until he retires at night, INA insurance is an unseen presence.

The steel in the razor he uses to shave in the morning is made by a company insured by INA. So is the clothing he dons, and the breakfast food he eats. His house is protected by the Homeowners Policy pioneered by INA. If it is Sunday,

[8]

the church he attends may well be covered by INA (which, besides being the largest underwriter of Roman Catholic churches, also insures a great many Protestant churches).

Chances are his car is insured by INA—and its manufacturer is probably an INA customer. The town through whose streets he drives buys its municipal government coverage from INA, and so does the school his children attend. On weekdays he is covered on the job by workmen's compensation insurance purchased from INA and eats his lunch in an INA-insured restaurant.

On the weekend he takes the kids to a zoo, which has an INA policy. He isn't worried by the crowds, for his children have their polio shots, produced in a plant under INA protection. After the zoo, there's time for a visit to a museum, for a look at an art collection and a Gutenberg Bible, all INA-insured.

After dinner the children are left with a baby-sitter (no, she isn't insured by INA—yet) while mother and father go to a concert. INA insurance protects the Stradivarius played by the violin soloist.

There's still time after the concert to switch on the television at home and watch the "Miss America Pageant," which also bears an unseen INA label. Then, with the kids asleep, there's time for Mom and Dad to talk—about vacation time (a trip to INA-insured Disneyland, or to Florida, where St. Augustine's Fountain of Youth is similarly protected). About college for the youngsters when they get older—a college insured by INA.

All this over coffee grown on plantations under INA's protection, with milk from a carton which displays a picture of Elsie the Cow, who likes INA almost as much as her spouse, Elmer.

And so to bed, after the lady of the house removes her

makeup made by an INA customer, with facial tissues manufactured by still another.

While she is busying herself so, her husband steals a
look at the INA-insured newspaper to see how his favorite
professional football team made out, another INA customer.

When finally day is done, he turns off a light made in a
plant covered by INA, with the power supplied by a utility
company that buys protection from the same underwriter.

This is the way it has been in the United States for 175
years and will be for many more. It's true that George Washington, who was President when Philadelphia was the nation's
capital, somehow got away from INA, but after his death the
company insured at least a barn at his Mount Vernon estate.
And Thomas Jefferson's home, Monticello, was covered by
INA.

Even a large part of the contents of the White House,
fittingly enough, were still insured by the company in 1967,
although it is strange to think that the company is older than
the residence of our Presidents. Another Washington building
covered by the company was the Octagon House, which was
occupied by James and Dolly Madison while the Executive
Mansion was being repaired after being burned by the British.

It seems only proper that so many historic places and
things should be insured by the company, which, besides being
the oldest stock insurance company in America, has an historical collection of its own valued at between $4,000,000 and
$6,000,000. Included in the collection are fire marks (plaques
put over the door of insured houses to identify the underwriter); very old side panels from fire engines, elaborately
decorated with portraits or scenes in the style of the early
Republic; many pieces of fire-fighting apparatus; marine paintings; ship models; records; documents; and other memorabilia
of the company from its earliest days down to World War II—

among them all of the directors' minute books from 1792, the first cash book, the first dividend book, stock certificates going back to 1794, and the first book into which the company's letters were copied.

Portraits of the company's presidents and directors are also part of the impressive collection, but a half dozen of the paintings have been a source of private embarrassment to the company ever since a vice president, going through the Louvre on a visit to Paris, spotted an art work that looked identical to the painting of one of the first INA directors, Michael Prager. On his return to America he reported the puzzling similarity, and a quiet investigation was launched. An independent art expert determined that the supposed portrait of Prager was actually a clever copy of the painting in the Louvre, which depicts an eighteenth-century marquis.

Further study indicated that the company's likenesses of John Ross and General Walter Stewart were almost certainly fakes, and those of John Barclay, Matthew McConnell, and Charles Pettit were at best questionable. All had been members of the first board of directors. The other portraits in the collection were all authentic.

Although the company's top management had nothing to do with acquisition of the fakes years ago, some senior officers still look sheepish when questions are raised about those six paintings.

The historical collection, fascinating though it is to students of Americana, can only hint at the spirit of the company, which has been the most important factor in INA's success. This mystique, according to the company's most vehement critic, enabled INA consistently to attract an unusually high caliber of employee.

There is nothing accidental about the pride that the company inspires and fosters in its people. Each generation of top management has articulated its business philosophy quite explicitly, and the emphasis has always been on the responsibilities of the company rather than on its privileges.

Thus, a statement of INA's "guiding principles" drawn up by Bradford Smith, Jr., chairman of the board and chief executive officer, and circulated in July 1966, said in part:

"We accept the obligation . . . imposed [on us by the free enterprise system] to operate our business in the public interest. . . . We will resolve all reasonable doubt as to policy conditions in favor of the policyholder. . . ."

The company was described as "an organization of people who are deeply conscious of their heritage, their public responsibility, and their aggressive commitment to progress and to the future. It is our job to adjust our service to changing public requirements and demands," for when these are "ignored or unsatisfied, we invite undesirable government intervention."

One part of the statement which might sound like a platitude to persons outside the insurance industry had much more meaning to the men in other companies. That sentence read: "We will be hard and aggressive competitors, all the while maintaining the highest ethical principles in dealing with others."

For nearly a century, from the mid-1900's to the end of World War II, INA could not be called a "hard and aggressive" competitor. On the contrary, it played a leading role in organizing associations of most of the insurance companies in this country in order to put an end to price competition. It was among a virtual handful of companies at the top of a power structure that held the industry in a vise. Because of a unique and baffling court decision, as we shall see in later chapters, this monopolistic industry framework was untouched long after federal antitrust laws had broken up most other domestic cartels.

This state of affairs ended—on paper—in 1944 when the United States Supreme Court overthrew the nineteenth-century decision and exposed the insurance industry to the force of federal law. When most of the other major companies tried to circumvent the new court ruling and to restore the old order, INA remembered its obligation "to operate in the public interest" and recognized that it could not adjust its "service to changing public requirements and demands" under the former state of affairs.

And so, virtually single-handed, INA plunged into what became a bitter war for independence. After about fifteen long years and hundreds of administrative hearings and court trials, which cost the company between two and four million dollars, the conflict was largely won by the company by 1960, although mopping-up operations were still being conducted as late as 1967.

It is difficult to find another example of an industry-wide combination in restraint of trade, technically a monopoly, that was successfully defied and shattered by one company, almost entirely alone.

In the course of the long struggle, INA introduced a host of new ideas in insurance, usually against the vigorous opposition of the most powerful elements in the industry. And by doing so it grew at a faster rate than the rest of the industry or the overall national economy.

With good reason, *Barron's*, the financial weekly, described the company as a "spry old underwriter" that "keeps ahead of the times."

"Venerable as it is, however," the periodical pointed out, "the company is one of the more innovation-minded concerns in the generally staid insurance business. For example, it pioneered the so-called Homeowners policies, providing all-in-one protection against theft, liability, and fire. Similarly, it was among the first to offer blanket liability coverage in the commercial and industrial field."

The other part of Bradford Smith's statement of principles, putting the policyholders' interests first, also proved to be more than a pious intention. So faithfully was it implemented that in one state where another large company had more than 1,000 complaints filed against it with the state insurance commissioner, INA had only eight, a record that earned the commissioner's praise. In addition, with every draft mailed out in settlement of a claim went a note from Smith asking the claimant if he was satisfied with the settlement and with the manner in which the claim was handled. Despite this invitation to protest, the company received only 332 complaints out of roughly 1,100,000 claims settled in 1966. Incidentally, the company paid out an average of $1,000,000 every day of the year, including weekends and holidays.

Of those who did complain, sixty-four felt that there had been unnecessary delay in settling their claims. The same number objected to the denial of their claims. Another fifty-three questioned the size of the proferred settlement or the amount allowed for repairs. Twenty were angered by failure to reply to their letters. Only four reported that they had been discourteously treated. The remaining 109, according to assistant vice president C. Sumner Katz, "included crank letters, telephone calls, inquiries from [state] Insurance Departments, etc., not subject to specific classification."

Such a small number of complaints speaks well not only for the company but also for the vast majority of people. As a matter of fact, the men most exposed to fraudulent claims, the claims men themselves, by reputation an untrusting, skeptical lot, seem to have the greatest faith in the honesty of most people. They are firmly convinced that dishonest claimants on any scale, from the motorist who insists that an old dent in a fender happened just the other day to the swindler who feigns a fictitious whiplash injury to his back, are a minuscule element in the population.

This belief is supported to some extent by repayments that are received by the company, usually from anonymous senders, fairly often. Such receipts are deposited by the company in a long-standing "Conscience Fund."

One day an envelope with no return address was opened in the home office mail room and more than $1,200 in currency tumbled out. There was no note and the sender was never discovered.

Early in 1967 the "Conscience Fund" file contained the records of eight payments, ranging from $900, $600, and $200 down to two $4 checks. Two of the checks had been sent in by priests at the request of persons they would not identify.

Occasionally there are notes enclosed with the checks. "Restitution for false insurance claim," read one scrawl. Another said, "Wasn't sure if I was entitled to a settlement that was made."

"An overpayment on a claim," said a letter received in INA's Oklahoma City office. "Just a little conscience money which I felt constrained to return. It rightfully belongs to your company."

One man, traced by the company to a Chicago address, said he had sent in $4 because he had been overpaid that much on an automobile claim in 1949. He gave no reason why he had waited until 1963, fourteen years later, to give the money back.

From Santa Rosa, California, came a rather large check and a letter that was longer than most. The unknown writer said:

"The reason for my action in this regard involves a claim I turned in to your company some time ago that I was not entitled to receive payment for, as my alleged loss actually did not exist.

"Sorry for whatever inconvenience this has caused your company but trust that the enclosed sum will at least make some restitution for your time and trouble."

Finally, a note from Dodge City, Kansas, said simply, "Thank you for your speedy adjustment and payment. There was an overpayment of $4 which I am now returning. Thank you."

It was a persuasive argument for fast and fair claims settlement.

2: Don't Give Up Those Ships!

 IT IS AN article of faith among INA men that the President and the Congress of the United States have been making liars of George Washington and Thomas Jefferson ever since those worthies occupied the posts of President and Secretary of State. And for more than a century and a half INA has been trying, in the words of a company publication, to make "honest men" of the two Founding Fathers. INA says that it is "deeply interested in restoring to the Father of His Country his fabled reputation for truth and veracity." The cost would be $5,000,000.

INA's crusade to polish the image of Washington and Jefferson came to the attention of Congress when it convened in January 1956. Veteran members of Congress were familiar with the matter, but the young members of both houses were somewhat puzzled to find Senate Bill 2880 among the hundreds of measures with which they were inundated.

Most of the other proposals, dealing with all the complexities of modern America, were quite clear to the legislators, but S.B. 2880 was altogether different. It required an understanding, not of current affairs, but of events nearly forgotten in the mists of time, going back to the administration of the first President and to a war of which most Americans know little or nothing.

Tongue in cheek, *The New York Times* called the bill "the most backward-looking legislation before Congress" while conceding that the measure's sponsors "maintain that the philosophy behind it is as progressive as it can be."

The philosophy was twofold but simple: that the Constitution of the United States must be upheld, and that the government ought to pay its just debts—two unarguable propositions, one might think, but history said otherwise.

For more than a century and a half the problem underlying S.B. 2880 had been argued over in Congress, the White House, and the courts without being resolved. If it hadn't been for the doggedness of INA, the matter would have been long forgotten. But the issue involved money that was owed to INA, and an insurance company can be as tireless in pursuing money to which it is entitled as it is in exposing fraudulent claims.

The story goes back to the closing years of the eighteenth century, when revolutionary France was at war for twenty-three years, off and on, with England and most of the rest of Europe, a conflict that finally ended on the low plateau of Brabant near a town called Waterloo.

There might appear to be little connection between an infant insurance company in America and the titanic struggle which engaged millions of men in the Old World in campaigns from Spain to Russia and Egypt, but there is very little that happens in this world that does not ultimately affect underwriters everywhere. The European conflict soon made its mark on the ledgers of the company that occupied a small brick building at 223 South Front Street (then numbered 119) in Philadelphia.

INA's involvement in the European war grew out of what was then the most important part of the company's business, its marine line. For ships insured by INA soon became victims of the struggle for power. All of the belligerents, and that included virtually every country in Europe, authorized privateers to prey upon enemy shipping and upon neutral vessels carrying "contraband" to hostile ports. In practice, anything that a neutral ship happened to be transporting was usually designated contraband, and it didn't matter what its destination was. The principal offenders were England, France, and Spain, but Denmark and even the Kingdom of the Two Sicilies seized what they could.

To the young American Republic, foreign trade was of vital importance, so the government deemed it expedient to reassure merchants, shippers, and underwriters. Jefferson informed them, "I have it in charge from the President to assure the merchants of the United States concerned in foreign commerce or navigation that due attention will be paid to any injuries they may suffer on the high seas or in foreign countries contrary to the law of nations and existing treaties, and that on their forwarding hither [to the government] well-authenticated evidence of the same, proper proceedings will be adopted for their relief." This was the first promise that led eventually to S.B. 2880.

A few months later Washington himself told Congress: "The vexations and spoliations understood to have been committed on our vessels and commerce by the cruisers and officers of some of the belligerent powers appeared to require attention. The proofs of these, however, not having been brought forward, the description of citizens supposed to have suffered were notified that on furnishing them to the Executive, due measures would be taken to obtain redress of the past and more effectual provisions against the future."

This was the second promise that was to lead to endless wrangling throughout the nineteenth and twentieth centuries.

Throughout the country people tended to favor either

the British or the French in the European conflict, and many Americans thought that before long we would be at war with one or the other. Under Washington's leadership the government began to fortify American ports and to build a navy. Meanwhile, diplomatic missions had been sent to London and Paris to try to bring about an end to the depredations against American shipping, and their efforts brought about a degree of improvement in the matter.

In March 1795, Washington called Congress into secret session to consider a treaty negotiated with the British by John Jay. Only the immense prestige of the President could win ratification of the pact, the provisions of which, when made public, so enraged the public that there were demonstrations against it in every city. Savage caricatures lampooning Washington were printed. Alexander Hamilton, known as the real master of the dominant Federalist Party, was stoned when he appeared in the streets. Jay was burned in effigy.

The judgment of history has been that the demonstrators were right. Jay's Treaty was close to a disaster. For a handful of British concessions Jay yielded a bucketful of American rights and demands. For example, Jay agreed not to export cotton in American ships, because he didn't know that cotton was an American product. The treaty said nothing about the vexing British practice of impressing American seamen into the British naval service, but the agreement did uphold the British in their violation of neutral shipping.

One of the few advantages of the treaty from an American point of view was that it did provide for indemnification of Americans whose ships and cargoes were unjustly seized by the British.

One unforeseen result of Jay's Treaty was the suddenly sharpened French hostility. Paris thought the pact showed that the United States had chosen to side with London in the

European war and reacted accordingly. The American envoy was compelled to leave France. The French government issued a series of decrees which amounted to a proclamation of warfare against American commerce.

From that point on, the French became the scourge of the seas, capturing American ships with a zeal that was reflected in the losses marked down in the books of INA and other underwriters. In one year, from June 1796, to June 1797, the French alone took 316 American ships as prizes.

There was "panic among American shippers," historian Alexander DeConde records: "Marine insurance jumped ten per cent overnight. Underwriters refused to insure vessels bound for French ports, requiring 'war premiums' for those bound for the British West Indies where French cruisers, or privateers, were taking a heavy toll from American shipping."

One victim was the schooner *Apollo*, for which INA had written a policy of $4,000 on the hull and $10,000 on the cargo before she sailed from New York, bound for Jérémie, a port in Haiti. On the high seas she had the misfortune to encounter the French privateer *L'Intéressante*, which took her into Santiago de Cuba as a prize.

The cargo was listed as "forty pieces of Madrass handkerchiefs, sixteen pots of pomatum, eighty-eight pounds of perfumed hair powder, sixty-seven barrels of herrings, twenty-seven barrels of menhaden, twenty-two barrels of prime beef, twenty-five barrels of prime pork, five heads [hogsheads?] of codfish, one hundred boxes of mould candles, forty large boxes of turpentine soap, twelve tierces of rice [a tierce was a forty-two gallon cask], fifty pairs of ladies' shoes, fifty hampers of best sweet oil, one hundred and one hams, twenty-four thousand twenty-two-inch shingles, fourteen casks of nails, four hundred empty coffee bags, twenty casks of old claret, fifteen casks of white wine, and forty-eight boxes of bottled claret."

Another loss was the schooner *Poll*. Benjamin Higgins

was skipper when she slipped down the Delaware from Phila-delphia, her destination La Guaira, the seaport for Caracas, Venezuela. INA had insured the hull for $1,625 and the cargo for $3,250; it is likely that other underwriters covered the balance of the risk. The *Poll* touched at St. Thomas but didn't succeed in reaching La Guaira. No sooner had she cleared the harbor of St. Thomas than she was chased "by a schooner under English colors" which was unable to catch her. Some time later, while almost at a standstill in a near-calm, the *Poll* was approached by a Danish ship, but it turned away for some reason.

Finally just a few hours out of La Guaira, the *Poll* was stopped by the French privateer *Bonaparte*, which put a prize crew aboard and took her into Curaçao, where her cargo was confiscated on the grounds that "she was laden in part with English manufacture."

Philadelphia's shippers were especially annoyed by one French privateer, the *Flying Fish*, which had enjoyed the hospitality of the port because it was understood that she preyed only on British shipping. After taking on water and provisions, she dropped down the river and out to sea. About a week later Captain George Dominick, master of the *Mount Vernon*, which INA had insured for $15,000, sailed for London. Within two days Dominick was back in Philadelphia, to report that his ship had been seized by the *Flying Fish* within sight of the Delaware capes. He had been put ashore by the French, but not before he had learned that they had a list of ships for which they were waiting, a list drawn up when the French were the port's guests.

The angered Philadelphians were somewhat embar-rassed later, however, when it became known that although the *Mount Vernon* had been insured and cleared as an American vessel, under charter to a merchant of the city, it was in fact a British ship, and had lately been purchased by an Englishman living in Philadelphia.

Don't Give Up Those Ships!

In a confidential memorandum to his own government, a French diplomat conceded that the privateers had been guilty of "acts of violence, brigandage, piracy" against American shipping. The French spoliations had also become a threat to the life of INA. Although premium receipts had exceeded losses by $123,162 in 1794, by $163,936 in 1795, and by $205,319 in 1796, the proportions changed radically in a short time. In 1799 losses outran premium receipts by $125,549, the following year by $42,257, and in 1801 by $224,000.

By the spring of 1797 John Adams had succeeded Washington as President, so the problem of the French spoliations was his. He wanted to avoid outright war if possible. Despite the public outcry in the United States against the French, Adams was able to write in a letter that he knew of nobody who was willing to go "to war with France lightly," adding glumly, "But she has already gone to war with us lightly. She is at war with us, but we are not at war with her."

He urged Congress to take additional steps to strengthen the Navy and protect our interests. One of the many measures soon enacted permitted American naval commanders to capture French privateers and warships.

The first American prize was taken off Egg Harbor, New Jersey, in July 1798, by the sloop of war *Delaware*, commanded by Stephen Decatur, Sr. After the *Delaware* captured a French privateer schooner, the *Croyable*, its skipper protested that his country and the United States were not at war. "The French have been making war on us for a long time," Decatur replied. "Now we find it necessary to take care of ourselves."

The growing but still small United States Navy was first concentrated in coastal waters and later in the West Indies, where the first battle between regular warships of the French and American navies took place. The engagement occurred February 9, 1799, off the island of Nevis, when the American frigate *Constellation* encountered the French frigate *Insurgente*. After a fierce fight in which twenty-nine French sailors and one American were killed, the French ship struck its colors.

In two and a half years of undeclared naval warfare with the French, the United States Navy took eighty-five French warships and privateers and lost only one American man-o'-war.

The changing fortunes of the sea war could be seen in the rates for insurance on shipping. In the summer of 1796, before the French reacted against Jay's Treaty, the rate for a vessel bearing cargo from the United States to a Caribbean port was about six per cent, but in six months the rate had doubled.

During 1797 premiums amounted to as much as twenty-five per cent of the value of ship and cargo, but in 1798 rates of thirty-three per cent were generally being quoted, and on one voyage to Jamaica an American shipowner paid a premium of forty per cent. In the first half of 1799, after our navy went into action in tropical waters, insurance rates were cut by at least half, and they were down to ten per cent by January 1800.

Nevertheless, when the French, now led by Napoleon, opened negotiations with the United States in an effort to end the undeclared naval war, they were impelled less by worry about the American successes than by a desire to prevent the Americans from making common cause with Bonaparte's major foe, Britain.

When the peace agreement, the Convention of Môrte-fontaine, finally was ratified by the Senate at the end of 1801, it contained provisions protecting American shipping from further interference, but the American negotiators had agreed to drop the claims of our merchants, shippers, and underwriters who had lost ships and cargoes to the French raiders.

The French proposal, accepted by our envoys, was, in

the words of one scholar, that "the United States would assume the responsibility of paying its own citizens for damages claimed."

At the time it was estimated that the claims ran to about $20,000,000. INA's stake alone amounted to $1,952,000, a sum far bigger than a struggling new company could afford. (Two years later a stockholders' committee found that half of INA's capital, in addition to all the premium income, was gone.)

Within two weeks of the treaty's ratification, the City Tavern, a favorite spot with shippers and underwriters not far from INA's office, was the scene of a meeting of businessmen who had incurred losses because of the French spoliations. A committee of seven was chosen to represent the group before Congress. Of the seven, four were directors of INA, including the chairman, Joseph Ball.

Nobody expected any difficulty in collecting the claims money. Although there was no question of the right of the government to bargain away the claims for the sake of the general welfare of the country, the Constitution protected those whose property had been sacrificed by the government. The Fifth Amendment, part of the Bill of Rights, said in part:

". . . Nor shall any person . . . be deprived of . . . property without due process of law; nor shall private property be taken for public use, without just compensation."

The committee presented its petiton to Congress, and a House committee promptly approved the claims as well-founded and recommended that they be paid from the Treasury.

It appeared that the matter was just about settled. In fact the controversy was just beginning.

That first bill was not passed by Congress, apparently because the claims could have caused monetary chaos. At that time the entire tax income of the government was little more

[25]

than $1,000,000 a year, about five per cent of the total esti-mated claims. (As it turned out, the claims actually amounted to some $5,000,000, still a vast sum for the fledgling nation.)

In the next Congress also a bill was reported out of committee, but failed of passage. And again in the next Con-gress. And the next. And the next. And so it went, on and on, in almost every Congress.

As Congress procrastinated, insurance companies which had suffered heavy losses in the French spoliations because of their trust in the promises of Washington and Jefferson began to collapse, until finally, of twelve insurance companies which had written marine policies during that period, only two sur-vived. One of the two was INA.

In 1826 President John Quincy Adams laid the full facts of the claims before Congress. A committee reported favorably on a bill, but neither the Senate nor the House passed it. Then the pattern kept repeating itself: introduction of bill, approval of bill by committee, but no action by either chamber.

By now the British had paid off the claims resulting from their ship seizures, a total of some $11,000,000. Spain paid $4,000,000. Even Denmark and the Kingdom of the Two Sicilies paid about $2,500,000 in all. In 1831 even France paid $5,000,000 for its depredations *after* 1800. The United States had forced other governments to pay, but it was still unwilling to pay the claims it had assumed in the Convention of Môrte-fontaine.

In 1832 the Rhode Island legislature asked Congress to pay the French spoliations claims. In 1835 the Maryland legislature did the same, but the bill was killed in the House of Representatives at Washington, despite its support by Senator Daniel Webster of Massachusetts, who had handled INA's claims against Spain.

Three years later organizations of merchants and shippers held simultaneous meetings in the major ports of

New York, Philadelphia, and Baltimore. The Baltimore rally sent a memorial to Congress that summed up the feelings of businessmen generally: if "private property is taken for public use," then "a just compensation must follow, if the Constitution and its provisions have not lost their weight."

Later that year the legislature of Connecticut urged passage of a compensation law. Two years later Maine did likewise, and in 1841 Massachusetts, Delaware, and Alabama followed suit. The only result was that a bill for payment reached third reading in the Senate three years later, only to die when Congress adjourned.

By that time most of the original individual claimants were no longer alive, and two generations of lawyers had occupied themselves with the case. More than a century later it would remind INA's general counsel, tall, witty Robert B. Ely, III, of a fictional lawsuit in Charles Dickens' *Bleak House*, of which the novelist wrote:

"*Jarndyce and Jarndyce* drones on. . . . Innumerable children have been born into the cause; innumerable young people have married into it; innumerable old people have died out of it. The little plaintiff or defendant, who was promised a new rocking horse when *Jarndyce and Jarndyce* should be settled, has grown up, possessed himself of a real horse, and trotted away into the other world. Fair wards of court have faded into mothers and grandmothers; a long procession of [court] chancellors has come in and gone out. . . . There are not three Jarndyces left upon the earth, perhaps, since old Tom Jarndyce in despair blew his brains out at a coffee house in Chancery Lane; but *Jarndyce and Jarndyce* still drags its weary length before the court, perennially hopeless."

And so it was with the French Spoliations (inevitably capitalized now, as befits an historic cause).

Finally, in 1846 Congress passed a bill to pay the claims, not in money, but in scrip for public lands beyond the Mississippi—to little avail, for President James K. Polk vetoed the measure. His veto message was a curious mixture of justifications: "The present is a period particularly unfavorable for the satisfaction of claims of so large an amount and, to say the least of them, of so doubtful a character." (Was he saying that debts shouldn't be paid if they were too big? And what made the claims of doubtful character, when a legion of Congressional committees and President John Quincy Adams had determined their validity?)

"If these claims be well founded," Polk went on, "it would be unjust to the claimants to repudiate any portion of them [but] this bill proposes to pay these claims not in the currency known to the Constitution and not to their full amount." (Was it better not to pay the claims at all?)

An attempt was made to override the Presidential veto. It failed of the required two-thirds majority that was needed. The shift of a single vote would have made the difference.

The case, like *Jarndyce and Jarndyce*, droned on.

In 1847 the General Assembly of Ohio protested that "in the continued delay of the United States, for the last forty-six years, to indemnify [French Spoliation claimants], that provision of the Constitution which declares that private property shall not be taken for public use without just compensation has been disregarded." Louisiana instructed its Congressional delegation to press for settlement of the claims.

Two years later the New York State Senate sent a message to the United States Senate expressing the opinion that it was "the bounden duty of the general government, without further delay, to make provision for the payment."

A few more years, and Congress finally did pass a bill to compensate the claimants, only to have it vetoed again, this time (in 1855) by President Franklin Pierce, a one-term Chief Executive. The substance of his veto message was that since the claims had been unpaid for so long, they must be unfounded. And somehow he managed to mix them up in his mind with the claims for French spoliations committed *after* 1800, and those claims, of course, had been paid.

The vote to override the veto was 113 to 81, less than the required two-thirds majority.

In the next Congress the Senate passed a French Spoliations bill, but the House did nothing. And again the years rolled on, with repeated unsuccessful attempts to get Congressional action. Nine more committees investigated the claims and recommended that they be paid, but nothing was done.

By 1885 INA's eighth president, Charles Platt, was in office. Several generations of company lawyers had been struggling with the French Spoliations claims. The government had grown much bigger and more complex. The Court of Claims had recently been established, and that indicated a new way to handle the case.

Congress passed, and President Chester A. Arthur signed, an act which provided that the Court of Claims was to "receive all proper evidence, historic and documentary," regarding the claims, to decide whether the claims were valid "according to the rules of law, municipal and international," and to "report all such conclusions of fact and law as in their judgment may affect the liability of the United States." In other words, the law did not provide for the payment of the claims, only for their investigation. Nevertheless, the Attorney General was instructed in the act to "resist all claims, by all proper legal defenses."

A two-year limit had been set for filing French Spoliations claims in the court, and when the period was up 20,000 had been recorded. INA and the other claimants were quite optimistic, because the Court of Claims, a year earlier, had ruled unanimously:

"It seems to us that this 'bargain' [the *quid pro quo* of the Convention of Môrtefontaine], by which the present peace and quiet of the United States, as well as their future prosperity and greatness, were largely secured, and which was brought about by the sacrifice of the interests of individual citizens, falls within the intent and meaning of the Constitution, which prohibits the taking of private property for public use without just compensation."

At long last, in 1891, Congress appropriated $1,304,095 (and thirty-seven cents, for an additional touch of the absurd) to pay some, but not all, of the French Spoliations claims, but little more than 100 ships had been disposed of by the Court of Claims, which still had a big backlog of cases.

Over the next fourteen years, three more appropriations bills were passed, so that by 1905 a total of $3,900,000 had been allocated to the claims covering 458 ships. But insurance companies were excluded from all but the first payout, in which the receivers for one defunct company got $12,860.

Since 1905 there have been no more payments, although the Court of Claims, in its final report, written in 1915, found that the government still owed $3,250,000 to French Spoliations claimants. President William Howard Taft asked Congress in 1910 to wipe the debt off the books, warning that the delay "injures the reputation of the government as an honest debtor," but Congress did nothing. During World War I the matter was forgotten, except, probably, by INA's lawyers, who never forget anything.

At a hearing of the House Committee on Claims in 1910, Bayard Henry of INA told the Congressmen:

"My family has been presenting these claims from 1800 down to the present time. One of my ancestors was the first president of the Insurance Company of North America, and from that time on, either as attorneys or as representatives of that company, we have knocked at the door of Congress for settlement. It has been over 110 years; I am of the fifth generation in pushing these claims, and I don't know whether I will be able to go on much further."

But there were other INA lawyers to take his place. In every generation of the company there was always at least one lawyer who became fascinated and indignant, poring over the musty old records of the claims. Edward M. Biddle carried the lance, and then Ely, and Barrett G. Tawresey, all very persistent men.

With every generation of lawyers, there has been a new eruption of the French Spoliations case.

In 1924 even President Coolidge, "Silent Cal," opened up (at the urging of an INA lawyer?) long enough to remind Congress of the French Spoliations: "The United States ought to pay its debts. I recommend action by the Congress which will permit of the payment of these remaining claims."

Nothing happened.

A decade passed, and then every year for about ten years Senator David I. Walsh of Massachusetts kept introducing bills to pay the claims. A vain attempt was made in the House of Representatives in 1949, and another in 1953.

Trying a new tack, INA's lawyers were back in the Court of Claims in 1954. The judges ruled that they didn't "have jurisdiction to pass upon the merits of the claim at this time." The Supreme Court declined to review the decision.

Subsequently identical bills were introduced in the upper house by Senator James H. Duff and in the lower chamber by Representative (later Senator) Hugh Scott, both of Pennsylvania. The Senate version was S.B. 2880: a bill to authorize the Court of Claims to hand down a final judgment after a trial in which every defense would be reserved to the government.

By that time the interest in the case, for both the government and INA, was in the principle, not the principal.

All unpaid French Spoliations claims could have been paid in 1956, and the expense to the government would have equaled the federal government's budgeted expenditures for only a quarter of an hour. And for INA, the claims due it were roughly the equivalent of one day's premium income.

As Congress considered S.B. 2880, Ely turned again to Dickens' *Bleak House* and read another excerpt about *Jarndyce and Jarndyce*: "Do I understand that the whole estate is found to have been absorbed in costs—and that the suit lapses and melts away?"

Perhaps. But the *Cleveland Plain Dealer* helpfully suggested: "Doesn't Uncle Sam have a few old boats around it could give the company as a token payment on the moral claim? . . . Uncle Sam ought to be able to sleep easier with the matter off his conscience. Especially since the claim, if interest were added, would total five million dollars or so."

Nevertheless, Congress turned down S.B. 2880, as it had all the previous efforts to resolve the dispute.

Ten years later INA's lawyers were still trying to devise a new strategy in the case.

"After all," as the *Plain Dealer* said in 1956, "you don't give up, after 150 years [or more] of trying."

3: Damned Nicholas

INSURANCE is almost as old as civilization. It goes back at least as far as Babylon.

In those days a trader whose caravan met with disaster could lose not only his shirt, but his family as well, for he was absolutely liable for any merchandise he carried for others. Besides the hazards of nature, the perils confronting caravans included pirates, barbarian raiders, and avaricious, semi-autonomous princes, and many caravans met with misfortune.

If the trader was unable to compensate the merchants who had entrusted their goods to him, they could take all his possessions and even sell his wife and children into slavery to get back the value of their wares.

Distressed by this state of affairs, traders turned to money lenders, who agreed to assume the risks of the caravan through loans that were repayable, at a high rate of interest, only after the goods had arrived safely at their destination.

Before long this practice had become so well established that it was given legal force in the Code of Hammurabi, 2,000 years before the Christian Era began.

From Babylonia insurance of this sort spread to Phoenicia and Greece, both of which applied the concept to their widespread sea-borne commerce. For a premium of eight per cent, a Greek in 324 could even buy protection from Antimenes of Rhodes against the loss of a runaway slave. When the Romans rose to dominance, they expanded insurance to include a form of life coverage. In medieval Europe, where the guilds of merchants and artisans controlled the economy, each guild also provided insurance for its members, including protection against fire, shipwreck, flood, theft, disability, old age, imprisonment, and lawsuits, whether the accused were guilty or innocent.

When the guilds were still at the height of their power, insurance as a purely commercial enterprise came into being. A banking house in the Belgian city of Bruges offered insurance on goods in the twelfth century, and in 1310 a strictly insurance company was chartered there.

By the middle of the fourteenth century, marine insurance was a feature of commerce in every maritime country of the Western world. In the fifteenth century a number of cities in Germany developed fire insurance as a communal undertaking.

The father of modern insurance is Nicholas Barbon, who lived in London from about 1640 to 1698. His full baptismal name was "If-Christ-Had-Not-Died-Thou-Hadst-Been-Damned Nicholas," but practical businessmen of his time preferred to shorten it to plain Damned Nicholas. (Colorful names ran in the family: his father is believed to have been Praise-God Barbon, or Barebone, whose name has come down in history because of the Cromwellian parliament of which he was a conspicuous member—"Barebone's Parliament.")

A physician who was better known as an economist, Damned Nicholas Barbon played a significant part in the rebuilding of London after the great fire of 1666, which destroyed 13,000 houses, ninety churches, and an immeasurable amount of merchandise and other property. In 1680 Barbon opened an office to write fire insurance on London houses at a premium of two and one-half per cent of the yearly rent for brick buildings and five per cent for frame structures.

Other men quickly moved into the fire insurance business, and within forty years coverages had been extended from houses to merchandise, furniture, and other valuables. By that time Barbon, who also founded a land bank, was dead, leaving a will instructing the executor *not* to pay any of Barbon's debts, which confirmed the belief of his creditors that he was indeed Damned Nicholas.

About the time that Barbon opened his fire insurance office, a number of businessmen, including some who patronized Edward Lloyd's coffee house in London, first in Tower Street and later in Lombard Street, decided that they would be willing to insure shippers against the risks of the sea. As time passed, those who needed insurance found it more convenient to go to Lloyd's, where they could talk to several insurers, than to go to a number of different offices.

Gradually, the insurers of Lloyd's evolved a unique organization to conduct the business in a more orderly fashion. The members of Lloyd's subscribed to policies individually, as they still do. A description of the ship and cargo was set forth on a paper, and each member who chose to accept a share of the risk wrote his name underneath, a custom which led to the word "underwriter."

By 1721 insurance had moved to America. John Copson opened an office in his house on Market Street (then called High Street) in Philadelphia to write "Publick Insurance on Vessels and Merchandizes." In an advertisement he promised, "Care shall be taken by the said J. Copson That all Assurers or Under Writers be Persons of undoubted Worth and Reputation, and of considerable Interest in this City and Province."

Four years later Francis Rawle of Philadelphia, in his

book on *Ways and Means for the Inhabitants of Delaware to Become Rich,* advised the "industrious Adventurer" to take a fling at marine insurance. But insurance was being written only by individual entrepreneurs in America until 1735, when the Friendly Society for Mutual Insurance was organized in Charleston, South Carolina, only to fail fifteen years later.

A more successful venture, limited to fire insurance, was organized in Philadelphia in 1752 by Benjamin Franklin. Sixteen years earlier he had encouraged the establishment of fire-fighting organizations similar to those to be found in small towns today. Each of the fire companies was really a private club, with its own uniforms, insignia, and social status. Every fire company owned its fire engine, which was filled by hand and pumped by hand.

There was great rivalry among the fire groups to see which could boast the best paintings on the sides of its engine. Some of the artists who painted the engine sides are highly regarded today, like Thomas Sully, two of whose engine sides are in INA's historical collection.

It was the success of the fire organizations that led Franklin to form a mutual fire insurance company named the Philadelphia Contributionship for the Insurance of Houses from Loss by Fire. Franklin was as versatile as he was brilliant, but his talents obviously did not include a gift for snappy names. Understandably, most people did, and do, refer to the Contributionship by its nickname, the Hand-in-Hand. Then as now, it offered perpetual insurance on only brick and stone buildings in Philadelphia and its immediate vicinity.

However, the Hand-in-Hand would not insure any building which had a tree next to it—this in the city William Penn had intended to be a "Greene Country Towne," a city whose principal streets included Spruce, Walnut, Locust, and Pine. In 1784, led by Dr. Benjamin Rush, whose great-grandson would be INA's tenth president, tree lovers finally rose up in rebellion against this bias of the Hand-in-Hand.

Dr. Rush was not one to put up with any nonsense in silence. A signer of the Declaration of Independence, a Revolutionary War veteran, and the nation's foremost physician, he spoke out bluntly against the anti-French war fever that gripped most of his fellow countrymen a few years later. "Honor! Dignity! Glory!" he growled. "How I hate the words when applied to kings or governments. To engage in a war in defense of either of them is nothing but duelling upon a national scale." The tree-loving protestors organized the Mutual Assurance Company for Insuring Houses from Loss by Fire, informally and logically called the Green Tree.

In the marine insurance field there were still no companies until the last decade of the eighteenth century. Before the Revolutionary War, individual underwriters issued policies on hulls and cargoes in the Old Insurance Office, within the London Coffee House at Front and High Streets, facing the wharves. Next door was another office maintained as a sort of agency for the New York underwriters.

During and after the war the insurance center of the city moved for some reason (perhaps the coffee house was owned by a Tory) to the City Tavern, the largest hotel in the city. Ship arrivals and departures and other matters of interest to mariners were posted in the tavern, which drew ship owners, masters, and businessmen with sufficient wealth to act as underwriters. There were about fifty men who wrote marine insurance, almost all of them as a sideline to other business activities, during the first decade after the war.

The immediate postwar period was one of economic depression, caused by the readjustment to peace, an unstable currency, and other factors. By 1781 there were only seven corporations in the country, and in the next ten years only twenty-five more were organized.

The first bank, the Bank of North America (from which INA later drew its name), was not founded until 1780, and only two more banks, in New York and Boston, had been established by the end of the decade. There were only three manufacturing concerns in the entire country. Seven out of every eight ships in American harbors flew foreign flags, mostly British.

To put it in economists' terms, the United States, like the underdeveloped countries of other continents today, was suffering from a lack of capital. Money was flowing out of the country. For example, the insurance market was primarily in London, because the American underwriters, joining together in a syndicate, could not write more than $25,000 coverage. The London underwriters, of course, were able to cover very large risks. And so money that could have been retained in this country to add to the national wealth went to England in the form of premiums.

This was also an inconvenient arrangement for those who bought insurance protection, for communications between Britain and America were slow, and claims could not be settled promptly by London.

The obvious solution was the supplanting of individual underwriters by an insurance corporation, but such an organization "was not suited to the insurance business before 1790," as economic historian Curtis P. Nettels has pointed out, "because the country lacked safe, long-term securities in which capital funds could be invested."

With the ratification of the Constitution, the nation had a responsible central government and a stable currency. One of the first acts of the new Congress was passage of the Funding Act of 1790, creating federal securities. On Wall Street brokers organized the New York Stock Exchange, one of the first indications that the national economy was beginning the fantastic growth that would, in another century, give the United States the highest standard of living in the world.

It was at this propitious moment that the promoter and the planner got together.

Damned Nicholas

The promoter was Samuel Blodget, Jr., wartime captain in the New Hampshire militia, postwar dabbler in the China trade, would-be speculator in real estate in the federal capital then being constructed on the Potomac, and, at the moment, manager of the Boston Tontine.

Very popular in the seventeenth and eighteenth centuries (and in the latter part of the nineteenth century in the United States), tontines took their name from Lorenzo Tonti, an Italian-born banker in Paris, who originated them. Basically, a tontine was a kind of lottery life insurance. The subscribers received dividends after a number of years and, in some versions, the last surviving subscriber received the principal of the fund.

The planner was Ebenezer Hazard, who would have been a remarkable man in any era. Born in Philadelphia January 15, 1744, at five o'clock on a Tuesday morning, he confirmed the saying that "Tuesday's child is full of grace." Although his father was a wealthy merchant, Ebenezer spent three adventurous years aboard British men-o'-war and privateers before the Revolution, having previously graduated from the College of New Jersey (now Princeton), of which his father was one of the original trustees. During the war and afterward, Hazard had served as surveyor of post offices and post roads and later as Postmaster General.

After 1789 he returned to private life as a merchant and broker in Philadelphia, where he also began the research which culminated in several histories, the most notable being *Historical Collections, consisting of the State Papers and other Authentic Documents intended as materials for a History of the United States*, still regarded as a basic source. He was an efficient, farsighted businessman, and an intelligent, reflective citizen.

Hazard and Blodget had known each other for several years when, early in 1792, the promoter wrote to the planner, inquiring about the possibility of selling some Boston Tontine shares in Philadelphia, whose population of 42,520 made it the nation's biggest city. Tontine shares hadn't been moving very well in Boston, which had less than half as many residents. So Blodget must have been happy to receive a reply that contained an invitation from Hazard to visit Pennsylvania to talk business.

While in Philadelphia, then the nation's capital, Blodget called on President Washington, on whose staff he had served during the siege of Boston in 1775. He asked the President to appoint him superintendent for the commission which was directing the work of designing and constructing the government buildings in the future national capital on the Potomac. After reading letters from owners of property in Federal City (now Washington, D. C.), the President did write favorably to one of the commissioners, describing Blodget as "certainly a projecting genius," but nothing ever came of the proposal.

Nevertheless, Blodget's trip was not fruitless. At Hazard's suggestion, he settled down in Philadelphia, changing the name of his enterprise to the Universal Tontine Association, and Hazard made room for him in his offices at Third and Chestnut Streets. The plan was to sell 50,000 shares in Boston and the same number in Philadelphia. At the end of twenty-one years the assets would be distributed among the surviving subscribers and the tontine dissolved.

After Hazard became secretary of the tontine, a number of leading citizens of the city agreed to promote the scheme, including John M. Nesbitt, a merchant; Jasper Moylan, a prominent attorney and leader of the famous Dancing Assembly; General Walter Stewart, federal inspector of revenue and surveyer of the port; Alexander James Dallas, secretary of the Commonwealth of Pennsylvania; and merchant Matthew McConnell.

Within fifty days of his arrival in Philadelphia, Blodget

met and married Rebecca Smith, daughter of the University of Pennsylvania's provost. She thought his promotional exuberance gave him a "comical look" even if it didn't sell shares in the tontine.

For the truth was that the tontine, even under its new name, was a failure. Despite a sales visit to Boston by Blodget and determined efforts by Hazard and his associates, only 187 persons had bought shares in the association by September, and it was clear that drastic action had to be taken. A meeting of the subscribers was called.

The meeting was held in the east room of the State House, better known today as Independence Hall. It was in that room that the Declaration of Independence had been signed and the federal Constitution had been drafted five years earlier. The minutes of the meeting, held on November 3, 1792, said:

"Tontines in general appeared to be in disrepute. Many who had subscribed were dissatisfied and were desirous that either the association be dissolved or the funds appropriated to some other use. . . . The idea of a general insurance company had been suggested, and appeared to meet with public approbation."

A committee headed by Nesbitt was appointed to look into the idea and report back to the subscribers in nine days.

On November 12, the committee endorsed the suggestion, and the meeting adopted a resolution "that the Universal Tontine Association be and is hereby changed from its original objects and converted into a society to be called the Insurance Company of North America."

INA was born, the first stock insurance company in the United States.

The company's name may have been suggested by Nesbitt, who was a director of the Bank of North America. According to the committee's outline, the new company would sell 60,000 shares of stock at $10 a share, to provide total capital of $600,000, an immense sum for a corporation in the condition of the American economy at the time.

To enable the former tontine subscribers to study the plan more carefully, the meeting was adjourned for a week. When the participants reconvened on November 19, the proposition was adopted unanimously, while in another building nearby the United States Senate was debating a communication from Secretary of State Thomas Jefferson regarding "an act making provision for the public debt."

At the Independence Hall meeting, Nesbitt, who was presiding from the famous "rising sun" chair in which John Hancock had sat during the Continental Congress of 1776, announced that a subscription book for stock buyers would be opened at Hazard's office.

This time Blodget was successful, for the good reason that he had a better project to sell. It had been agreed that the company would not come into being until 40,000 shares had been sold, but that goal was reached in just eleven days.

The shareholders were a mixed group: a shipowner's name was followed by that of a ship carpenter; there was a stable keeper, a cobbler, and a stationer; one man was a clerk in the War Department and another was secretary of the United States Senate. And, as one might expect, there were bankers, merchants, and lawyers.

In order to elect officers and directors, the stockholders met on December 10. Blodget received the highest number of votes—4,136—which was not as much an indication of the general esteem in which he was held as of his energetic efforts in lining up proxies. The next highest number of votes was for Joseph Ball, owner of an iron works and a director of the Bank of the United States. Then came Nesbitt, McConnell, Moylan, merchant and shipowner Charles Pettit, Mayor Thomas L. Moore, General Stewart, and another shipowner and merchant, John Ross.

The next day the board held its first meeting, at the City Tavern. Nesbitt was elected president and Hazard secretary. The board voted a number of committees into being to split up the work, and one of the committees leased the South Front Street building to be INA's first home. The rent was put down in the books as £ 100 a year (equivalent to $266), although Congress had thrown out the English money system more than a year earlier in favor of the dollar. Of course the Hand-in-Hand was even more conservative; it kept accounts in pounds, shillings, and pence until 1815.

The offices were opened for business on December 15. William Coulthard was employed as clerk at $500 a year. There was one other employee, the porter John Valentine Cline. Pettit wrote to Nesbitt, "John Valentine Cline . . . has been in my service the greater part of the last twenty years. He now comes to offer his services to the insurance company." The board set Cline's pay at £ 6 ($10) a month plus "an hint of a douceur at Christmas in case of good behavior." For some reason, the porter was always called Valentine, never John.

Although the company's founding plan had authorized it to write life, fire, and marine insurance, the first two were largely neglected at first. The failure of the tontine, which was, after all, a form of life insurance, probably dampened the enthusiasm of the directors for that line of business, and there was formidable competition in the fire line from the Hand-in-Hand and the Green Tree. Moreover, most, if not all, of the directors had a good deal of experience in marine underwriting. Perhaps most important, the opportunities for profit were greater in the marine line.

Several policies were written on the first day of business. Policy No. 1, issued "for Conyngham, Nesbitt and Company," was on the ship *America*, James Ewing, master, "at and from Philadelphia to Londonderry." The ship was valued at $12,000, and INA accepted a risk of $5,333.33 on it at a premium of two and one-quarter per cent, or $120, plus a charge of fifty cents for the policy. Policy No. 2 covered the cargo aboard the *America* to the amount of $3,200 at a premium of $72.50.

Another of the directors, John Leamy, took out Policy No. 3, on the brig *Margarita* bound for New Orleans "with liberty to touch and trade at" Cape François on the island of Hispaniola (now Haiti).

The largest premium on the first day was $280.50 for a policy on the ship *Friendship*, commanded by Samuel Hubbel, covering a voyage planned to take nine months, "at and from Alexandria in Virginia to Falmouth in Great Britain, to trade between Europe (without the straits [*i.e.*, Gibraltar]) and America . . . commencing this day, and to continue until the ship's arrival at any safe port in the United States."

The premium almost certainly would have been greater if the ship had been going past the Straits of Gibraltar into the Mediterranean, for the corsairs of the North African coast were taking a heavy toll of shipping at that time.

Although the office was open for business only during the latter half of December, premiums for that period totaled $6,663.92, two-thirds of the premiums being in the form of notes, an early form of installment payment. Obviously the directors were satisfied that the company was off to a good start, for the minutes of their meeting on February 22, 1793, said in part:

"The president informed the board that the managers of the Dancing Assembly had found a lot to build on, which they thought would accommodate both them and the insurance company; and proposed that the insurance company should unite with them for the purpose of building . . . each to advance six hundred pounds. . . . Agreed that Mr. Nesbitt and Colonel Pettit be a committee to meet Mr. Moylan and endeavor to devise a plan for building for the accommodation of the insurance company, with a view at the same time to the accommodation of the Dancing Assembly."

It was a mere formality, of course; Moylan, as an INA director, was present at the board meeting, as were Pettit and Nesbitt. The exclusive Dancing Assembly is now the oldest organization of its kind in America.

Nine days earlier, taking note of the outbreak of war in Europe after the proclamation of the republic in France, the company began writing a new clause into marine policies: "It is mutually agreed that this insurance is not made against any risque or loss occasioned by war; but only against such risques and losses as are usually insured against in time of profound peace."

Today it would be called a war-risk clause.

In the following month the company engaged the services of two lawyers, Jared Ingersoll and Edward Tilghman. Ingersoll, Attorney General of Pennsylvania, was Colonel Pettit's son-in-law.

Although Ingersoll and Tilghman were asked to review the company's standard policy phraseology, the company turned to Alexander Dallas, who had been associated with Hazard and the others in the tontine, when they wanted their petition for incorporation drawn up.

The petition had been submitted to the legislature just three days after the company's office was opened. It pointed out that the company would help to keep money in this country, that its large capital would protect policyholders against the failures that were so common among individual underwriters, and that the public could have greater confidence because it would be easier to sue a corporation than an individual.

Not surprisingly, the private underwriters joined together to urge the legislature not to permit INA's incorporation. The company fought back with "memorials from a number of merchants, ship owners, insurers, and citizens . . . praying that the company styling themselves the Insurance

Company of North America may be incorporated." The word battle moved into the columns of the newspapers and dragged on.

One opponent of incorporation argued that insurance corporations in England had corrupted British officials, concluding, "I therefore sincerely hope the legislature of this state will not establish a precedent of so dangerous a nature, and which may eventually destroy the constitution of the country."

On the other hand, an advocate of the proposal reminded newspaper readers that the company's founders all had excellent reputations. They were not likely to act less honorably as directors of a corporation, he said. Besides, incorporation would not give the company a monopoly; individual underwriters could still continue to do business.

After a month of inaction by the legislature, the company's board decided to prod the lawmakers indirectly by applying to the state of Delaware for permission to incorporate. The tactic worked. The Pennsylvania legislative committee which had been considering the company's application voted a favorable report. Among the reasons it advanced for approving the petition were these:

"That insurance cannot be so well conducted by individuals as by an incorporated company, for want of that identity which would enable such a company to be sued in case of loss, where justice could be had more speedily than in suing every separate underwriter. . . . That solidity is also to be considered, which it is impossible to attain with certainty with private underwriters, whereas this company's proposed capital of six hundred thousand dollars in the public funds will be a sufficient guarantee to those who employ them. [And] that already the charges of insurance have been considerably abated since the establishment of this company, whereby a great saving to the mercantile body is effected. . . ."

With the committee's approval, a bill of incorporation was introduced in the legislature on April 1, 1793, but when that body adjourned ten days later no action had been taken.

And then an epidemic of yellow fever struck Philadelphia. Bonfires were burned and muskets discharged in the belief that this might help to purify the air. All manner of preventive measures were taken. People smoked tobacco, took snuff, sprinkled vinegar about, and had their physicians bleed them. Doors and windows were kept tightly shut, despite the stifling heat. And still people sickened and died, until there were not enough hearses to carry all the dead.

Yellow fever epidemics like this were not uncommon in American cities at the time, and they always led, as this one did, to a general evacuation of the city. President Washington and all the other top government officials left. Trenton was invaded by panic-stricken men, women, and children from down river. The exodus included most of INA's directors, and meetings of the board had to be suspended because a quorum could not be obtained.

Through it all, Ebenezer Hazard remained in the city with his family. In a letter to his friend, geographer Jedediah Morse, on September 20, Hazard gave a vivid description of Philadelphia in the grip of the epidemic:

"The disease has spread all over the city, and if we may judge from the number of funerals, its malignity has not abated much. Great numbers of the citizens have shut up their houses and fled into the country; so few are seen in our streets and so many houses are shut that every day has the appearance of Sunday.

"Business is almost entirely at a stand[still]; almost every countenance is gloomy, and when two persons meet, 'Have you heard of any new deaths today?' is among the first questions that are asked; our physicians differ in sentiment both about the nature of the disorder and the mode of treating it, and have added to the general distress by publishing their contradictory opinions in the newspapers.

"Such are the apprehensions of the contagion, that a friend dares not visit a friend who is sick . . . and carry the disorder to his own family. No friends attend at funerals, except perhaps two or three, who keep at a distance from the body . . . accompanied by three or four Negroes who bury it. No clergyman attends, no ceremony is made use of, but the putrid corpse is committed to its kindred earth, and covered up as expeditiously as possible.

"Our situation has rendered such sights as these both frequent and familiar to us—yet they are distressing. How are the widows—how are the orphans multiplied! This city truly mourns. . . . There are bitter drops on the cups of many . . . but we have among us some who can say of the Lord, He is our Refuge, and our Fortress, our God, in Him will we trust. . . .

"Divine protection has hitherto preserved the lives and health of my family, and I cannot say that we feel much alarmed on our own accounts; but we cannot help being distressed for others. . . ."

Medicines grew scarce, and so did food, for farmers were afraid to go into the stricken city. The closed shops and houses were plundered by mobs of hungry people.

Hazard wrote to Nesbitt on September 23:

"The situation in our neighborhood I find has become truly alarming . . . and it does not appear necessary to attend longer at the office as so little business offers. . . . Mr. Coulthard went a few miles into the country on Saturday afternoon and intended returning this morning; but as it is now one o'clock, and I have not yet seen him, I fear he is sick. There are no directors whom I can consult on this occasion. Thus situated,

I have concluded to remove the books and papers, for the present, to my own house. . . ."

Coulthard was indeed sick, but fortunately he soon recovered. A few days later Hazard, too, fell ill, but he also was back on his feet in a short time.

Yet through it all the indomitable Hazard kept track of what was happening to ships insured by the company. Despite a severe coastal storm, the ship *Betsey* had arrived safely. However, the *Flora*, insured for $5,000, probably received some damage, and the *McClenachan* was on shore; we are seven thousand dollars on vessel and cargo."

By October 24 Hazard was able to report, "All accounts agree that the sickness has very much abated." A week later he wrote to Nesbitt, "People are beginning to return to the city, but I think they are too hasty." And Nesbitt agreed; he had no intention of going back to Philadelphia "before next week or some rain to wash the streets."

The next day, November 1, there was what Hazard described as "a charming rain." He hoped it would "enable our citizens to return soon without risque; a good frost after it will do the business."

People began moving back to a city in mourning. About 5,000 had fallen victim to the disease, or one in every nine inhabitants.

Despite the epidemic, the company continued to prosper. In the first six months it had received $62,114.33 in premiums and $3,276.20 in interest, and there had been only two losses, both in the same storm: the ship *Industry*, driven ashore at the mouth of the Delaware, with ten passengers and the crew of a lifeboat drowned; and the cargo of the sloop *Betsey*, pounded to pieces on a shoal near Sandy Hook, not far from New York harbor. The losses totaled $4,515.74.

In the second half of the year, premium receipts came

to $151,350 against $19,474 in losses. Two semi-annual dividends, each of six per cent on paid-in capital, were authorized.

The business had already outgrown the company's quarters, so the offices were moved to 107 South Front Street, at the corner of Walnut.

In December the legislature reconvened, and by now, with a year of business behind it, the new insurance company had proved itself; so well, in fact, that a second group organized a company and applied for incorporation, not in addition to INA, but in place of it. The rival organization was headed by Thomas Willing, merchant, ship owner, and president of the Bank of the United States, and it included George Latimer, speaker of the Pennsylvania House of Representatives.

On January 31, 1794, the legislative committee considering the matter voted a resolution praising insurance companies in principle and recommending incorporation of *both* INA and the rival group, which would be called the Insurance Company of the State of Pennsylvania.

The competing companies now raced for the honor of being first to get a charter. The Pennsylvania Company's bill passed the House a day ahead of INA's, but both bills passed the Senate on the same day and were sent back to the House for a vote on amendments.

The difficulties in INA's bill were straightened out three days ahead of the other, and Governor Thomas Mifflin signed the act incorporating the Insurance Company of North America, on April 14, 1794, four days before its competitor (although the Pennsylvania Company did not actually begin doing business until the following October).

Finally the Insurance Company of North America was firmly established. It had begun as the pace-setter. Now it had to maintain its leadership.

4: A Business of Risques

FORTUNE magazine once described INA as a company that "drips with tradition." The rich patina of tradition worn by the company today was largely acquired during the nineteenth century as the company confronted the uncertainties of life in a young, rapidly growing and changing country. "The early history of this company is closely interwoven with that of the nation itself," according to insurance historian William D. Winter, himself the chairman of the executive committee of the Atlantic Mutual Insurance Company of New York, which dates back to 1825.

During most of that period INA slowly, and sometimes painfully, built a reputation for soundness, dependability, and fairness in the fire and marine fields, having dropped life insurance after 1817.

The company's mere survival is remarkable, for by 1804 there were forty insurance companies in the United States, just twelve years after INA began business as the first; and hundreds of other insurance companies were established in the following decades, all but a handful of them collapsing, usually with disastrous losses to policyholders and investors, as a result of the recurrent financial crises, the city-wide conflagrations, the wars, and the technological revolutions that marked the nineteenth century.

Like Ebenezer Hazard, who clung stubbornly to his post of duty in Philadelphia through the yellow fever epidemic, the early men of INA set the style for their successors by their tough-fibered determination.

Thomas Tingey, who was a director of INA in 1794, was typical. In 1799, he was in command of the sloop of war *Ganges*, a former merchant vessel fitted with twenty-four guns and commissioned as a United States Navy ship, when she was stopped and boarded by an officer from the English frigate *Surprise*, a forty-four gun warship. The British officer demanded surrender of all Englishmen on board, the customary ruse by which English officers took American seamen by force to serve on British warships. Captain Tingey was the first American commander to resist this sort of abuse. "A public ship carrier has no protection but her flag," he told the British officer. "I do not expect to succeed in a contest with you, but I will die at my quarters before a man shall be taken from the ship." Nonplussed by the unexpected belligerence of Captain Tingey, the English withdrew without taking any men and without a fight.

The British interference with American shipping so aggravated relations between the two countries, which a dozen years earlier had both been fighting the French, that Congress declared war on Great Britain in 1812, a war in which the United States enjoyed a surprising number of victories at sea while suffering a series of dangerous defeats on land. Despite its successes in isolated sea battles, the United States Navy was too small to protect our shipping, and so the war had a devastating effect on our foreign trade.

"The commerce of the United States has been swept from the ocean . . . while the commerce of England has greatly increased," the *Portland* (Maine) *Gazette* lamented. "When insurance on British vessels can be made for three or four per cent, it could not be made on United States vessels short of fifty per cent."

For a company still struggling to stay alive, the war and the years of ship seizures and losses preceding it were heavy blows. After an initial period of prosperity, INA began to lose money on marine insurance in 1799, and it was not until 1804 that premium receipts exceeded losses. At that point the company's capital was down to $300,000, half of the original amount, and there was no surplus.

The lack of money made it impossible for the company to profit from a sudden boom in American shipping during the first decade of the nineteenth century, and many other concerns that had entered the insurance field began to compete energetically. Although the capital fund had been restored to $600,000 by the middle of 1806, the marine line lost money again the following year.

No marine insurance was written in 1808 because of the government's embargo on foreign trade, but that was followed by three years of limited profits, counteracted by three years, including the war period, that forced the company to dip into its capital again.

During this time the company had become increasingly active in the fire insurance line, in which the percentage of profit was greater although the actual amounts were much smaller. Like the Hand-in-Hand and the Green Tree, INA had a fire mark, a metal symbol put on the house of every policyholder. Because the insurers contributed financially to the fire-fighting companies, it was assumed that the volunteer firemen might be more zealous in combating the flames at a house sporting the fire mark of a supporter.

Today INA's historical collection includes 117 fire marks from companies in eighteen states. INA's first fire mark, adopted in 1794, was a crude, six-pointed star, discarded in

1796 when the company chose an eagle rising from a rock, a design prepared by Claudius F. Legrand.

Until INA started writing fire insurance, a policyholder could buy protection only for buildings, not for their contents. The company's bold decision to begin "insuring goods, wares, and merchandises in dwelling houses, warehouses or stores and upon buildings, against the risque arising from fire" was one of the most striking early manifestations of what would be a notable company tradition, innovation, the pioneering of new forms of insurance to meet new needs.

William Beynroth bought the first fire policy, issued December 10, 1794, "on German dry goods" in his house at 211 High Street, Philadelphia. The rate was three per cent. Beynroth valued the goods at $8,000, so his premium, for three years, was $72 plus $2 for "badge and policy," the "badge" being the fire mark. In return for paying in advance, Beynroth received a discount of $8. Lawrence Herbert, who purchased the second policy, insured for only one year, which disqualified him for a discount.

In 1795 INA established other precedents by printing 5,000 advertising handbills and, later that year, by offering to insure "brick or stone houses within ten miles of the city." Less than a year passed, however, before the company realized that its limits were still too parochial; it decided to write fire insurance on property anywhere in the country, and within another twelvemonth INA's life mark was on buildings from New Hampshire to Georgia.

Almost from the beginning, arson was a problem. The board of directors in 1797 authorized "a reward of from one hundred dollars to one thousand dollars for discovering and prosecuting to conviction the person or persons who set Mr. Sperry's store on fire [in New York], as there is some reason to suspect that the fire was not accidental."

Even before the company was organized, the frontier

had begun the relentless movement West that would not stop until it reached the ocean on the other side of the continent. Following Daniel Boone, an endless line of pioneers in wagons was crossing into Kentucky through the Cumberland Gap, and thousands more were moving westward in flatboats down the Ohio River. Kentucky's 1790 population of 73,677 had more than trebled by the dawn of the nineteenth century. In the same year that saw the founding of INA, Kentucky achieved statehood.

For some reason that is unclear today, the imagination of one member of INA's board, Alexander Henry, was kindled by the vision of the opening of the West, although it is believed that he himself never got beyond the environs of Philadelphia. On October 6, 1807, Henry made an eloquent appeal to the board to follow the pioneers by establishing an agency beyond the Alleghenies.

Apparently his fervor impressed the board, for it named him chairman of a committee to "consider the benefit and propriety of extending insurance against fire generally to other cities and towns in other states beyond what it is now customary to make." It is not surprising that the committee reported favorably on the proposal.

The first place chosen for an agency was Lexington, the principal market town of Kentucky, site of the first state legislature and home of Henry Clay. A prosperous local merchant, Thomas Wallace, a trustee of Transylvania College, the oldest educational institution west of the mountains (founded in 1780), was appointed INA's agent.

Appointments quickly followed for agencies at Louisville and Frankfort, Kentucky; Washington, Pennsylvania; Cincinnati, Chillicothe, and Steubenville, Ohio; Nashville, Tennessee; and Wheeling, Virginia (later West Virginia).

This is acknowledged as the beginning of the unique American Agency System. Today there are more than half a million independent insurance agents in the United States, part of a tradition begun by INA.

The first agents had severely limited powers. They could solicit fire insurance and survey properties offered as risks, but the decision to accept the risk and at what rate was made at the home office until the time of the Civil War.

Through correspondence from the home office, the new agents quickly learned that the company insisted on meticulous examination and selection of properties offered for insurance, the process that came to be known as underwriting. One agent was told:

"Your survey of Mr. Cramer's property and the buildings in which it is contained is very minute and satisfactory, but the risk is of a nature which we consider as being among the most hazardous, inasmuch as that printers and book binders are generally in the habit of working by candle light, surrounded by combustible matter and the business too often entrusted to boys and other inconsiderate persons. Books and stationery are also considered very hazardous not on account of their combustible quality but the difficulty of removal in case of fire and being so very susceptible of injury by water.

"The property being contained in wooden buildings, also serves to increase the risk; which I am of opinion cannot be taken under 1¾ per cent for one year on a sum not exceeding ⅔ of the whole value of the property."

Another modern concept, "moral hazard," or the reliability and character of the prospective policyholder, was touched on in another letter which said:

"It is desirable in all cases of insurance on *personal property in particular* [original emphasis] to know something of the moral character of the assured. . . . You will therefore confer a favor by giving me a confidential hint where circumstances may in your opinion require it."

'Spry Old Underwriter'

A polished patina of tradition characterizes the
oldest stock insurance company in the United
States, affectionately described by a modern
financial periodical as a "spry old underwriter."
INA was already a half century old when hand
pumpers like this were built about 1830. This
model, like the other memorabilia in this
group of illustrations, is in the company's
historical collection.

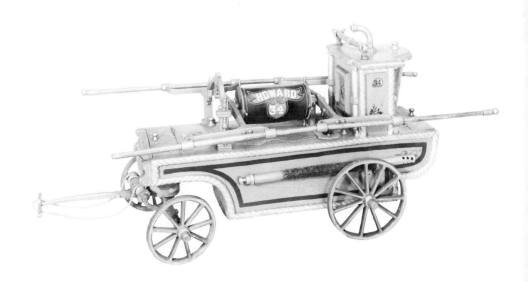

Early fire companies adorned paneled sides of their engines with paintings, like these showing Benjamin Franklin. UPPER LEFT: a head, based on 1783 portrait by Joseph Sifrede Duplessis (artist unknown, c. 1830). BELOW IT: Franklin and his son William performing famous electrical experiment with kite (unknown, c. 1830).

RIGHT: wearing helmet of Union Fire Company, which he founded in 1736 (c. 1850, signed "Chas. W. Wright"). FACING PAGE: at the age of 17, in front of Second Street Market in 1723 (attributed to David Rent Etter, c. 1830).

Three of the engine sides that decorated apparatus of New York fire companies. RIGHT: Americus No. 6 Fire Engine Company painting shows Venus being born of the sea (probably painted in 1849 by John A. Woodside, Sr.). BELOW: Lexington No. 7 Fire Engine Company panel depicts Battle of Lexington (by M. Betsch, probably painted about 1849). Eagle No. 13 Fire Engine Company side had popular patriotic motif (artist unknown, c. 1863).

From the policyholders' point of view, one of the most distinctive INA traditions took shape at this time, as a letter to an agent in Reading, Pennsylvania, indicates. Acknowledging receipt of a report from the agent regarding a recent fire there, the company told him:

"We are much gratified to find that our loss is not likely to be so fatal as we at first apprehended; and indeed it is questionable whether we are in strictness liable for any damage Messrs. O'Brien's goods may have sustained in the removal of them. . . . As it may have been a prudential measure, however, we are not at all inclined to make any difficulty in the settlement."

As time passed, this attitude was crystallized into an explicit company philosophy for claims settlements, which can be stated succinctly in three parts: first, to pay all just claims as quickly as possible; second, to resolve reasonable doubts in favor of the policyholder; but, third, to resist all unjustified claims as vigorously as possible.

The disinclination to split hairs would have pleased Ebenezer Hazard, but he had retired from active participation in the business by the time of the Reading fire because of his ill health and his desire to devote more time to his scholarly pursuits.

There had been many other changes around the board table. Blodget, beset by financial troubles, resigned to try to recoup his fortunes through his real estate promotions in Washington; he failed, and three years later was thrown into debtors' prison. Nesbitt's firm, Conyngham, Nesbitt and Company, went bankrupt shortly before his death, which spared him the embarrassment of seeing INA dun Conyngham for money owed to the insurance company.

New faces in the company's offices included a young lawyer, Joseph Hopkinson, who was also something of a poet.

During the undeclared naval war with France, Hopkinson wrote words for his friend, Gilbert Fox, the actor, to sing to the music of "The President's March," believed to have been composed nine years earlier by Philip Phile. Fox sang Hopkinson's song as the finale to a comedy, *The Italian Monk*, at a performance in the New Theater in Philadelphia April 25, 1798. The song was an immediate success, widely reprinted under the title "The New Federal Song." Today it is a patriotic favorite under its modern title, "Hail, Columbia." There have been Hopkinsons associated with INA ever since Joseph's time.

The men who succeeded the first leaders of INA were worthy of their predecessors. John Inskeep is typical of the kind of man that the company has always been able to draw upon. A captain in the New Jersey militia during the Revolution, he bought a tavern in Philadelphia when peace came and later opened a china and glassware business. Elected a city alderman in 1799, succeeding John Barclay, who was one of the original INA directors, Inskeep became mayor of Philadelphia in 1800. (John Wharton, another INA board member, had occupied the mayor's office just before him.)

Inskeep also was at one time associate judge of the Court of Common Pleas. As a judge he freed on a writ of habeas corpus a slave who had been brought to the city by United States Senator Pierce Butler of South Carolina. Although Inskeep was not trained in the law, his ruling was upheld on appeal. In 1806, at the age of forty-nine, Inskeep became the fourth president of INA.

One of Inskeep's first acts as president was to inform the stockholders that, premium receipts having exceeded losses, he intended to invest the net gain in order to improve the company's financial strength. This meant there would be no dividend, although only one dividend had been paid in the past seven and a half years. Nevertheless, the stockholders approved Inskeep's decision, passing a resolution thanking "the president and directors for their good management and attention to the concerns of the company."

Thus another INA tradition began to take form: conservative management of the company's funds to provide against the bad years that were sure to come from time to time.

Despite Inskeep's frugal administration of the company's money, there was nothing stingy or small-minded in his sentiments regarding the company's responsibilities as a corporate citizen. A year after he became president, the calamitous Embargo Act, which cut off all foreign trade, was put into effect by the federal government in the woefully mistaken belief that England and France, which had been interfering with our shipping, needed commerce with us more than we needed them.

In a matter of weeks insolvent-debtor notices filled the newspapers. In every city and hamlet throughout the country advertisements of sheriffs' sales covered post offices and the doors of courthouses and taverns. Thirteen hundred men were imprisoned in New York alone at one time because, ruined by the Embargo, they were unable to pay their debts; in most cities the jails were not big enough to hold all the debtors.

"A traveler who saw the city in this day of distress assures us that it looked like a town ravaged by pestilence," the nineteenth-century historian John B. McMaster recorded. "The counting-houses were shut or advertised to let. The coffee houses were almost empty. The streets along the waterside were almost deserted."

Unemployment was widespread; the plight of the jobless was pitiful. In this community crisis, INA, despite the losses that it was suffering, contributed $500, a great deal of money in those days, to a program of relief work.

After fifteen months, the Embargo was eased, but the march of events of which it was a part was carrying the country toward the War of 1812. At one point during that conflict,

Philadelphia itself felt endangered. On August 24, 1814, the British captured Washington and set fire to the Capitol, the White House, and the Navy Yard. The government fled, and the enemy fleet sailed up Chesapeake Bay to attack Baltimore. It appeared that Philadelphia would be next.

As the townspeople hurriedly prepared makeshift defenses, INA's board of directors met briefly. "The president proposed taking into consideration the propriety, under present circumstances, of making preparation for the removal of books, papers, and effects of this company for safe keeping from injury which may be done thereto, should the enemy enter this city," the minutes of the meeting reported. "Whereupon he was authorized to adopt such means, and at such time as he may think fit. . . ."

With relief, the Philadelphians learned that the British had been halted with heavy losses outside Baltimore, having failed to reduce Fort McHenry during the bombardment that inspired Francis Scott Key to write "The Star-Spangled Banner." On October 14 the British sailed down the bay, on their way to Jamaica. The threat to Baltimore and Philadelphia was ended.

With the national capital in ashes and the government's coffers virtually empty, President Madison appealed to INA's old lawyer, Alexander James Dallas, to come to Washington as Secretary of the Treasury. For two years during that critical period in our nation's history Dallas served in that post, in which he succeeded in restoring the public credit. Simultaneously, he served for one year as acting Secretary of War.

In 1817, a year after leaving government service, Dallas died, which was a double blow for his old associates at INA. For not only did they miss an old and valued friend, but they also lost the benefit of his keen financial acumen at a critical time, when the boom-and-bust roller coaster that was the

American economy in the nineteenth century was about to plunge into its first crisis.

The panic of 1818–1819 did not mark the first economic depression; there had been seven before it, beginning in 1762. But 1818–1819 was the first major national banking crisis, the visible evidence of the Industrial Revolution in what was still essentially an agricultural country. "Nearly all the manufacturing establishments of the country were broken up, their owners ruined, and their property sold at enormous sacrifices," Joshua Gilpin wrote in 1819. Banks failed everywhere.

At such a time, the stockholders of INA could be grateful for its prudent management, for the company was able to pay a dividend of ten per cent in 1818, ten per cent in 1819, nine per cent in 1820, eight per cent in 1821, and ten per cent in 1822, by which time the Northeast had largely emerged from the depression.

The rest of the century was shaken by violent up-and-down fluctuations. During the latter part of the 1820's and most of the 1830's, the country enjoyed a great expansion of the economy, only to suffer a financial and monetary crisis in 1837, followed by a general collapse in 1839–1840. The next crash was in 1854, with another in 1857 that left a lingering effect until the Civil War boom. There was a postwar depression, a major collapse in 1873, another in 1884, and an historic panic in 1893. All in all, it was a trying time for anyone and especially for men entrusted with the conservation and productive use of other people's money.

In the first half of the century INA, like all other insurance companies, had to dip into its capital during bad times to meet its obligations to policyholders. No law required insurance companies at that time to maintain adequate reserves, although INA did set aside, from time to time, a small part of its profits in order to prepare for the inevitable rainy day.

However, in 1832 the directors adopted a definite policy

of retaining "a larger surplus than usual," having come to the conclusion that "the amount of undecided premiums" was "inadequate to any heavy demand."

Although the surplus had grown to $47,311 in January 1837, it proved insufficient when the panic struck that spring. Again the company had to take from its capital, until five years later only half the original $600,000 was left, and the company officially reduced its capitalization to $300,000, "what it is really worth."

Most of the other companies went under. Of the relative few that survived, only one other company remained a joint-stock operation; the other survivors had turned themselves into mutuals.

As a result of the collapse of the other companies, Massachusetts became the first of a number of states to pass laws requiring fire insurance companies to maintain reserves sufficient to fulfill their contracts. Having already started a program of building its surplus, INA needed little prodding in this direction. By 1849 its surplus had grown to $200,000. The company never had to touch its capital again.

In the marine line, the effects of the War of 1812 lasted for more than twenty years. Finally, during the early 1830's, the American merchant marine began to recover, and the phenomenal success of the clipper ships, which were built in this country, gave our shipping industry a significant boost for about a decade after 1843.

The rise in American-owned tonnage entering our ports was impressive but deceptive, for its proportion of the total of all vessels clearing United States' ports in foreign trade dropped from ninety per cent in 1821 to seventy-one per cent in 1860. The decline of the American merchant marine, hastened by the Civil War, continued until, toward the close of the century, "less than ten per cent of the overseas commerce of the United States was carried in American vessels," according to Winter, who added:

"As trade follows the flag, so, too, marine insurance protection, which is but one element in the conduct of trade, is ordinarily furnished by citizens of the same flag, with the result that marine insurance was diverted from the American market."

The change from sail to steam played a major part in the deterioration of the American merchant marine, for our shipping industry was reluctant to shift to steamships and our shops apparently had difficulty producing the large iron frames and big steam engines needed for the transatlantic trade. For INA, however, the steam engine opened a new market for insurance, the river traffic.

Before steam, the flatboat or the equally slow-moving raft was the usual means of transportation on the vast Ohio-Mississippi-Missouri river system, and losses were heavy, in large part because it was easy for the numerous river pirates to overtake the sluggish craft. The heavy loss record had caused INA to lay down a general rule against insuring river traffic. But the first steamboat on the rivers "struck the knell of [the] river pirates," as Paul I. Wellman has pointed out. About the time steam came into general use the *Cincinnati Gazette* said: "The invention of the steamboat was intended for us."

Now INA felt it could afford to accept risks on inland waters. An agent was appointed in St. Louis in 1849 specifically to handle this line of business, although he was permitted only to insure cargoes, never ships. Part of his instructions read, "You may adopt the same rates of premium which the companies of your city are charging, not submitting to any reduction for the purpose of securing business. The latter is bad policy."

That philosophy, too, has remained as a part of INA

tradition: to charge the policyholder the lowest premium which would return a reasonable profit to the company, but not to reduce rates to an unprofitable level in order to get the account.

A year before the appointment of the St. Louis agent, the Mexican War had been brought to an end. INA's only loss in that war was $7,500, its policy on a ship which was burned after it had run aground off Tampico.

The Gold Rush drew ships to San Francisco. Although many of the ships never sailed out the Golden Gate once they had entered the harbor—at one time 500 vessels rode at anchor there, their crews having deserted to go the mine fields—INA profited by the huge movement of ships.

Another who profited was a twenty-year-old Philadelphian, Charles Platt, son of a ship owner in the China trade. He was in Hong Kong when the Gold Rush started.

"Here am I," he wrote to a friend from the British colony in China, "living on board the *Heber* in this beautiful harbor, attending to her being loaded for the 'Land of Gold.' Excitement continues and numbers are going. I myself would like to go for I think fortunes are to be made there. But as I can't leave very well now, I have contented myself with shipping to the extent of my ability all sorts of things—hats, chow chow ware, etc. . . ."

In another letter from Hong Kong to a Philadelphia friend, Platt outlined his "ideas of life," apparently in reply to a question in a previous letter:

"What are they? An income of about $3,000 per year clear, a nice little place with a few acres around it, near a city but not so near as to be in its way for 'improvements'; pleasant society in the neighborhood, not too much, but *enough*! A house, tasty and neat, with arrangements of its 'internals' to suit my taste, and now to come to the all important part, a good library of books, not bought in a heap but chosen by myself. Chairs fit to sit in, to read the said books. A billiard table for recreation; with one or two horses, and finally, last of all, but far from least, a wife to my taste and of my own choice to grace the whole."

Such unexciting goals, in a youth of twenty, help to explain why another Philadelphian, Owen Wister, said his townsmen's worst vice was moderation. Obviously young Platt, who eventually became INA's seventh president, did not "go native" in the Orient.

When the Civil War erupted in 1861, Platt was secretary of the insurance company, having joined it the previous year. Before Fort Sumter was fired on, the company had already inserted a war-risk clause into its marine policies, relieving INA of any losses arising out of the conflict unless an extra premium was paid.

The first INA-insured vessel to fall victim was the bark *Rowena*, captured by the Confederate raider *Jeff Davis* a month after the fall of Sumter. Soon other raiders were roaming the high seas, searching for Northern prizes. The Confederate cruiser *Alabama* set sail from the British Isles, destroyed the American whaling fleet off the Azores, then took nine prizes as she sailed toward America. Two hundred miles off New York the *Alabama* turned south, overtook and burned two Union merchantmen, and before long was reported wreaking havoc along the courses followed by ships bound from Northern ports to California or China.

Now Platt proved that, staid or not, he was capable of considerable ingenuity. Most of the marine underwriters were reluctant to insure a ship departing, say, for Europe if the *Alabama* had recently been sighted along that course.

But Platt took a different view of the matter. Considering that news of the raider was at least a week old, and sometimes as much as two months old, when it was received in Philadelphia, he reckoned that the cruiser would not dare remain in the area, for Union men-of-war were scouring the seas for it. Therefore the latest course on which the *Alabama* was known to have been lurking ought to be the safest.

Of course the theory applied only to outbound vessels, but it did work. After sixteen months, the *Alabama* had sailed around the world and seized forty ships, but not one of them was insured by INA. By the end of the war, INA's losses to the Confederate raiders totaled $11,169, compared with $36,971 for another company, $16,397 for a second, $48,934 for a third, and a whopping $1,653,889 for a fourth company.

Platt's salary was raised 150 per cent, and he was given a bonus of $1,600.

The war also affected the company's fire insurance. As early as 1855, when the debate over the extension of legal slavery in new states was at its height, the board had decided to tighten the wording of the "clause in our fire policies designed to protect the company from loss in event of fire resulting from foreign invasion and civil commotion."

As secession spread early in 1861, INA refused to renew policies written through the New Orleans office and later cancelled policies in Washington, Baltimore, and St. Louis. No new business or renewals were accepted from any agency in the South except the office in Lexington, Kentucky.

To compensate for the business that would be lost in the South, the company launched a vigorous campaign to expand its work in the North and the West. To facilitate the drive, INA decentralized its operations to a considerable extent, dividing the country into regions: the Pennsylvania State Central Agency (1861) and the Western Department (1864), which consisted of thirteen Midwestern and Plains states. After the war, other departments were organized, the Eastern in 1868 and, in 1875, the Southern and the Pacific Coast.

As in the War of 1812, Philadelphia was threatened briefly in June 1863, when Lee drove into Pennsylvania. INA contributed $2,000 to the war chest and limited office hours to two hours a day as its employees enrolled in the militia and helped throw up hasty breastworks. The scare ended July 5, when it was learned that the Southern Army had retreated after the Battle of Gettysburg.

After the war, the English underwriters invaded the American market in force. With large surpluses they were able to cut rates in order to woo customers away from the American companies. Many of the American marine insurance companies went out of business; those that also wrote fire insurance generally abandoned the marine field. A few companies clung almost desperately to marine insurance.

But INA had grown to the point where it could compete in the tough struggle with the London insurers. In 1872 the company realized a profit of more than a quarter of a million dollars on marine premiums of $1,232,437.

One reason for the company's prosperity was its attention to detail and its persistence in ferreting out all the facts about claims. When the officers and crew of the British bark *L.E. Cann* arrived in Philadelphia in 1882 aboard a schooner which had found them in an open boat fifty miles off Brunswick, Georgia, INA had a natural interest in their story, for it had issued a $60,000 policy for the vessel.

According to Captain Brooks' account, his ship, bound from Mexico to New York, had been so battered by rough weather in the Gulf of Mexico that its planks had separated, letting water in faster than the pumps could draw it out. So the ship had been abandoned shortly before the arrival of the schooner.

Checking the records, an INA claims man found that four other ships abandoned at sea had carried cargoes insured by the consignors of the freight aboard the *L.E. Cann*. Although a British court, convened at INA's request, found Captain Brooks blameless, the company kept a salvage tug at

[67]

sea, searching for some trace of the lost vessel. Three times the tug returned, to report no success, and three times it was sent out again.

Finally the wreck of the *L.E. Cann* was found on Cape Lookout, North Carolina, where it had run aground. The hulk was towed to Norfolk, where the hold was pumped out and the cargo, water-soaked but intact, examined. Although the manifest listed the cargo as rubber, vanilla beans, deerskins, coffee, and tobacco, the inspectors found that it largely consisted of 106 bales of broom grass, 151 bales of old rags, 210 bales of bones, 185 bales of sand, and a pile of scrap metal.

It was also discovered that ten holes had been bored in the hull below the water line. When news of the derelict's examination leaked out, the captain disappeared.

Not fraud, but conflagrations troubled the company's fire underwriters during this period. These immense fires, which often destroyed most of a city, were recurring events during the nineteenth century.

In 1835 nearly 700 buildings went up in flames in a single holocaust in New York City. Ten years later a fire left 1,000 buildings in Pittsburgh in ruins. Most of St. Louis burned in 1851. Portland, Maine, was almost totally destroyed in 1866. On October 8, 1871, a blaze that started in Mrs. Jeremiah O'Leary's stable on the West Side of Chicago, fanned by a strong wind, swept across the city; two days later, when the fire had burned itself out, it was found that 17,450 buildings, valued at $200,000,000, had been wiped out, leaving 100,000 persons homeless.

The Chicago fire forced sixty-eight insurance companies into bankruptcy, and eighty-three other companies settled claims only in part. INA paid its claims, totaling $650,-000, in full, one of fifty-one companies to do so. But the company's willingness and ability to pay its losses in full brought in a great deal of new business, especially from people to whom the fire had been a forceful reminder of the importance of insurance. "We have obtained [in ninety days] a business which under ordinary circumstances would have required ten years to secure," Platt said.

A year later the company was struck a more serious blow. Flames were discovered in a four-story granite building in Summer Street in Boston on November 9, 1872, but the fire could not be contained. After two days of the inferno, more than 600 buildings had been gutted, for a loss of about $75,000,000. Twenty-five insurance companies collapsed; all the rest paid their claims. The heaviest loss was INA's— $988,530.

The following January the company passed a dividend for the first time since 1855. Within five years, however, INA was able to increase its capitalization to $2,000,000 and to report "the largest surplus over all liabilities [$2,426,626] of any American insurance company, and equal to that of any foreign company."

On the eve of the company's centennial, the report to stockholders pointed to an average annual dividend during that first century of 12.4 per cent. As recently as 1860, the report said, "the total income from fire and marine premiums was $500,000 while it is now over $5,000,000; the entire properties of the company were $1,100,000, while they are now yearly $9,300,000."

In a very short time the company's strength would be tested more painfully than ever before, and it would need those financial resources to meet an almost overwhelming catastrophe.

5: San Francisco: Earthquake or Fire?

IN 1944 an independent research organization questioned New York insurance brokers to find out what companies they favored, and why. One man said that he gave his business to INA and a few other companies because he had a strict and simple rule of thumb, to deal "only with those companies who paid in full after the 1906 San Francisco earthquake."

That INA did pay in full can be credited in a large measure to the integrity and the courage of one young man, Sheldon Catlin, who had been an INA employee for only seven months on April 18, 1906.

At 5:12 that morning the ground shifted horizontally an average of ten feet and vertically as much as four feet along 210 miles of the California coast lying over the San Andreas Fault in the earth's crust, causing damage for thirty miles on both sides of the fault. The worst damage occurred in what Will Irwin called "the gayest, lightest-hearted, most pleasure-loving city of this continent, and in many ways the most interesting and romantic"—San Francisco.

San Francisco: Earthquake or Fire?

In a sixth-floor suite of the Palace Hotel the great Enrico Caruso, who had sung the part of Don Jose in *Carmen* a few hours earlier, scrambled into clothes and ran into the corridor. John Barrymore, at a friend's home, saw a collection of Chinese glass utterly shattered. Cornices dropped into the streets, and in a few places entire walls of buildings toppled. A steel telephone pole sliced down on a dairy wagon in Mission Street, killing the driver. The streets had humps and holes where none had been before. Twisted steel rails had snapped. Like a madman's fountains, broken mains spouted water. The City Hall was in ruins, and the four floors of the wooden Valencia Street Hotel had crashed down into a splintered, dusty mass of men, women, wooden floors, furniture, plaster walls, window glass, and metal plumbing.

All in forty-eight seconds.

For more than an hour all communications with the city were cut off. Then the first excited bulletins flashed over telegraph wires across the country. For little more than sixty minutes the staccato messages told of a city in shambles with fires springing up in many places. Then the line went dead.

Almost two hours later telegraph keys began clicking again. The lines had been restored to Oakland across the bay from the stricken city, and scraps of information, rumors, unconfirmed reports, and random intelligence clattered into newspaper offices throughout the country.

The nation's attention was focused on San Francisco, and the fragmentary and hearsay character of most of the news about the catastrophe for days after the quake only whetted everyone's interest. Few people, except those who had friends and relatives in San Francisco, were more anxious for the latest news than insurance men. They shared the general concern for the victims of the disaster, and in addition they were apprehensive about the possibility of huge losses.

However, as the days wore on, the newspaper accounts

[71]

indicated that the fires were simply consuming the rubble of buildings already demolished by the temblor. Because fire insurance does not cover earthquake damage, it appeared that the insurance companies would not be hit hard. Only if the fires spread to buildings relatively untouched by the earth tremor would the underwriters be liable.

In the INA home office that day, seventy-seven-year-old Charles Platt, who had become president in 1878, told his associates not to worry. Reminding them that the company had survived the conflagrations in Chicago and Boston and a half million dollar fire in Baltimore just two years before, Platt said, "We don't intend to let San Francisco frighten us."

A telegram went out to INA's department managers over Platt's signature: "If the entire city is destroyed our surplus and contingent fund will not be exhausted. Our losses will be as promptly paid as they can be adjusted."

About two weeks later Platt sent a statement to the press:

"We have already wired our representatives [in San Francisco] to draw at sight on us to pay every claim proved. This shows how we stand. But, of course, where buildings have been destroyed by the earthquake and not by fire no insurance will be paid. If the building was shaken down and the ruins then swept by fire, a compromise will be reached and a just portion of the insurance will be paid. In the case of buildings blown up by dynamite by civil or military authorities, we are exempted by a clause in our policy, but I think the companies will pay insurance as the buildings were destroyed in an effort to stop the fire."

On the same day Catlin, who was a special agent in INA's Pittsburgh office, was called to Philadelphia and told to go to San Francisco to handle the settlement of claims. He was told to use his judgment and to consult with, and follow the same general practices as, the representatives of "the leading and best companies."

San Francisco: Earthquake or Fire?

INA's policies in San Francisco totaled $3,740,000, but two associated companies also had risks there: the Alliance Insurance Company (more or less a subsidiary, organized in 1904), $1,296,000, and the Philadelphia Underwriters (in which INA had a half interest, having helped to set up the company in 1895), $712,000.

On the day Catlin left for California, INA's home office assumed that the maximum loss for each of the companies would be a little more than half of their total risks there. This was only a guess, of course, for no direct word had yet been received from the San Francisco office.

The day after Catlin left, a wire from special agent J. K. Hamilton arrived in Philadelphia: "Our loss estimated from city premiums about three million. No message from you." Another telegram from him estimated the Alliance's loss at about $600,000.

In Philadelphia astonishment and dismay greeted Hamilton's dispatches. They could only suppose that he was overlooking the distinction between fire damage, for which INA was liable, and earthquake damage, for which it was not.

As Catlin traveled west, other insurance companies, involved in INA's San Francisco risks through reinsurance (i.e., agreements through which the other companies accepted a portion of the risks), began to put pressure on the home office to discourage the company from taking too liberal a position on claims settlements. One company bluntly informed Platt that "this company will pay only such losses as it may be legally liable for," thus excluding "any loss or damage by fire or otherwise, occasioned directly, or indirectly by earthquake or other specially exempted perils."

Most of the other companies which urged INA to be "reasonable" were more subtle. They believed, as Platt and INA vice president Eugene L. Ellison did, that fire damage in San Francisco could not amount to more than half the total toll.

[73]

Perils: Named and Unnamed

The first shock came May 5 in a letter from Catlin written the day after his arrival:

"I find that the earthquake damage is comparatively slight in San Francisco, the great loss being occasioned by fire. We can count upon very little salvage."

Incredulous as Eastern insurance executives were at the news (for representatives of other companies were sending similar reports), they could find confirmation in an eyewitness account by Jack London published in *Collier's Weekly* on May 5. The first two sentences of the famous novelist's article said, "The earthquake shook down in San Francisco hundreds of thousands of dollars' worth of walls and chimneys. But the conflagration that followed burned up hundreds of millions of dollars' worth of property.

"It was dead calm [out on the bay]," London wrote. "Not a flicker of wind stirred. Yet from every side wind was pouring in upon the city. East, west, north, and south, strong winds were blowing upon the doomed city. The heated air rising made an enormous suck. Thus did the fire of itself build its own colossal chimney through the atmosphere. Day and night this dead calm continued, and yet, near to the flames, the wind was often half a gale, so mighty was the suck."

The fires raged through San Francisco for three days. When they finally had burned themselves out, a quarter of a million persons were homeless. Three hundred and fifteen persons were known to have lost their lives and 352 more were reported missing, few of them ever to be found. The inferno had destroyed 28,188 buildings in 522 city blocks, covering an area of more than four square miles. The property loss was estimated at some $400,000,000.

The great destroyer had indeed been fire. After the earthquake, as historian Oscar Lewis has written, "although San Francisco was badly shaken, the damage was not irreparable. Had there been no aftermath of fire, all traces of the

[74]

disaster would probably have disappeared in a few months. . . . The great majority of buildings sustained only superficial damage [from the temblor]."

The lack of water, because of broken mains, was the most important factor in the city's inability to contain the flames, but the insurance companies had every reason to believe the percentage of fire damage would be high. For in their files they had copies of a report from the National Board of Fire Underwriters (to which INA and every other major company then belonged) stating that the congested district of San Francisco was "unmanageable from a fire-fighting standpoint," and concluding:

"In fact, San Francisco has violated all underwriting traditions and precedents by not burning up; that it has not done so is largely due to the vigilance of the fire department, which cannot be relied upon indefinitely to stave off the inevitable."

That report had been written just eight months before the catastrophe. Now "the inevitable" had happened, and Sheldon Catlin, making his way through the tent cities that housed the homeless, sent a message to be put on the telegraph wires in Oakland. The telegram arrived in Philadelphia at nine minutes before midnight on May 6: "Estimate North America [INA loss] $4,400,000 gross, $3,200,000 net. Alliance $1,200,-000 gross, $1,100,000 net. Salvage estimated ten per cent including earthquake."

If that were not sufficiently explicit for the home office, Catlin spelled it out in a following letter. "I understand," he wrote, "there were no buildings of any particular value which collapsed before the fire. Those which did were those of greatest age, poorest construction, and least value."

An INA employee of less than a year, he laid his career on the line in two outspoken sentences:

"There has been generally published a report that the

companies might insist on deducting forty per cent from face of policies for earthquake damage throughout the city. My individual opinion is that any such average ratio would be absolutely unjust to assured."

The telegram and the letter caused consternation in Philadelphia. If Catlin's estimates were correct, the Alliance's liabilities were double its assets; it would be wiped out. Many other insurance companies had sought refuge in bankruptcy, but that was not the INA way—and even if the Alliance were only a sort of left-handed subsidiary, it was still an INA company. So Platt called a meeting of the Alliance directors and they agreed to his proposal that another three-quarters of a million dollars be paid into the company through an assessment. Thus the Alliance could pay its San Francisco losses in full.

The question remained: *Would* INA and its subsidiaries pay losses dollar for dollar, or would it make a standard deduction from the face value of all San Francisco policies?

As many other companies increased their pressure on INA to join with them in resisting full payment, the vice president, Ellison, wrote to Catlin asking him to check with the representatives of "the best companies" to see what they were doing. But Ellison, to his credit, also told Catlin, "We fancy that any company that will refuse to pay for losses [fairly] adjusted . . . will soon be in bad odor."

As the claims poured in on Catlin, who had set up headquarters in a house on the edge of the burned district—a thousand claims were filed within fifteen days of his arrival— he clung to his estimates and to his stand against a cut in payments. He asked the home office to send him two strong men who were expert adjusters. And he continued to throw cold water on any inclination of the home office to overstate damage from the earth tremor.

"The damage by earthquake has, in my opinion, been greatly overestimated in Eastern reports," Catlin said. "From what I have seen as well as from careful investigation from the most reliable sources, I cannot see how there could have been over a ten per cent general damage at the outside. It is to be regretted that I cannot give you more encouraging figures but must, of course, tell you the truth as it appears to me. . . .

"It looks very much as if the weaker companies and even some of the larger companies which have been very hard hit are doing what they can to *maximize* the extent and amount of the earthquake damage . . ."

In a subsequent letter he wrote:

"There are a number of independent adjusters here from the East and it looks as if they were acting under instructions to make as much as possible out of the earthquake damage. I am not trying to minimize the earthquake damage. I wish I could prove it to have been fifty per cent, but I can only report the situation as I believe it to be. Some of the representatives of companies very close to your office entirely disagree with me, whether from disinterested motives or not I cannot say."

But he was able to name five highly respected companies which were paying off in full, or taking no more than two per cent discounts for cash. The companies ("they include some of the best," he conceded) which were deducting a substantial percentage from the face value of all policies were taking advantage of those most in need of money, Catlin asserted in still another letter.

"It is comparatively easy, with those small policyholders who need the money badly, to obtain these reductions by paying immediately," he said. "But when it comes to the larger ones who can resist it they will demand full settlements and I think they will get them. There is simply no doubt that some of the oldest, fairest, and most liberal companies are, in the face of such tremendous losses, adopting tactics which they never used before in order to save themselves."

One can see Catlin at his desk, writing to Philadelphia, determined to stand firm for fair and honest treatment of the policyholders but beset with anxiety about the reception his uncompromising reports were getting in Philadelphia, for he still had received no clear directive. In the absence of orders to the contrary, he began, on his own initiative, paying claims in full "where there are no earthquake or other complications," as a few of INA's best competitors were doing.

Finally Ellison sent what he described as tentative instructions to Catlin, with orders not to make them publicly known. His distaste for publicity was well founded, for what Ellison had in mind was a good deal less than Catlin regarded as fair treatment of claimants. Ellison suggested that Catlin follow the same practice as the representatives of the other companies which were paying only part of the value of each policy. He did not specify what ratio should be used, but many of the companies were deducting forty to sixty per cent. Ellison's justification must have sounded lame even to him:

"It is our duty to our companies to see that our policyholders bear some portion of the burden. We are called upon to make good losses for which we received no consideration from our policyholders, whether they suffered from the earthquake or not."

His reasoning was odd, to say the least.

Toward the end of his letter, Ellison said, "We are not at all fearful of any bad results that may come by reason of compromise settlements." By compromise settlements, of course, he meant partial payment. And if it were true that the company was not afraid of public reaction to this stand, then the company had a great deal to learn about public opinion, as it would soon discover.

On May 31 high officials of nearly a score of insurance companies, including INA, met in New York to agree on a common approach to payments. The meeting resolved that only claims which did not involve any earthquake damage would be paid in full. All others would be settled by "reasonable compromise," a phrase that meant a deduction of between ten and fifty per cent. In a letter informing Catlin of the decision, Ellison, apparently uncomfortable in his own mind about the whole affair, added somewhat apologetically, "We beg to assure you that we have no idea of dealing unfairly with our policyholders. At the same time it is only right that we see that the interests of the company are fairly guarded."

He concluded by asking Catlin if he felt unable to "honorably follow" the meeting's scheme.

While the letter was still on its way to Catlin, the newspapers published and vehemently criticized the resolution, and it immediately became manifest that the public as a whole regarded the plan as an attempt by some insurance companies to welsh on their obligations. Nevertheless, Ellison sent a wire to Catlin eleven days later recommending that one-third be sliced from the value of every policy in "reasonable compromise" cases.

With those instructions in his pocket, Catlin went to a meeting of representatives of 107 companies in Oakland. Men from three companies said their home offices would not agree to go along with any partial-payment plan. Catlin must have longed to join them in their repudiation of any across-the-board deduction, but he was now bound by his orders from Philadelphia. Instead, when a vote was called, he cast his ballot reluctantly with the "shavers," as he disdainfully referred to the partial-payment group. The "shavers" won the vote by a two-to-one margin.

But Catlin had fought for his principles too hard to yield now. As soon as the meeting was over he and two adjusters who had been sent to join him in San Francisco, J. C. Johnston and H. N. Friedley, went together to the telegraph office and sent a wire to Philadelphia, all three signing it. They reported they had voted with the "shavers" but only "under instructions." Then they added, "Our judgment [is] against it. North America [*i.e.*, INA] apparently only solvent company supporting resolution. People here know company solvent and will not accept reduction as they will from others."

This was the first evidence that Johnston and Friedley shared Catlin's strong feelings about the proportion of loss that could be fairly attributed to the earth shock.

No sooner had their telegram arrived in Philadelphia than a reply came by wire from Ellison, saying just what Catlin wanted to read, "We leave this matter in your hands."

At last, thanks to Catlin's stubborn defense of principle over expediency, INA was committed to doing the right thing.

From a public relations point of view, it was too late, however. Ellison had said the company didn't fear the consequences of its cut-rate stand. Now he had to eat his words. Newspapers across the country reported the partial-payment decision of company representatives at the Oakland meeting. Many journals took care to print the names of the companies voting in favor of one-third deductions, including INA, of course. A San Francisco newspaper headlined: "71 Companies [it should have been 61] Will Bunko the Policy Holders— Thus Far Only Thirty-two Insurance Concerns Make Pretence to Honesty."

From every part of the country INA received letters of condemnation. In response to a plea from the head of the company's Western Department, which really covered the Midwest, Platt sent a telegram to the New York *Journal of Commerce* and the *Chicago Record-Herald*, saying that "all reports" that INA "has proposed to settle its San Francisco losses on the basis of a flat reduction of twenty-five per cent, or any other per cent, are untrue." In a word-for-word literal interpretation, what the wire said was true.

In fact, however, INA might very well have gone along

with the proposals of other companies for a percentage cut, if it hadn't been for Sheldon Catlin.

When it was all over, INA had paid claims of $3,260,000 and Alliance, of $1,032,000, figures astonishingly close to Catlin's first on-the-scene estimates.

Catlin, who had been married just a short time before he was sent to San Francisco (he took his bride along with him), was afraid he'd be fired for his highly ethical but expensive stand. Instead, Ellison sent him a $500 bonus. Four years later Catlin was elected assistant secretary and in 1916, ten years after the San Francisco fire, he became a vice president, a post he held until his retirement in 1941.

To this day, San Francisco publications make reference from time to time to the way the insurance companies handled claims in 1906. Twenty-seven companies out of 113 paid in full, many of them taking a one or two per cent discount for cash. INA was one of that group.

6: The Conservative Revolutionary

SHORTLY AFTER Benjamin Rush became president of INA, during World War I, he had occasion to attend for the first time a meeting of the National Board of Fire Underwriters. Walking into the large room, Rush made a circuit of the still-empty room in silence, peering at the portraits of former officers of the board, each painting much like the others—a very elderly man, very substantial and impressive in appearance, dressed in a black broadcloth suit with a heavy gold watch chain displayed across his vest. Finally Rush spoke.

"There are too many gray beards here," he said. "Too many old men."

During his tenure at the head of INA, his own company, despite its hoary past as the first and therefore the oldest stock insurance company, began a revolution that overthrew most of the old ways of life in the entire industry, shaking many of the superannuated standpatters out of the seats of power in which they had been dozing, and fought, virtually singlehandedly, a successful war to break the restrictive bonds of a monopolistic system which INA had helped to bring into being in the first place.

The Conservative Revolutionary

Paradoxically, that upheaval was instigated by a profoundly conservative man, for Benjamin Rush was the epitome of the Old Philadelphian, a member of one of the few truly aristocratic groups in America. As Kitty Foyle's father said in Christopher Morley's novel, "Those folks are so pedigree . . . they hire someone to drive the Rolls for a year before they use it, so it won't look too fresh."

Rush's father, Colonel Richard Henry Rush, raised and commanded the Sixth Pennsylvania Cavalry during the Civil War. The colonel's father was Richard Rush, a lawyer and statesman who had a remarkable record of public service under six Presidents (Madison, Monroe, the second Adams, Jackson, Van Buren, and Polk), and ran unsuccessfully for Vice President in 1828. Beginning as comptroller of the United States Treasury, he served, among other posts, as Attorney General, Secretary of State, Secretary of the Treasury, Minister to London, and Minister to France. Among his major contributions to history were his roles in resolving the boundary dispute between Canada and the United States and in persuading Monroe and John Quincy Adams to proclaim the Monroe Doctrine.

The most notable of all the ancestors of INA's Rush was his great-grandfather, for whom he had been named: Dr. Benjamin Rush, physician, scientist, reformer, philosopher, politician, and government official. A good-hearted, passionate, inventive, well-informed, and able man, Dr. Rush was also vain and opinionated and spent a good part of his life in hot water because of those weaknesses.

Acclaimed by history as the first great American doctor, the Philadelphia-born and Edinburgh-trained physician was a pioneer in humane treatment of the mentally ill, but was so sharply criticized in his own time for his unrestrained enthusiasm for phlebotomy (blood-letting) that he had to sue one of his antagonists for libel; Dr. Rush won an award of

$5,000 as a result of the trial. He founded the first American anti-slavery society in 1774, and what was probably the first joint-stock company, the United Company of Philadelphia for Promoting American Manufacturers, a cotton goods business, the following year.

One of the first American public figures to advocate political equality for women (on health grounds!), he signed the Declaration of Independence and joined Washington's army as Surgeon-General. In 1799 he was Treasurer of the United States Mint. He carried on this distinguished public career, which earned him the intimate friendship of such men as John Adams and Thomas Jefferson, while practicing and teaching medicine. "Every man is public property," he said. "His time and talents—his youth—his manhood—his old age— nay more, his life, his all, belong to his country."

And he lived up to that code.

Dr. Rush's great-grandson was born in Chestnut Hill in 1869 and, for some reason not indicated in the available records, quit school at fifteen to enter business. His first job was office boy with a firm of Philadelphia marine insurance brokers, Curtin and Brockie.

By the time he was twenty-one he was an "average adjuster," signifying not that his work as an adjuster was just average, but that he specialized in marine losses involving "general average." In maritime law, "general average" has to do with "a sacrifice to avert a common peril." In other words, if one shipper's cargo had to be jettisoned for the safety of the vessel, all the other shippers with goods aboard would share the loss.

At twenty-five, Rush was manager of the Curtin and Brockie average adjusting department when he resigned to join INA as assistant to president Charles Platt at a salary of $3,000 a year, a good deal more than his pay at the agency. The extra money meant that Rush could marry a girl from

Stamford, Connecticut, which he did just six weeks after taking the new position.

A short time later INA salvaged a canned-goods shipment, with which it seemed the company was stuck, for all the labels had been washed off the cans. Lunching at a Horn and Hardart cafeteria, as usual, Rush suddenly got an idea. He approached the restaurant chain's purchasing manager and sold the cans.

It would take a good deal more than a clever salvage sale, however, to improve INA's marine results, for that year, Rush's first with the company, the marine line's losses exceeded premium receipts by more than half a million dollars, making it the worst year for marine insurance in the company's history. In later years Rush said that all he could think was, "If this keeps up, I'll be out of a job before long."

Before going to work for INA, Rush had heard that the company was a good resource for reinsurance on poor risks. It occurred to him that if INA were reinsuring poor risks, it might explain a good deal about those huge losses. But determining the facts was harder than one might expect. The plain truth was that INA and other companies simply did not know what types of business were running at a loss.

Marine business was divided into fourteen classifications, eight on the basis of routes, five dealing with kinds of cargo, and one for reinsurance. However, profit and loss figures were not kept by classification, but for all marine policies. There simply wasn't enough information on which to analyze the loss problem.

So Rush, who had been working for INA about eighteen months, started digging into the records of premiums and losses on every single transaction. A clerk in the marine department, Henry W. Farnum, became interested and joined him in the work, and then a nineteen-year-old clerk, Thomas R. Young, was pulled in on the team.

Perils: Named and Unnamed

As the research went on, the three found their regular work was suffering, so they put aside the survey during the day and worked on it every night in the office when everyone else had left. It took weeks, and then months, as the three men, who had now broken the marine business down into 198 categories, went back over the records for the past five years in each category.

The analysis was close to completion when Platt sent Rush to Europe to study marine results there. On his return, Rush said the European marine underwriters were not doing as well as their fire counterparts, but they were showing better results than the American marine insurers because they were skimming the cream of the business. He suggested that, for the time being, INA should virtually abandon marine operations in Europe to devote more attention to marine underwriting in this country.

Now he was able to tell Platt that he had reliable figures that would show how the domestic marine insurance could be made to produce a profit. Platt asked him for a report in writing to be put before the board of directors.

Pointing out that INA's losses were only part of a generally adverse underwriting experience in marine insurance, Rush said one reason for this was the decline of the American merchant marine, since steamships, mostly built abroad, took much of the profit out of sailing vessels. As sailing ships became bad investments, "many owners withdrew from business, others let their vessels down until they were finally lost from neglect, and others knowingly destroyed them in order to collect the insurance money."

Even steamships were not necessarily profitable investments, Rush said, because technological improvements had been introduced at such a rapid pace that obsolescence was hastened, and "many steamers built not ten years ago . . . are of no more value as investments than would be a stagecoach line between Philadelphia and Pittsburgh."

[86]

Another reason was competition. The "enormous profits" which had been made in marine insurance "between the years of 1860 and 1890" (the last profitable year) had brought many underwriters into the marine business, and this multiplication of insurers had brought about "the fiercest competition," manifested in rate wars, a reluctance to resist questionable and even fraudulent claims, and a willingness to go along with "these admittedly vicious conditions" for fear of losing business.

Marine insurance could be made profitable again, according to Rush, if INA's board and officers had "the courage of their convictions to avoid the bad business and to hold fast that which is good."

Rush suggested five remedies:

First: Stop reinsuring good business. INA, he showed, had been losing money by reinsuring good risks, so that other companies profited from them instead of INA. He suggested the company set up its own Reinsurance Account for good risks.

Second: Drop business that was unprofitable "by reason of vicious conditions which we by ourselves cannot reform." If conditions improve in those lines, INA could always re-enter the market. On the other hand, he advocated retaining any type of business "which has become unprofitable solely through a temporary reduction of rates below the paying point, but which otherwise is in a sound, healthy condition." Not only would he keep that business "as far as possible," he "would re-insure it with those companies whose competition is responsible for the reduction in rates," thus giving them "the necessary object lesson as to the unwisdom of their actions."

Third: Extend and improve the marine classification system. Although he didn't say so, he meant to do this by using the categories he had developed in the course of his research.

Fourth: Go after small accounts to a much greater extent than in the past and avoid "the business of all well-organized trusts," because the resources of monoplies "are so great that they have no need of marine insurance, and in my experience they never engage in it except when they know that they can make a profit from their underwriters."

Fifth: Put the preceding recommendations into effect "without haste" but "without delay," and pursue this course "steadily and consistently until the end sought is attained."

The first result of Rush's report was to improve his own profit picture. One month after he submitted the report he was named second vice president in charge of the marine business. Now it was up to him to prove that his plan would work.

"A young revolution . . . hit the office," one of Rush's associates said. The losing petroleum business was dropped. Most cotton and sugar shipments no longer would be insured by INA. Premiums on unprofitable lines were raised by as much as a hundred per cent. The new classification system, with 198 categories, was put into use. Only doubtful risks were reinsured. INA would only accept reinsurance on good risks.

Premium volume for marine business declined twenty-five per cent, but Rush had expected that, since premium volume is really no indication of profit or loss. Any company willing to write any risk at very low rates can build premium volume, but losses will grow faster.

With Platt's steady support, Rush stuck to his guns despite protests from many old customers and even from one or two directors. Rush had warned Platt that it would take five years to prove his plan, and that the first two years would be bad, and he was right about the latter. In 1899 the company's net loss on marine business reached $764,412, but 1900 produced a profit of $241,513, and the following year the marine profit was $360,447.

The 1900 profit was the first in the marine line in six years, and the company continued to enjoy favorable results until the outbreak of World War I.

Model of hand-drawn hose
reel truck was probably made
about 1880 to be used as
salesman's sample.

LEFT: detail of fire engine side from Americus
No. 6 Fire Engine Company of New York
shows motto, "We Lend a Helping Hand."
Fire marks, like those on this page, were
placed on buildings to show who insured them.
ABOVE: fire mark (1752) of the Philadelphia
Contributionship for the Insurance of Houses
from Loss by Fire, usually referred to as the
Hand-in-Hand. BELOW IT: fire mark (1784) of
the Mutual Assurance Company for Insuring
Houses from Loss by Fire, called simply
the Green Tree.

Fire mark of INA issued in 1796 took the place
of the company's first fire mark, which was a
six-pointed star. This mark identified property
insured by policy 447, two buildings in
Southwark, one of them "a factory for staining
paper hangings." Property was owned by
William Poyntell and Samuel Law. INA was
first to insure contents of buildings as well as
structures themselves.

Platt's confidence in Rush was justified. Rush's stature in the company grew steadily. When Platt died in 1909 at the age of eighty, Ellison was elected president, and Rush became senior vice president.

"Rush was an awful tough man to work with," an INA executive, now retired, who first met Rush in 1908, recalled recently. "I felt very close to him and I was devoted to him, but I can't say he was easy to work for. He wasn't.

"Partly it was his manner. He struck many people as being gruff and abrupt. Personally, I always thought that it was just a cover-up for shyness.

"He had an impelling urge to do the right thing. No expedients—they were out the window. Well, usually the right thing to do is the hard thing to do [like Sheldon Catlin's firmness in San Francisco], so Rush's lieutenants were sometimes troubled by it."

That urge to do the right thing fit together so well with INA's tradition of fair dealing with policyholders and claimants that its reputation was greatly enhanced as Rush rose in influence. It was so, for example, in 1912, when 2,340 souls sailed from Southampton, England, on the maiden voyage of the White Star liner *Titanic*, a ship so unsinkable, everybody agreed, that the disbursement (*i.e.*, total loss) insurance was written at a premium of only three-eighths of one per cent. This meant, in the case of INA, that its share of the insurance cover had brought in $187.50 in premiums by April 14, three days before the ship was to have arrived in New York harbor for the first time. That day the *Titanic* struck an iceberg and sank, carrying 1,595 people to their death in the icy waters of the night.

Most of the $5,566,820 insurance on the vessel had been written in England, but INA and one other American company had a very small part of the coverage. INA's share was $50,000, handled by the New York brokerage firm of

Johnson and Higgins. When a clerk at the brokerage house took the policy out of the file there, he saw that it had not been signed by a representative of INA, which meant that it was invalid. Henry Farnum, manager of INA's New York office, telephoned Rush. "Sign that policy immediately and put it into effect," Rush snapped.

Earlier that day—the day the news was flashed to an unbelieving world—Rush strode out of his office to ask one of the marine underwriters, "How much did we have of the *Titanic?*"

"Fifty thousand," he was told.

"Why didn't we have more?" he demanded.

"That's the kind of man he was," Ludwig C. Lewis, who knew Rush, once said. "He was looking at it as an underwriter would have considered it *before* it sailed. It should have looked like a good risk, and he wanted us to write as many good risks as we could. And he wasn't a man to waste time crying over a loss if it had been properly underwritten."

Earlier that year INA had paid a $20,000 claim on the cargo of a tramp steamer, the *Montoswald*, which had sailed from Baltimore on February 20 bound for Hamburg. The ship was never seen again. Some time later the widow of the ship's captain turned over to the London Board of Trade a letter from her husband, which the Chesapeake Bay pilot had mailed for the skipper after seeing the vessel clear Cape Henry, heading into a gale. The letter said:

"My dear Lizzie,

"By this time you will have heard that we are loaded for Hamburg, and no doubt we will come to [Newcastle-on-Tyne, the ship's home port]. I will be glad when we get home; coming to Baltimore I was three days in the ice, and we have had the same thing coming down [Chesapeake Bay].

"I want you to keep this letter as evidence, in case anything happens to the ship, as I wanted the ship dry-docked in New York and the owners would not allow it; as it is now we have twelve feet of water in the forepeak, and we are not out of harbor yet. Goodness knows whether we will reach home or not, but don't expect us any time, as I cannot give you any idea when we are due. We have the sailors at the hand pumps now, so what it will be when we get out of the bay I don't know. . . .

"Your affectionate husband,

"G. Stannard"

The letter prompted an official investigation, as a result of which the owners were compelled to refund the insurance, and new regulations tightening inspections of ship for seaworthiness were put into effect.

Two years later, in 1914, Rush and his daughter arrived home from a visit to Europe. They had left the Continent just in time, for six weeks later World War I broke out. Although history dwells largely on the land war, that was also the greatest naval war the world has known since the Napoleonic wars ended in 1815. Marine underwriters had no experience in modern naval warfare to guide them.

Fortunately, INA's marine policies, unlike those of most other companies, already included a war-exclusion clause, inserted on Rush's orders ten years earlier during the brief war between Japan and Russia. "Not that I thought a general war likely," he explained later. "The truth is I could conceive of no such thing as a general war. Nevertheless, it occurred to me that *should* such a war break out suddenly, it might cost us a million dollars. So I put the clause in."

When the World War did occur, Rush decided that INA, in order to plan its course of action, would have to guess which side was going to win the war. "Without hesitation," he wrote afterward, the company "chose France, Great Britain, and their allies, as much on account of their belief in the righteousness of their cause, as on account of their known maritime superiority."

There was a subjective factor, however, which operated

then and a quarter of a century later, at the approach of World War II. That factor was the admiration and sympathy for the British which Philadelphians generally harbor, evidenced, among other things, by the popularity of cricket there until very recently (three well-known suburban clubs are still called cricket clubs). This Anglophile sentiment was even stronger at INA, for American marine underwriters, as a result of years of friendly business dealings with Lloyd's and other British insurers, feel a good deal of kinship with them.

In the first month of the war, as the New York *Journal of Commerce* reported, "insurance rates [were] chaotic and quotations the highest ever known." Most American marine underwriters avoided insuring German or Austrian ships by quoting inordinately high rates, but none of the companies was able to calculate what the proper rates should be for other vessels. By August 14 the *Spectator*, an insurance journal, was saying, "Practically no [marine] insurance is being written."

On the same date, at the request of top leaders of commerce and industry, a bill to create the Bureau of War Risk Insurance was introduced in Congress, and about two weeks later it became law. Under the act, the bureau was empowered to do what the insurance industry could not dare hazard, insure American ships and cargoes against loss or damage by war if coverage could not be obtained from insurance companies at reasonable rates. The British government offered the same financial protection to vessels flying under its flag.

Drawing on Charles Platt's strategy in the Civil War, INA insured ships departing on voyages along tracks where German surface raiders had recently struck, the company assuming that the predators would be elsewhere by the time the insured vessels got there. The theory worked almost as well as it did in the Civil War. It was not until late in the winter of 1914–1915 that INA suffered its first loss to a German raider. When the sailing ship *William P. Frye*, en route to

England with grain, was captured and sunk by the *Prinz Eitel Friedrich*, INA paid a claim of $10,000.

The event which aroused most Americans emotionally was the sinking of the Cunard liner *Lusitania* off Ireland without warning by a German submarine. There were 1,924 persons aboard, and 1,198 perished, including 63 infants. Among the dead were 114 Americans. INA had a share of the insurance cover; it paid a claim of $21,740, the second loss caused by a U-boat.

In January 1917, Germany announced a policy of unrestricted submarine warfare, and in the next few weeks three American ships were torpedoed, leading to a declaration of war by the United States on April 6. Now vessels were going to the bottom at an increasing rate: 368,000 tons sunk in January, 540,000 in February, 593,000 in March, 881,000 in April. Insurance rates to the British Isles and to the Mediterranean went as high as twenty per cent.

Some American companies withdrew from the marine market, and it was suggested that INA do likewise, but Rush objected. The company's position of leadership would be impaired for years if it withdrew, he said. Besides, it was the company's duty to continue underwriting marine risks when its country was at war. By the fall of 1917 ship sinkings had diminished significantly. The crisis was over.

The fire side was mainly concerned with sabotage during the war. The worst disaster of this kind, caused by German agents, was the explosion of 2,000,000 pounds of munitions in the arsenal of Black Tom Island, New Jersey. Several workmen were killed, and $22,000,000 worth of property was destroyed, INA's insurance share of the loss being $132,000. Enemy saboteurs also were responsible for a munitions blast at Kingsland, New Jersey, which cost the company $76,000. Many years after the war, German reparations compensated INA for those two losses.

During the war, in 1916, Eugene L. Ellison died of a heart attack at his desk. Rush, then forty-six, was elected president to succeed him. John O. Platt, a nephew of Charles Platt, became senior vice president.

A handsome, vigorous patrician, Rush was once described by *Fortune* magazine as a "gentleman with a precise and orderly mind, an exquisite tailor, and a reputation in his business for personal integrity and for being one of the best marine-insurance men in the United States."

On the surface, he appeared to be the antithesis of his illustrious forebear; the old doctor had been one of the founders of what became the Democratic Party; his descendant was a Republican. The ancestor was exuberant, outgoing, reckless, argumentative; the modern Benjamin Rush was restrained, introvert, prudent, diplomatic.

Nevertheless, beneath the reserved shell of the twentieth-century Rush there lingered more than a spark of the eighteenth-century Rush, who, with his friend Ingersoll, as sociologist E. Digby Baltzell has observed, formed a team "often branded" by "their fashionable families and friends" as "radical nonconformists."

The new president of INA, too, had no use for customs and conventions that fettered the present with outmoded ties of the past. INA should be "more concerned with today and tomorrow, than it is with yesterday," Rush once said.

When Rush reached the top of INA, such a man was badly needed, for, although it was a sound, solid company, it was slipping into a slough of stodginess. It was no longer aggressive.

The company's problem was spotlighted very neatly by C. R. Tuttle in a conversation with T. Leaming Smith soon after Rush became president. Tuttle had just become manager of the Western Department with headquarters in Chicago; Smith was a marine underwriter who rose to vice president before his retirement in 1946. Having just come to INA from another company, Tuttle told Smith, "[INA] is considered to be a very well behaved cat. It will eat a mouse if you put it in its mouth, but it won't go across the street for one."

Fortune said the same thing in somewhat different fashion: "[INA] was dignified, cautious by tradition, not given to novelties. It was very High Church as insurance companies go. This was before the gaudiest days of United States salesmanship. A company could still be both High Church and big. But in order to [grow], Rush's company couldn't remain . . . High Church. It had to become Low Church and even evangelical. It had to compete with the evangels of the great era of salesmanship."

But Rush didn't want to throw the baby out with the wash water. He was anxious that INA, despite the modernization that he had in mind, retain the virtues of which its men had always been proud. So he called in the company's men from the field in order to talk with them. He told them to continue making generous settlements, to avoid hair-splitting and technicalities, and to resolve doubts in favor of the insured. "Do the right thing and not the technical thing," he said, giving voice again to that "impelling urge" to maintain the highest standard of ethics, no matter how hard it might be.

To the assembled employees, Rush set forth his philosophy of insurance in nearly the same words he used two decades later in an address to the Newcomen Society:

"The first duty of our organization is to the policyholder rather than to the stockholder; to the body politic rather than to the body corporate; to those who are served rather than to those who do the serving. In fact, the whole insurance machine exists for the benefit of the community in general and the policyholder in particular."

Within that framework, changes had to be made in

INA's operations to keep pace with the times. For World War I made it clear that the United States was now a world power, which vitally affected the insurance industry, and particularly the marine line. And even before the war, the United States had been transformed from an agricultural country to an industrialized society. Economic historians Thomas C. Cochran and William Miller point out:

"By 1893, New England alone was producing manufactured goods more valuable per capita than those of any country in the world." In the manufacture of timber and steel, the refinement of crude oil, the packing of meat, the extraction of gold, silver, coal, and iron, the United States surpassed all competitors.

"America had more telephones, more incandescent lighting and electric traction, more miles of telegraph wires than any other nation. In specialties like hardware, machine tools, arms, and ammunition, she retained the leadership assumed before the Civil War, while her pianos as well as her locomotives had become the best in the world."

That transformation vastly expanded the need for insurance and especially for new types of protection. The insurance industry in the United States and abroad had developed new policies to meet these needs. In 1840 fidelity bonding was introduced; in 1845, accidental injury; in 1864, travel; in the 1880's, public liability; in 1885, burglary; in the 1890's, title and credit; in 1897, workmen's compensation; and in the early years of the twentieth century, that peculiarly American insurance with the contradictory name, inland marine.

Because of a crazy-quilt of state laws and industry self-policing regulations (which will be discussed in the next chapter), fire and marine insurance companies were hamstrung in the kinds of policies they could write. In the closing years of the nineteenth century, casualty companies had arisen to fill the vacuum. At least one major American fire and marine company had set up a casualty affiliate in order to free itself from some of the restrictions hindering the parent company.

Most fire insurance men were contemptuous of the casualty business. Rush himself once said he had heard fire underwriters refer to casualty insurance as "a lowdown business of ambulance-chasing that no decent fire insurance man could be expected to soil his fingers with." But Rush, in whom the pragmatist was always warring with the traditionalist, and winning, took a favorable view of casualty.

In 1920 he decided that INA should have a casualty affiliate. On the recommendation of the board of directors, the stockholders voted unanimously to increase the capitalization of INA by raising it to $5,000,000 (from its previous level of $4,000,000), as the first step. One of three tellers of the stockholders' vote was Alexander J. Dallas Dixon, a grandson of Alexander James Dallas, one of the original shareholders of the company.

The additional money was used to fund a new, wholly owned subsidiary, the Indemnity Insurance Company of North America, which opened for business with a capital of $1,000,-000 and a surplus of the same. The Indemnity specialized in the casualty field: automobile, workmen's compensation, fidelity and surety bonds, public official bonds, contract and supply bonds, lost securities bonds, bonds required by courts for various purposes (such as executors' bonds), burglary, personal accident and liability, and many other coverages.

Because of industry and state rules, each company was limited as to the number of agents it could have in a town. INA, like other large companies, circumvented this rule by building what was called a "fleet" of "pups," or subsidiary companies. The Alliance and the Philadelphia Underwriters had been established at the turn of the century, but INA held only a half interest in the latter. Now INA bought complete control and turned Philadelphia Underwriters into a new entity called the Philadelphia Fire and Marine Insurance Company.

INA also obtained another subsidiary by forming a holding company, the Securities Company of North America, which in turn purchased control of the National Security Fire Insurance Company of Omaha, Nebraska, the holding-company device being used because of legal barriers to one fire insurance company's owning another fire company. Finally, in 1930, INA bought the Central Fire Insurance Company of Baltimore.

Meanwhile, the American merchant marine had grown tenfold during World War I. Peace found the United States a real competitor of Great Britain, for the first time in more than half a century, in the carrying trade. Congress and the Administration wanted to maintain our maritime strength, but that meant the domestic market for marine insurance had to be enlarged and freed from domination by the London underwriters. At the request of the government, Rush and two other marine insurance leaders, Hendon Chubb and William R. Hedge, devised a plan for three American Marine Insurance Syndicates. This fulfilled expectations in providing a market with much greater resources than had been available before.

However, new problems reflecting the postwar disorganization of society and the changing values and mores of the Roaring Twenties arose, most of which are still with us. Theft and pilferage achieved massive proportions. Careless packing and improper handling caused increasingly heavy losses.

Nevertheless, the friendly attitude of our government toward the merchant marine, added to the withdrawal of companies which had suffered losses in marine underwriting, gave stability and growth to the American marine insurance market, and even during the terrible Depression of the 1930's the marine line continued to thrive.

As always, there were losses, some of them spectacular. INA lost $319,000 on the *Caserta* when it ran aground leaving Palermo for New York loaded with silk in 1920. The English Channel was the graveyard of *L'Atlantique*, which burned for a total loss of $11,000,000 in 1933, with INA paying out $240,000.

The most memorable marine loss during that period was a cruise ship that sailed from Havana to New York in 1934. A new luxury liner, it was sometimes called a floating Waldorf-Astoria, although some mariners called it a jinx ship because of a number of minor mishaps. But the skipper said his passengers were "safer here than they would be crossing Times Square." But nobody, not even the captain, was safe aboard the *Morro Castle*.

On the last night of the cruise, September 7, the captain collapsed at the farewell party he was giving for the 318 passengers, and a few minutes later an officer announced that he had died. All further festivities were cancelled. A few hours later, shortly after 2:30 in the morning, the ship's crew discovered fire coming from a port ventilator amidships.

From that point on, matters went from bad to worse. The crew did not know how to contain or fight the fire properly. With a twenty-mile-an-hour wind blowing, the ship maintained a speed of eighteen knots, thus fanning the flames with a forty-one mile wind. The lifeboats were not filled and lowered properly by the crew, and the radioman was not authorized to send an SOS until the fire had destroyed the ship's electrical system, although he was able to get out one message on an emergency transmitter. Fourteen minutes earlier a freighter seven miles away had radioed a query to the Coast Guard: "Any news of a large ship afire off Sea Girt?" Its crew had seen the flames through the foggy night.

When it was all over and the still smoldering *Morro Castle* had beached herself just 100 feet from Convention

Pier at Asbury Park, it was found that 134 persons had perished, most of them by drowning after leaping into the water from the burning ship. INA's men, shaken by such a disaster so close to home, found that their own company's share of the loss on the hull and the tobacco cargo totaled $200,000. They supported the government in its campaign to tighten safeguards and standards.

During the 1920's and 1930's the inland marine line also kept growing. The risks covered by INA indicated some of the changes taking place in American life: the brand-new, streamlined trains, *City of San Francisco* and *City of Los Angeles*, for example, two gleaming beauties that drew people to railroad stations just to see this new thing called streamlining. And there was the Kentucky Derby winner, Bold Venture. And the Holland Tunnel, the first vehicular tunnel under the Hudson River.

Even the biggest single inland marine loss of that period reflected a feature of our society, the fantasy life of the movies, which were at the peak of their popularity (with not a thought to television, now only a little more than a decade in the future) when a fire destroyed motion picture film at the Consolidated Film Industries in Los Angeles at a cost to INA of $180,000.

Casualty insurance for INA was rough sledding at first. In its first fourteen years, the casualty subsidiary managed to lose $8,500,000. A lesser company might have given up, but instead, in 1933 INA brought in an outsider, John A. Diemand, who had long experience in casualty underwriting, to run the subsidiary. He went to work righting things, with the result that by 1935 the Indemnity was earning a profit.

By its very nature casualty underwriting is likely to involve some strange risks. Being a casualty man is like being asked to gamble in high stakes in a different and wholly new game every day. For example, the Indemnity was asked by an airplane manufacturer to insure it against anything, including action by our own or other governments, that might prevent it from delivering eighty warplanes to China. Despite Japan's war with China and the danger that Washington, having passed the Neutrality Act, might enforce it in Asia, the Indemnity wrote two performance bonds for the manufacturer. With this assurance, the aircraft company built and delivered the entire order, the last plane being shipped three months before Pearl Harbor was attacked.

A legal, rather than military, problem was the battle between the radio networks (there was still no television) and the American Society of Composers, Authors, and Publishers, usually referred to by the acronym ASCAP, in 1940. The dispute was over royalty arrangements covering the broadcast use of songs written by ASCAP's members. The two major networks, the National Broadcasting Company and the Columbia Broadcasting System, joined with the National Association of Broadcasters in boycotting ASCAP-controlled songs in setting up a rival organization, BMI (Broadcast Music, Incorporated), which is still, like ASCAP, very much alive today.

The refusal of broadcasters to use ASCAP music lasted for several months, and during this time ASCAP carefully monitored all broadcasts, checking for possible copyright infringement. Advertising agencies, performers, broadcasters, and others needed financial protection against possible lawsuits for infringements, so the Indemnity wrote a policy for a half-million dollars covering such a contingency.

During the interbellum period of two decades, INA, like other companies, was hit by a number of large claims, including five disasters in a single year (1927) and two quarter-million dollar losses in 1934, from the Schenley Distillery fire in Louisville and the Chicago Stock Yards blaze.

But small claims were beginning to add to the company's administrative expenses. One $10,000,000 school district account was divided among thirty-five agents in a Western city, and the agents split the account among fifty companies, one of them INA. When the school board filed a $12 claim for wind damage to a schoolhouse roof, INA's share of the loss (if it can be called that) came to two cents. But it cost INA $7 in labor, stationery, and postage.

The frivolous nuisance claims began to flow in, the first trickle that would turn into a flood inundating every insurance company. For example, one policyholder, garbed in overalls, sat on a lighted cigarette and filed a claim for fifty cents.

But the biggest problem facing the fire insurance business was not the petty claim, expensive and annoying though that might be, but the rigid system that was strangling freedom of enterprise in the industry.

7: Business That Isn't Commerce?

 FOR MOST of the first half of this century, the insurance industry had been an economic fossil. Long after the Sherman Antitrust Act marked the beginning of the end of *laissez-faire* in American life, insurance executives were able to go on doing business in the autocratic, nineteenth-century manner, immune, as few other businessmen were, from the threat of government prosecution.

While the Oil Trust, the Tobacco Trust, and other combinations "in restraint of trade" were being attacked and dissolved in the federal courts, the insurance companies were routinely and publicly regulating competition, fixing prices, enforcing uniformity in coverages, establishing the level of agents' commissions—in short, doing nearly everything the law frowned upon in other businesses.

All of this resulted from a highly improbable decision by the United States Supreme Court.

It began very early. Back in 1819 the Salamander Society was set up by insurance companies to control rates charged to policyholders and commissions paid to agents in New York. By mid-century the insurance companies were beginning to come together in national organizations.

The insurance industry was not alone in this. In many, perhaps most, lines of endeavor the same sort of process was taking place. The "recurrent pattern of nineteenth century business" has been described by economic historians Cochran and Miller:

"Under [price-cutting] pressure [from competitors], weak producers always surrender. Unable long to sell at a loss, they soon go out of business. They either close . . . or sell . . . to salvage what they can for investment in some more promising venture.

"To the perseverance even of the most economical producers, however, continued losses and depletions of capital also set a limit. And when, from the gossip of the trade, they learn that their competitors would also like to put a stop to ruinous below-cost sales, they meet to seek ways and means to end cutthroat practices.

"Competition is thus curtailed or abandoned. Price agreements replace price wars. Markets are divided among former competitors. Trade associations are formed to enforce fair-trade practices, to see that parties to new agreements do not break the rules."

This was monopoly, of course, not in the sense of domination of an industry by one or two giants, but in regard to restraint of trade.

In 1866, twenty years after an abortive earlier attempt, the insurance industry, hard hit by two years of heavy losses followed by a $5,000,000 conflagration that burned a half-mile triangle in the heart of Portland, Maine, organized the National Board of Fire Underwriters, which claimed to be the first national trade association. The founders of the National Board expressed their objectives in a four-point statement:

1. To establish and maintain, as far as practicable, a system of uniform rates of premium;

2. To establish and maintain a uniform rate of compensation to agents and brokers;

3. To repress incendiarism and arson by combining in suitable measures for the apprehension, conviction, and punishment of criminals engaged in this nefarious business;

4. To devise and give effect to measures for the protection of our common interests and the promotion of our general prosperity.

Through the work of the National Board, premium rates rose all over the country, and the insurance companies prospered. Looking back a century later, in the social, political, and economic environment of our times, it is easy to decry those monopolistic practices, but such an attitude oversimplifies a complex problem.

In fact, the industry combinations represented, not greed for bigger profits, but an understandable desire for mere survival. Hundreds of insurance companies collapsed during the last century because wild competition had depressed rates below the break-even point, and every time an insurance company failed, it was a misfortune (and sometimes a tragedy) for policyholders as well as stockholders. An insurance policy is only a piece of paper unless the company is able to pay any claims that may be charged to it; the solvency of insurance companies, then as now, depended on adequate rates, and in the economic jungle of the nineteenth century, the only way to obtain and protect profitable rates was through monopolistic combinations.

Control of industry conditions through insurance company agreements was far-reaching at times. Thirty-seven companies drew up in 1868 a document which came to be known as "the Chicago Compact." It provided that no company would continue to do business through any agent who wrote a fire policy at a rate lower than the National Board's; that no other National Board member company would have anything to do with such an agent; and that any agent who placed business with a non-Board company would be cut off from all business dealings with any Board company.

During some periods local or regional organizations regulated the industry, more or less. To enforce their edicts, the controlling bodies were authorized to examine the books of companies and agencies. Every policy that was written had to be submitted to "stamping offices," which put their seal of approval on the documents if they conformed to rate and coverage restrictions. Because of "public and legislative enmity," in the words of William Hamlin Wandel, the stamping offices later were called "inspection bureaus," an innocuous label that concealed their true function.

At least one regional association even required member companies to submit "all daily reports, endorsements, and cancellations" for examination.

After 1890 this sort of thing was outlawed for almost all industries by the Sherman Antitrust Act, but not for insurance companies. Their immunity went back more than two decades to a curious tangle of circumstances.

In 1868 Samuel B. Paul, who represented four New York insurance companies in Petersburg, Virginia, objected to the large personal bond required of agents for non-Virginia companies. After he wrote a fire policy without filing the bond, he was convicted of violating the state licensing law.

But more was at stake than the license violation of one Petersburg agent. In many states there was growing agitation for laws covering agents and companies. To the National Board of Fire Underwriters, it seemed that Samuel B. Paul's predicament might offer an escape from these state threats.

The National Board paid the expenses for Paul to appeal his conviction to the United States Supreme Court. The arguments for Paul were that Virginia's law encroached on two provisions of the federal Constitution, one granting to the citizens of each state all the privileges and immunities of citizens in the other states, and the other investing Congress with the power to regulate commerce among the states.

A favorable ruling, it was felt, would protect the insurance companies from onerous state laws, especially if a moderate federal act covering the industry could be passed.

By unanimous decision, handed down on November 1, 1869, the Supreme Court held that a corporation was not a "citizen" in the constitutional sense. More important, the court asserted that "issuing a policy of insurance is not a transaction of commerce" and that insurance contracts "do not constitute a part of the commerce between the states."

Not interstate! Not commerce!

The National Board's legislative committee told its companies sarcastically:

"When [the committee members] remember that underwriting owes its inception to the necessities of commerce, and is today one of the principal safeguards and promoters, they feel constrained to admit that the language of the decision, in which it is declared that underwriting is in no sense an element of commerce, is in conflict with the irresistible convictions of common sense.

"Your committee would not, however, bespatter the judicial ermine with suggestions drawn from so humble and unpopular a basis of judgment as common sense confessedly is."

Thus it was that the insurance industry found itself exempt from federal legislation when Theodore Roosevelt led the trust-busters into battle.

In the meantime, the states attempted to break up the restrictive insurance organizations by means of "anti-compact" laws.

"The attacks on control associations have been attacks

on 'the trust' and on any forces antagonistic to the free play of competition," Wandel wrote in his authoritative study, *Control of Competition in Fire Insurance*. "Competition was, and still is in some places, supposed to assure the most economical conduct of the business and to protect the innocent public against excessive rates. In the combination of companies was seen monopoly and consequent excessive rates and profits."

The first anti-compact laws were passed in 1885, and over the years about half the states enacted similar legislation. But by 1944 the anti-compact laws had been repealed in all but two states. The repeal of the state laws can be traced to two causes: the relentless lobbying of the insurance companies and the demonstrated ineffectiveness of the statutes.

The industry associations found many ways to circumvent the laws. When the Ohio law went on the books, for example, the regional organization sent a letter to all agents piously exhorting them to obey the law but warning them that they must continue to maintain the association's rates if they wanted the member companies to continue writing insurance in Ohio.

In Missouri the agents formed an "Underwriters Social Club," with a stamping department, a scheme quickly crushed by the courts, which described it as "a plain, palpable, but bungling pool, trust, agreement, combination, confederation, and understanding, organized to avoid said anti-trust statute."

A popular form of evasion was to pass a resolution that the rules of the organization regulating the industry were "advisory" instead of "mandatory," adding that it was "understood that members are under the same moral obligation to observe such recommendations as if they were mandatory."

Possibly the most common method for handling the problem posed by the anti-compact laws was "one of ignoring, quite deliberately, the statutory provisions," as Wandel, an advocate of rate-fixing associations, put it.

Sometimes, when non-member companies caused a real pinch by their competition, the organization would wage a rate war against its rivals. Thus, resorting to what it called "a little rate fight," the National Board's New England committee was able to drive out non-member competitors in 1875.

With eighty-five to ninety-five per cent of all insurance companies included in the organizations, non-members had very little hope of standing up against such an onslaught.

As time passed, the system became more tightly organized and coherent. By the 1930's the industry was dominated by the Insurance Executives Association, composed of men regarded as "the first rank." (The IEA, in turn, was ruled by its "Committee of Fifteen," presidents of the biggest companies.) Someone had referred to the IEA's rulings as "imperial decisions."

The lines of control radiated downward from this group to the National Board of Fire Underwriters and to similar national organizations for inland marine, casualty and surety, and multiple-location insurance, and four regional associations.

At any level, these organizations had the power to fine, to expel, to give orders regarding almost every external facet of the operation of the business. If a company resigned or was thrown out, it might lose all its agents, for they knew that they could not write policies for any other member company if they cooperated with a non-member. In some lines, a company in the system was forced to agree not to reinsure a company that was an outsider.

Up to this point, the insurance industry could be compared fairly with many of the other combinations in restraint of trade, except that the others began to fade or change in form after the turn of the century.

Monopoly in the insurance industry, however, had two unusual aspects. The first was that the biggest companies did not use their obvious power, as they could have, to grab most of the market and drive the smaller companies out of business. "No one group of companies has a substantial share of the total non-life insurance market," economist Roy J. Hensley reported in a 1962 study of the industry. And another economist, Simon N. Whitney, who carried out a two-volume investigation for the Twentieth Century Fund, found that "at the end of 1955 . . . the four largest fire and casualty companies had only nine per cent of the assets of their industry."

The second peculiarity of the monopolistic structure in the insurance industry was that the companies apparently resisted the obvious opportunity to squeeze exorbitant profits from the public. Between 1921 and 1945 the statutory underwriting profit for the industry never exceeded 7.4 per cent and usually was much lower, even going down into the loss area for ten of those twenty-five years, according to Hensley. Profiteering was not the motive for the tight control of the industry.

The purpose of the system was to throttle competition, and in this it succeeded phenomenally. This tended to discourage ambitious, energetic young men who had an understandable desire to make a name for themselves by bringing in new business. INA's Robert O. Young recalled working in his early days with the company in Missouri under "a gentleman of the old school" who approved of the system without reservation.

"One time I was trying to get some business out of an agency," Young said. "I had made friends with a young lady there and she had promised to transfer all the business of one of our competitors to our company. I came back to the office, quite happy about it, and told my boss. He was quite upset and told me to go back and tell her not to transfer any of this business. We didn't want to get business this way, he said, and we weren't about to take business away from a competitor who hadn't done anything except maybe he hadn't made friends with the right people."

Another incident occurred in Peoria, Illinois, about 1933. After INA assigned field men and technical representatives to evaluate all the properties owned by the Roman Catholic Archdiocese there, the archbishop placed all the insurance with the company.

"Well, it was considered that this was an unethical activity," Young said. "All of our competitors called a protest meeting and kicked us out of the organization for unethical conduct. But I heard that the 'unethical' part of it was not what we did, but the fact that we got in there and did it before we told anyone else we were going to do it. They didn't have a chance to catch up."

The industry organizations had a rule for all occasions, and there was, and is, a plethora of organizations. "Perhaps no business is so addicted to organizations as is insurance," commented Professors Albert H. Mowbray and Ralph H. Blanchard. They pointed out that 151 pages of the *Insurance Almanac* was devoted to listing industry associations, and the list wasn't complete.

The men at the top, in the Insurance Executives Association, had immense power, and they ruled like monarchs in the Age of Absolutism. It was said that on the golf course everyone was expected to step aside to let the president of a fire insurance company tee off first, though other foursomes might have been waiting at the first tee to begin their games.

At one time, when Congressional investigators began looking into the insurance business, a fire insurance president said to John A. Diemand, then president of INA, "Why shouldn't the public accept the edicts and decisions of the presidents of the fire insurance companies without question?"

"And what is so sacrosanct about the president of a fire insurance company?" Diemand asked.

Recalling the incident later, he said, "I thought I was going to get my throat cut."

For INA, the straitjacket of inflexible, intricately detailed rules promulgated by the fire insurance organizations became increasingly irritating, although the company had helped to establish the system in the first place. Its purpose then had been to bring stability into a chaotic situation. Now the pendulum had swung too far the other way, from anarchy to dictatorship.

It was probably inevitable that Benjamin Rush would grow restive, for his background was in marine underwriting, which has always operated in complete freedom from regulation, by government or by the industry. By its very nature marine insurance must have the utmost flexibility, for no two risks are alike, and the underwriters are in constant competition with London insurers who operate without restrictions.

In 1929, nine years after he had established the Indemnity as INA's casualty subsidiary, Rush withdrew it from membership in the National Bureau of Casualty and Surety Underwriters when the organization objected to a revolutionary new automobile insurance plan he wanted to put into effect. A forerunner of the "Safe Driver" plans widely publicized thirty years later, it enjoyed considerable success.

The casualty men of INA, like the marine underwriters, were more independent—"free-wheeling," it was sometimes said—than their fire colleagues, probably because the liability field was still so new.

"The casualty business, with its simpler and more flexible setup, was better adapted to changing conditions," said John O. Platt, whose background was in the fire line. "Less hidebound by tradition, it met its problems better than fire."

As early as 1920 INA indicated its dissatisfaction with the fire insurance bureaucracy by supporting a proposal to let insurance companies, whether fire or casualty, write any kind of coverage except life.

Five years later, in a speech to the Insurance Society of New York, Rush dwelt on "the necessity for a greater flexibility in the rating of each individual risk," which could only be taken as a criticism of the organizational structure in fire insurance, for that was the source of the ratings. Pointing to Great Britain, where uniform ratings did not exist, Rush observed, "Practically no complaint is heard [there] of any unjust rate discrimination—free competition takes care of that, and could be relied upon to take care of a similar situation in the United States."

The use of the phrase "free competition" could be considered nothing less than an act of defiance to the other men who controlled the fire insurance business. To them "competition" was a dirty word. The president of one of the industry regulatory organizations, reviewing the 1929–1934 period, the depth of the Depression, said it "caused some [companies] to forget their obligations and the simplest of the proprieties, engaging in business-getting—I will not dignify it with the name of competition."

Although his company was a member of the controlling inner group, Rush persisted in his appeals for the relaxation of stringent, outmoded rules. In 1932 he said:

"Insurance . . . will attain a higher position in the confidence of the public, in proportion to the measure of the completeness of its service to the public . . . in providing that particular form of coverage which the needs of each individual insured require, as cheaply and with as little red tape as possible. To do this, it must change some of those laws and practices adopted many years ago which are no longer applicable to modern business conditions."

As mild and reasonable as that stand might seem to an outsider, the industry leaders recognized it as an outright attack on what Rush considered to be their standpat attitude.

Finally, in 1939, Rush, then sixty-nine years old, outlined to a conference of the company's field men his opinions about many of the things he thought were wrong with the insurance industry. Arguing that "the whole insurance machine exists for the protection of, and service to, the policyholder," he said, "I am afraid there are still a good many men in the insurance business who allow their own personal and temporary interest to obscure this basic and cardinal fact."

Again, as he had been doing for two decades, Rush called for "multiple line charters" to permit one company to write any kind of insurance, with the possible exception of life. This would be to the advantage of the insurance customer, who would have one policy covering all of his hazards, instead of perhaps a dozen or more policies.

"He would not run the risk (as he now does) of falling between two stools, and failing to protect something on which he desires protection," Rush said. "It would, in the long run, cut down the cost of insurance for him in that it would only require the executive force of one company instead of two as is the case at present."

Agents were ready to accept the multiple-line concept, Rush said, but he added:

"I regret to state that most of the opposition comes from the fire insurance companies and casualty insurance companies themselves. They will tell you . . . that it cannot be done in America, and this in the face of the fact which they know, that it has been done successfully in Great Britain for more than forty years . . . [Their real objection is] that certain officers of the casualty companies and the fire companies feel that they might lose their jobs. As a matter of fact, they won't lose their jobs. They would merely have to have a paymaster with a different name.

"In line with this . . . comes the drawing up of broad coverages in one policy for the convenience of the assured. In Great Britain you can cover most of the hazards that are covered by fire insurance, inland marine insurance, and casualty insurance in one document. . . . Think how convenient this would be to the average policyholder."

Next Rush sharply criticized the insurance companies for "the obstinacy with which they stick to the full coverage standard fire form." Again he made a comparison, drawing on his experience as a marine underwriter:

"In marine insurance, whatever degree of coverage you want, from absolute all-risk policies up to total loss only, you can get, paying the correct rate for each class of coverage. You can get an excess-of-loss policy on any excess you choose—you pay your money and take your choice.

"In the fire insurance business, such a thing does not exist, and most of the fire companies are opposed to it because they feel they would get less premium, which might be true. [But] I do not believe it, because when the assured wants a special form he goes over to the London market and gets it, and that premium would stay over here were it not for the obstinacy with which fire insurance men stick to their present forms.

"How would you feel if you went into a tailor shop to order a golf suit [this was in the days when plus-fours were usually worn by golfers] and the tailor refused to make you any other kind except an old-fashioned frock coat with waistcoat and trousers to match? This is the equivalent case to that taken by the fire insurance managements today."

Inequities in commissions to agents then came under attack by Rush. Life insurance commissions averaged five per cent—a reasonable figure, he felt—and ocean marine commissions ten per cent; but the inland marine commission ran from fifteen to twenty-five per cent; the average casualty commission was twenty per cent; and the fire commission, twenty-two per cent.

To "take one-fifth out of every dollar for insurance protection, and pay it out for the cost of putting the business on your books is too high," he insisted. Such a high cost of acquiring business put a company at a competitive disadvantage and invited "a political investigation of the cost of fire and casualty insurance."

As a solution, Rush suggested commissions "graded on the amount of trouble and expense to which the agent was put to secure and service the business," augmented by a "contingent commission on profits to the agent," which would, he argued, do a good deal "to improve the agent's judgment in the selection of risk."

Finally, Rush turned to loss prevention.

"I will not live to see it," he said, "but I think the time will come (at least I hope it will come) when the largest proportion of companies' expense goes for loss prevention, so that we should really insure against loss. In other words, an insurance policy bearing with it, as it does, the insurance company's prevention service will be a guarantee that no preventable loss can occur. . . . I cannot help but feel that it is one of the biggest opportunities that the companies have in their hands today."

That speech foreshadowed many of the major developments in the insurance field over the following three decades, but few men in the industry, particularly among the leadership, shared Rush's vision, then or later. Instead they noted, with some bitterness, his blunt denunciation of what he deemed their business myopia.

The speech was not quite a declaration of war, but many saw in it an ultimatum for reform.

8: Preparation for the Battle

 BENJAMIN RUSH's blast at the insurance hierarchy was also his swan song. Two months later, on March 16, 1939, he resigned the presidency after twenty-three years as chief executive officer and became chairman of the board, a post created so that the company would not lose his services. John O. Platt succeeded him as president.

During Rush's presidency the company had prospered, despite one of the worst depressions in the nation's history. From 1916, when Rush took the helm, to 1939, INA's capital had increased threefold and its surplus tenfold; annual premium income had risen four hundred per cent and earnings on investment income five hundred per cent. The Indemnity, writing casualty lines, had been organized in 1920 with assets of $2,000,000; now its assets were more than $30,000,000.

"These material gains are outstanding," Platt said at a testimonial dinner for Rush, "but the thing I like to realize with pride and gratitude is that no one has ever been asked to do anything that did not square with his instinctive feeling of fair dealing."

The new president had gone to work for INA in 1891,

as a seventeen-year-old office boy. At the time of the great Baltimore conflagration which destroyed seventy blocks in 1903, Platt was a "special agent," as the job was then called. With two adjusters to help him, Platt cleaned up the company's Baltimore claims in six weeks and returned to Philadelphia with voluminous notes on the ability of various types of construction to resist flames, observations which were later included with those of others in a 130-page study published by the National Fire Protection Association.

Sixteen years after joining the company, Platt became an assistant secretary and three years later second vice president in charge of fire business. Upon the death of his uncle, Charles Platt, in 1916, when Rush was elected president, the younger Platt was made senior vice president. The fire branch continued to be his primary responsibility until he was elected INA's tenth president.

A lean, handsome man, Platt was gentle and dignified. Despite the shyness that made him seem unusually reserved, most of the people at INA viewed him with genuine affection, a reflection of his own courtliness and consideration for others. "I would say Mr. Platt was the most gracious man I ever knew," John A. Diemand later recalled.

(The mother of Geoffrey Stengel, the company's secretary-treasurer at the time of its 175th anniversary, was Platt's cousin, but Stengel did not go to work for INA until long after Platt's death in 1947.)

To a man as diffident as John Platt, the burdens of the presidency of a company like INA must have made every day a trial by ordeal, especially since his immediate predecessor was an executive as aggressive and strong as Rush. There is a company legend, undocumented but apparently well founded, that Rush proposed Platt for president with the private condition that he would occupy the post for only two years. Apparently Rush, in elevating Platt, was expressing both his devotion to the long-dead Charles Platt and his real fondness for John Platt. There were probably days, when perhaps a difficult decision involving personnel had to be made, when the sensitive Platt regarded the post as less of an honor than an affliction.

No man was ever more alive to INA and the part it had played in the country's history than Platt, however. He was once described by *Fortune* as "the chief mouthpiece of [INA] tradition." One day he and Diemand went to one of the annual meetings of the National Board of Fire Under-writers. The speeches they heard "were all pitched to the past glories," according to Diemand; "what we did in San Francisco, in the Chicago fire, the Boston fire, the Baltimore fire."

On the way back to Philadelphia, Platt asked Diemand, "Well, what did you think of that?"

"I'm disappointed, Mr. Platt," his companion replied.

"Why?"

"Because they haven't said anything about the future," Diemand said.

It was one measure of the vast difference between the two men.

In 1941 Platt became vice-chairman, the only person ever to hold that title in the company's history, and Diemand was elected president.

"The night before I was elected president of the company," Diemand said, "[Rush] called me on the telephone: 'Would you come up for a few moments?' I went up and we had a little talk. He was telling me what I should do—never get into a fight with your directors; if you believe in a thing, stick to it; don't get a swelled head.

"Then, leaning over to me, the tears running down his cheek, 'John,' he said, 'remember this is a good company.'

"I said, 'Mr. Rush, we'll keep it a good company and try to make it a better company.' "

In many other companies, the lachrymose scene would have been fantastic, even ludicrous, but not at INA, which has always inspired an unusual passion among its men.

The eleventh president of INA, hand-picked by that old patrician, Rush, represented a sharp break with the aristocratic tradition of the company. Diemand was a self-made man. Orphaned in childhood (his mother died when he was four, and his father when he was six), Diemand had graduated from Girard College, a unique establishment founded by a legacy from the eighteenth-century banker, Stephen Girard, for "poor, white, male orphans."

His first job was with an engineering magazine, but he really wanted to go to work for the Pennsylvania Railroad in its engineering corps. (Years later he would sit across the INA board table from M. W. Clement, president of the Pennsy.)

While he was waiting for the railroad job, a friend who had sold typewriters to Girard College visited him.

"He said, 'Listen, you've got a few days here. How would you like to go down to an insurance company, the Philadelphia Casualty Company, and demonstrate a typewriter?'" Diemand remembered.

"That was February 8, 1904. I went down to demonstrate the typewriter. At the end of the first week I hadn't heard from the railroad, so I went to the head of the insurance company and I said, 'Dr. Keeler, suppose I wanted to stay in this business. Would I have a job?'

"'You've got one now,' he said."

In 1913 the largest company in Europe, the Zurich Insurance Company of Switzerland, which was just starting to do business in the United States, hired Diemand, who by that time was head of the Philadelphia company's claims department, to head the Zurich's claims operation in Chicago. Four months later he was put in charge of Zurich's production (*i.e.*, sales) and underwriting activities in Chicago, and then, a year and a half later, he was transferred to New York and given all the territory east of the Allegheny Mountains. By 1933 Diemand was executive vice president in charge of the Home Indemnity Company.

When Diemand took over INA's casualty affiliate, the Indemnity, in June 1933, the Depression lay like a blight on the land. Fifteen million were jobless. In the past three years, 5,000 banks had failed, wiping out 9,000,000 savings accounts. There appeared little hope for the economy.

And it was up to Diemand to save a company which, by the end of the year, would have lost $8,500,000 in fourteen years, more than $2,000,000 of it in 1933 alone.

The impulse must have been well nigh overwhelming to do something—anything—in a hurry, for Diemand knew that Rush and the board of directors wondered whether the Indemnity was worth saving. Nevertheless, Diemand took no precipitate action. Loading a box full of Indemnity records, he took them to the Maine woods. In September he returned with a plan for rehabilitating the whole casualty operation. Rush told him to go ahead and do what needed to be done.

Fortunately, Diemand had one old friend on whom he could depend, Herbert P. Stellwagen, who had been secretary-treasurer of the National Bureau of Casualty and Surety Underwriters until he joined the Indemnity as an assistant vice president in 1929.

A Phi Beta Kappa alumnus of New York University who had served in the Army in France in World War I, Stellwagen had testified on rates and rating methods before legislative committees in more than half the states and taught insurance courses in Columbia University's extension division. A conscientious, compassionate man given to understatement, Stellwagen was able to enforce discipline without ruthlessness.

As he once told a group of field men, he was not "so constituted as to act the heavy boss." He found "it hard to

get the Simon Legree complex." He added, "We value association on an informal, pleasant basis, and we will continue that
way," although "we are businessmen engaged in an exacting
business." During his long career with INA, he evoked warmth
as well as loyalty from his men.

An experience of Edwin H. Marshall indicates how
Stellwagen was regarded by his men, and why. During World
War II, Marshall, then assigned to the company's New York
office, was given the responsibility for underwriting a new type
of coverage, war risk accident insurance.

"Within a few months we had losses that accumulated
to over a quarter of a million dollars on the book of business
that I was writing in New York, and we had earned premiums
of about $25,000," Marshall said, "so at that point we had a
1,000 per cent loss ratio. Well, I was an underwriter responsible
for making a profit, but here I am losing money faster than
you can imagine. And sweating it.

"So one afternoon, when Mr. Stellwagen was visiting
my boss in New York, I walked over to them and described
the figures on the business, which I am sure they were aware
of as well as I was. I expressed my dismay and asked, 'What
do I do now?'

"Mr. Stellwagen, without batting an eye, said, 'Take the
rubber bands out of your knees, Marshall, and go back and
write more of the business.'

"It was characteristic of the courage and foresightedness
of the man. He'd made a decision and this was a field of insurance that he felt we could find our way in. Naturally, he
knew that fortune could go against us at first, but not in the
long run, for the decision was sound. And he knew that here
was a young underwriter who needed reassurance that management was behind him, that the world wasn't collapsing on
him."

At the time Diemand assumed the leadership of the

Indemnity, part of that company's trouble was that most of the responsible executives, with the exception of Stellwagen, had fire, rather than casualty, backgrounds. As Stellwagen put it:

"Casualty insurance people had to deal with deferred liabilities; fire people dealt with losses easily measurable and easily settled, physical damage which could be ascertained. In such casualty claims as bodily injury cases, whether automobile or other liability—indeed, in workmen's compensation—cases could not be resolved for many years, and so we casualty men were accustomed to consider the setting aside of reserves for our losses as being paramount in our minds."

But the man who headed the Indemnity before Diemand, being a fire man, did not comprehend the need for unusually large reserves, and neither did Rush, who had been trained in the marine end.

"When the Depression hit," Stellwagen explained, "we found ourselves under-reserved as to losses. So we began to pay for dead horses, as we say; as we went on, we found that cases reserved for $1,000 cost $20,000 when they were settled, and so on. I fear that Mr. Rush thought that was deliberate and willful mismanagement, whereas it was ignorance of the true situation."

The saying that "a new broom sweeps clean" was not very applicable to Diemand's reform of the Indemnity, for there were very few dismissals, although two or three men were fired. One manager of an out-of-town office was found to have contributed to the failure to maintain proper reserves; because he had a contingent commission on his profit, he "influenced the reserves downward" in order to show a profit. Reserves cannot be counted as profit until the claim (if it is less than the reserve) is paid, so higher reserves meant lower profit figures.

As a result of Diemand's new ways of doing business

—cutting loose from unprofitable risks, adding more profitable lines, eliminating waste—the Indemnity finally showed a profit for the first time in 1935, just a year and a half after the new boss took over. No new money had been put into the company; Diemand had to work with what he found at hand.

The Indemnity remained out of the national casualty bureau. Ironically, it was only a matter of months after Stellwagen left the casualty bureau in 1929 to work for the Indemnity that his company resigned from the organization.

A few friends sent him letters protesting the decision, and some anonymous person mailed him a clipping of an insurance journal article reporting a speech he had made; across his picture the unknown correspondent had scrawled a phrase imputing canine antecedents to Stellwagen. One insurance company in another state, which had provided surety bonds required for the Indemnity to do business in that state, cancelled the bonds. Another company made a special effort to woo away the Indemnity's most valuable agents. But most of Stellwagen's casualty colleagues in other companies remained friendly.

Although the casualty underwriters were more flexible in their types of coverage than the fire insurance men, Diemand and Stellwagen did have at least one brush with the rest of the industry. It had been the custom in all casualty companies to write a separate policy for every bit of public liability protection bought by a policyholder.

"Mr. Stellwagen and I decided that was a lot of hokum," Diemand said. "We would write a blanket cover. Well, we did, and some of the casualty boys visited me and wanted me to withdraw it because, they said, I was just making it easy for the mutuals. As a matter of fact, we figured we were taking business away from the mutuals by that act. We got away with that all right."

Diemand had been at the Indemnity only about six months when Rush tested him. At the time, Diemand was changing the Indemnity's reinsurance agreements with the London underwriters. Representatives of the London brokerage house came to Philadelphia and Rush sent for Diemand.

"John," he said, "I want you to cancel all those arrangements you are making."

"Now, wait a minute, Mr. Rush," Diemand protested, as he launched into an explanation of what he was doing and why:

"We are getting it at less commission and so on. Everything is met."

Rush listened, then said, "That's all right with me. Now go ahead and do whatever you want to do."

When Diemand moved into the president's office, Stellwagen became executive vice president of the Indemnity. He remained in charge of INA's casualty business until his retirement in 1963, at which time the board of directors declared in a resolution: "He has made great contributions to the progress, stature, and reputation of [the company]." The resolution said Stellwagen "had earned the respect and affection" of everyone "for his integrity, his wisdom, his understanding, and his leadership." After 1963, Stellwagen continued to serve INA as a member of the board.

The marine business, after Diemand's elevation, remained the primary responsibility of vice president T. Leaming Smith, backed up by G. Brinton Lucas, who rose from secretary to vice president in 1943. To them fell a large share of the company's involvement in World War II, which will be described in a later chapter.

The most sweeping changes occurred in the fire branch during the transition from Rush through Platt to Diemand. In 1940, during Platt's presidency, vice president Sheldon

Catlin of San Francisco renown, retired, and this line of business became the responsibility of vice president John Kremer, whose great-great-grandfather, Simeon Toby, was president of INA's first competitor, the Insurance Company of the State of Pennsylvania.

The most far-reaching personnel change in the fire line occurred in 1943, when Bradford Smith, Jr., was elected vice president in charge. A native Philadelphian, Smith attended Dartmouth in 1923. After going to work for INA in 1929, he was elected an assistant secretary in 1936 and fire secretary in 1940.

In the years that followed, Smith would be the company's field general in the front lines during its war to revolutionize the industry. And when that war was largely won, he would undertake equally revolutionary changes within the company itself, transforming it from top to bottom, molding it into a progressive organization utilizing the latest technological advances in order to meet the challenge of a changing America.

None of this could be foreseen in the industry, or even in the company, at the beginning of Diemand's presidency. At that time the man who tended to attract the most attention, after Diemand himself, was one of the most colorful and controversial men in the company's history, Ludwig C. Lewis.

"Wig" Lewis was perhaps best described by one of his critics as "that difficult and dynamic man who did a great deal for the company." Short, stocky, with the scrappiness, quickness of mind, and restless energy of a terrier, Lewis was wont to say he wasn't engaged in a popularity contest, and he acted as though he believed that profoundly. He once told of a meeting that he and Francis F. Owen, INA's resident vice president for the West Coast, had with the president and vice president of another insurance company.

"The difference between you and me," Lewis told the other company's vice president in his usual blunt fashion, "is that when I say I'll do something, I do it; when you say you'll do something, you may do it."

"My God!" the tactful Owen groaned, according to Lewis' account.

To his admirers as well as his critics, "Wig" was "a character," a vivid personality that some could never forget and others never wanted to forget.

"How many people come to the office in a leather vest— you know, one of those comfortable vests with shotgun-shell buttons?" one who remembered him fondly asked. "Well, that's what 'Wig' did whenever he felt like it.

"And how many people, when they make martinis, would set up five glasses, pour gin in four of them and vermouth in the fifth, and then dump it all in the shaker?

"Everything he did was a little bit different from the way anybody else would do it."

His mind raced along at such a pace that his tongue and his pen simply couldn't keep up with it, so Lewis tried to boil down his thoughts into an abbreviated form to save time. The result was that most people found him incomprehensible at least part of the time.

" 'Wig' always sat down and started in on you as though you knew what he was talking about," Diemand said. "When he'd begin talking away a mile a minute, I'd say, 'Wait a minute, "Wig." You're in the middle of it. I want to hear it from the beginning.' "

Obviously it was easier for the president to do than for one of Lewis' subordinates. INA men around the country got used to receiving long-distance telephone calls that left them bewildered. One day an executive in one of the company's Western offices picked up the phone and heard Lewis' voice.

"That stuff coming through OK, fellow?"

"I still don't know what he was talking about," the field man confessed fifteen years later.

Another executive bumped into Lewis in an elevator at the head office. Lewis turned to him and barked, "That fellow can't do that, can he?"

"Damned right he can't," his startled associate replied, not having the foggiest idea whom or what the conversation, if it could be called that, was about.

"Good!" Lewis said.

Even when it was clear what Lewis was talking about, he could be enigmatic. One executive who was being hired tried to tell Lewis about his background and experience.

"We know more about you than you know about yourself," Lewis declared.

"I still don't know what he meant," the man said twenty years later.

Another executive hit on one method for catching up with Lewis' speeding mind.

"After 'Wig' gave me directions I found confusing," he explained, "I would stop in to see Mr. Diemand for a chat about things. Then it would all become very clear because I realized that Diemand had told 'Wig' what he wanted done, and 'Wig' had been trying to tell me. It just didn't come out the same way when 'Wig' talked in that shorthand fashion of his. I would do what Diemand wanted done and 'Wig' would say, 'That's great.' He'd recognize it."

Lewis was all drive. He couldn't sit still and quietly converse; he had no small talk.

In "Wig's" life, there were two loves. The first was his wife, a woman of considerable charm, with a mind as keen and quick as his own. She was confined to a wheelchair for many years by chronic illness, and even Lewis' most severe critics found his devotion to his wife touching.

His other love was the company, whose welfare occupied his busy mind night as well as day. It was not uncommon for an executive to receive a telephone call in the evening from Lewis, to discuss a business problem. This could be vexing to a man who wanted to relax with his family and forget the tensions of the day. The solution hit upon by one executive was to say to Lewis, when he telephoned, " 'Wig,' I have just had two martinis, and I don't think I should talk business."

"All right, my boy," Lewis would say, understandingly, and hang up.

Although Lewis was a martinet who despised mediocrity, he could be compassionate and forgiving about human errors, whether they occurred in a man's business activities or his personal life, if the man honestly acknowledged his mistake. But he loathed alibis.

"If you went in and tried to weasel out of a mistake," an associate recalled, "he was absolutely intolerant, absolutely unforgiving as long as a man would not face up to what was going on."

In his singlemindedness about the company, Lewis was regarded by some as unnecessarily harsh in his dealings with people. But he always backed up his men with the same loyalty he expected of them.

He had a deep feeling about the responsibility of the company to its employees. For example, one man in the field suffered terrible burns when his hotel bed caught fire, probably from a cigarette carelessly dropped. Lewis learned that the man had been drinking and came to the conclusion that perhaps the man's job contributed to the tensions that made him drink. Therefore, Lewis insisted that the company was liable for all of the man's medical and other expenses for the rest of his life. The man underwent a series of plastic surgery operations which cost the company thousands of dollars beyond the ordinary expenses of caring for a person totally disabled.

On the other hand, Lewis could be sharply cutting in

his criticisms of people, even when others were present. As a group of men left Lewis' office after uncomfortably witnessing the dressing-down one of their number had received, somebody threw an arm around the man's shoulder and said, "welcome to the club."

Unquestionably, as Diemand put it, " 'Wig' had his idiosyncrasies."

Ten years after Lewis' retirement, a senior executive, looking back, said, "He kept us all on our toes and stirred up. He didn't let people sit back and put their feet on the desk and snooze."

"He was a difficult man to work for, in many ways," another concluded, "but he certainly taught us a tremendous discipline. If you came through it, you were a very special person. As for his impact on the company—well, I think, as many do, that his contributions were unique and important."

A member of an old Philadelphia family which had at one time engaged in the China trade, Lewis dropped out of the University of Pennsylvania to go to work for INA in the marine department in 1909. After serving in the air arm of the Naval Reserve in World War I, he began to concentrate on inland marine business, which he built over the next two decades into a major revenue-producing branch of the company.

From coverage of goods in transit by rail, the company moved in the 1920's into the growing movement of freight by trucks. Between 1920 and 1928 Lewis was able to double premium volume. Bridges were insured beginning in 1925, and so were all manner of things having nothing whatever to do with matters marine, ocean or inland: jewelry, for example; trophies; race horses; works of art; and merchandise being purchased on the installment plan.

In 1931 Lewis and executives of four other companies took the lead in organizing the Inland Marine Underwriters Association "in recognition of the need for sounder methods and reasonable uniformity of contracts," as one insurance text puts it.

Actually, the success of inland marine, in other companies as well as INA, had brought the wrath of the fire and casualty companies down on the heads of the marine underwriters. This might have been predicted, for inland marine policies cut across the rigid walls that had hitherto divided the insurance business into fire, marine, and casualty.

As Bradford Smith, Jr., put it in an address in 1953, the "broad and realistic" inland marine policies satisfied a public need, by offering all-risk protection "as distinguished from the traditional named-peril method for a cash value determined at the time of loss." Moreover, "a host of special [inland marine] coverages" were offered, "all outside of the underwriting imagination of fire and casualty underwriters who were limited in their view and scope by their training and background, by the rules of their own trade associations, and, to a considerable extent, by law."

To make matters worse, from the point of view of the fire and casualty men, marine underwriters writing inland marine contracts had far more freedom in setting rates. As fire premiums fell off during the first years of the Depression, complaints about inland marine encroachments were lodged with the state insurance commissioners, as a result of which the three branches of the industry appointed a group to study the problems.

The group emerged from its deliberations with a "Nationwide Definition and Interpretation of the Insuring Powers of Marine and Transportation Underwriters." To enforce the Definition, the industry in 1933 established a "Joint Committee on Interpretation and Complaint."

An immediate result of these developments was that Lewis' inland marine business had to turn over $1,000,000 in premiums to the fire and casualty divisions of the company, scarcely the sort of thing to make a man of Ludwig Lewis' temperament think well of the way the insurance industry had compartmentalized itself.

About that time Lewis and Diemand, who had just moved into the top post at the Indemnity, were introduced. "I'll never forget my first meeting with him," Diemand chuckled many years later. "He said, 'What good did the Indemnity ever do this organization?' And I said, '$7,000,000 or $8,000,000 worth of loss, that's what it did. And you know why.' "

On that apparently inauspicious note began an increasingly close association of the two men.

As Diemand's star rose, so did Lewis'. In 1940, when Diemand was elected to the board of directors in preparation for his elevation to the presidency the following year, the company decided to abolish the Western Department, which covered the Middle West from Chicago. The Eastern Department had been eliminated in 1926 and the Southern in 1932, but everyone dreaded the shutdown of the Western Department, for it was ruled by C. R. Tuttle.

An autocrat of the old school, Tuttle (known irreverently throughout the company as "King Tut") had built the Western department into a satrapy that was nearly autonomous. To go to Chicago and tell Tuttle that his domain no longer existed was a task so formidable that nobody wanted it.

"Who did Mr. Rush indicate was the man—of this whole big organization—to go out there and tell Mr. Tuttle that we were disbanding his Western department?" Diemand asked.

" 'Wig' Lewis, of course. 'Wig' was assigned to do that job, and the job was done. It took a fellow with a great deal of muscle, and 'Wig' did it. And out of it some awfully good men were placed in positions where they could grow, an advantage denied to them under the previous type of management."

Elected a vice president in 1937, Lewis retained that title after Diemand became head of the company.

"I didn't make him an executive vice president," Diemand said, "but he had all those powers, plus."

Lewis became Diemand's "great lieutenant." As one associate put it: "There can be greatness in a lieutenant and of a different variety than that of the chief. 'Wig' had the guts to do what had to be done. His greatness was in interpreting and carrying out Mr. Diemand's ideas, in getting things done. Many of the things that were done were accomplished against the resistance of many people in this company, who were not used to the new concepts and didn't want to change. 'Wig' saw that it got done."

Sweeping changes were coming, and Diemand now had a top management team that was in tune with them. The Insurance Company of North America had often been referred to by some of its liveliest competitors as "the sleeping giant."

Now the giant was about to awaken.

9: The World Turned Upside Down

THE TRAIN of events that led in the end to an overwhelming upheaval in the insurance industry began in the mid-1930's, and it was started by a handful of insurance executives who were, ironically, devoted to preserving the network of organizations that tightly controlled the insurance industry.

Before they were done, these men, none of them INA representatives, plunged the industry into a scandal that had national repercussions.

The affair had its genesis in 1929, when the state insurance superintendent of Missouri tried to prevent a rate increase and the companies obtained an injunction preventing state interference with the new rates. Pending outcome of the litigation, the federal court ordered the excess in premiums impounded; by 1935 this fund amounted to about $9,500,000. A separate hoard of nearly $2,000,000 was impounded by the state court in a related action.

In 1935 the impounded funds were still being held, so an insurance executive in Chicago, working through a St. Louis insurance agent, offered a $750,000 bribe to Thomas J. Pendergast, the one-time saloon bouncer who had risen to become political boss of Kansas City, Missouri. It was agreed that Pendergast would see to it that Missouri's new insurance superintendent, R. Emmet O'Malley, a Pendergast henchman, signed a "compromise" settlement of the dispute under which the impounded funds would be released, eighty per cent going to the companies and twenty per cent to the policyholders.

Few of the 122 insurance companies that had an interest in the impounded funds knew about the bribe. They had simply been billed by the Chicago insurance executive for expenses in connection with the litigation. As one biographer of Pendergast later put it, "The insurance executives simply made out a check to their trustee for some necessary expenses, and what he did with it was his business."

Nobody cares more about maintaining a reputation for rectitude than an insurance company executive, and officials of the companies which had become unwittingly involved in the scandal were probably more stunned and upset than anyone else when they learned about the affair after it had resulted in a federal investigation. The companies assisted in the inquiry by persuading the St. Louis man to divulge the whole story to a grand jury.

In the end, all of the impounded money went to the policyholders, by court order, and the companies were fined. Pendergast, who had received his last bribe payment on April Fool's Day in 1936, went to prison in 1939, and so did O'Malley, both of them having failed to pay income taxes on the bribe money.

The case attracted an enormous amount of publicity, none of it good for the industry. But it was only the beginning.

As one might have expected, the Missouri authorities took a somewhat jaundiced view of the insurance industry for the next few years. Its operations were scrutinized with unusual zeal and increasing frustration. Finally, in 1942 Attorney General Roy McKittrick of Missouri went to Washington with a complaint. Despite his state's antitrust law, he said, fire insurance companies were still fixing rates, and there didn't seem to be much he could do about it, partly because most of the companies' home offices and almost all of the "advisory" organizations that controlled the business were located outside the state.

Attorney General Francis Biddle and his trust-busting aide, Thurman Arnold, agreed to test the decision the Supreme Court had rendered seventy-three years before, that insurance was not interstate commerce.

About the same time, a hotel and a department store in Georgia protested to the Department of Justice that they were unable to buy fire insurance at competitive rates. The government decided in its test case to move against the industry organization covering Georgia and five other Southern states. This was the South-Eastern Underwriters Association, to which INA and 197 other companies belonged.

The SEUA had long been a bone of contention in the states where it had jurisdiction. As early as 1915 the governor of North Carolina told the legislature:

"The rate of insurance which the people of the state must pay and the rules regulating the insurance business are now fixed by the South-Eastern Underwriters Association. This monopoly controls the insurance of the South. There is no competition."

And in 1928 a special commission appointed by the governor of Virginia to investigate insurance rates asserted:

"The state of Virginia in fire insurance rates is at the mercy of the South-Eastern Underwriters Association, located at Atlanta. . . . There is no competition in insurance rates in this state. . . ."

The indictment returned by a federal grand jury in 1942 made a number of specific charges against the SEUA and its member companies. They controlled ninety per cent of the fire insurance and "allied lines" sold by stock insurance companies in the six-state area. Premium rates and agents' commissions were set by the SEUA. To enforce the rules and to compel customers to buy only on SEUA terms from member companies, the group employed boycotts and other forms of coercion and intimidation. Reinsurance, essential to small companies and important even to large ones, was denied to non-member companies by the members. An agent who persisted in representing a non-member company was almost certain to lose the right to represent SEUA concerns. Even customers who bought from non-SEUA companies were threatened with boycotts.

The government concluded its accusations by charging that inspection and rating bureaus, as well as agents' associations, had been drawn into the conspiracy.

INA and a few other companies which had been trying to break through the straitjacket of industry restrictions might have been expected to hail the government's action. Instead, they joined in the legal defense: the INA board authorized the contribution of funds to help meet the legal expenses, and president Diemand served on the committee of the Insurance Executives Association which selected the lawyers who would fight the indictment.

There were probably two reasons for this reaction. First, like everyone else in the industry, INA saw the possibility of chaos if a successful prosecution resulted in the elimination of the right to make rates through rating organizations on the basis of the combined experience of all companies. Second, they were shocked and angered by the fact that the government had obtained a criminal indictment instead of filing a civil case.

("To think that it was done by a Biddle!" one old Philadelphian on INA's staff exclaimed incredulously. And the company's general counsel, Edward M. Biddle, managed to write a lengthy discussion of the case without ever mentioning the Attorney General's last name, despite several references to that Main Line apostate.)

Even the Attorney General saw some justification in the industry's indignation at being accused of a crime. "I think it is pretty hard on insurance companies," Francis Biddle told a joint Congressional subcommittee in 1944, "that after seventy-five years of the government's not taking any action, their activities should now suddenly be declared criminal; and, therefore . . . we would consider filing bills in equity rather than criminal procedures, so the companies would have an opportunity of amending their practices, because it would be unfair to send a man to jail for something he considered legal."

The mood of the industry leaders was best described by *Fortune*: "The great men of the fire and casualty insurance business are, without exception, unspectacular citizens who rarely get their names in the newspapers, never if they can avoid it.

"None but the *crème de la crème*, the real churchgoers of the fire insurance business, were brought up on the Washington carpet. They couldn't have been more surprised if they had been arrested on suspicion of being Episcopal vestrymen."

The indictment, the magazine went on, "for conspiratorial practices in which they had openly and even piously engaged" for so long gave this industry the impression of "a world turned upside down."

Nevertheless, bolstered by the memory of all the previous Supreme Court rulings on insurance, the SEUA offered only one defense: insurance was not commerce, and therefore insurance companies were not required to conform to the Sherman Act's standards of business conduct.

The federal court in Georgia agreed with this argument. Dismissing the indictment, the district court held:

"If there is to be any overruling of the long line of clear and thoroughly considered decisions of the Supreme Court, acquiesced in for seventy-five years by Congress and administrative agencies, it will have to be done by the Supreme Court itself or by Congress."

But the matter did not end there. The Department of Justice appealed the lower court's ruling to the Supreme Court.

Now the industry, although it had every reason to expect another favorable ruling on the basis of past decisions, grew uneasy. After all, times *had* changed, even if the structure of the industry gave little indication of it. President Franklin D. Roosevelt's New Deal administration had been in office for nearly a decade, and it had wrought many transformations in American life, most of them apparently irreversible.

Since 1932 Prohibition had been repealed; a system of federal insurance of bank deposits had been established; the National Labor Relations Board had been set up to adjudicate collective bargaining disputes; farm prices had been propped up by federal support; the Securities and Exchange Commission had been called into being to govern transactions in stocks and bonds; the Tennessee Valley Authority and the Rural Electrification Administration had put the government into the power business, and the Social Security Act, into insurance —the list seemed endless.

Then, too, the New Deal, midway through Roosevelt's second term, had suddenly gone in for trust-busting as no previous administration ever had done, not even the first Roosevelt's. In the five years after Thurman Arnold's appointment to the Department of Justice in 1938, he instituted forty-four per cent of all the anti-monopoly actions undertaken by the government in the half century since passage of the Sherman Act. He was obviously not an opponent to be underestimated.

Finally, the Supreme Court itself had changed. Traditionally conservative, the court had struck down so much legislation by 1937 that President Roosevelt had made an ill-advised and unsuccessful attempt to "pack" the court, whose justices had been tagged "the nine old men" by two newspaper columnists. Despite the failure of Roosevelt's plan, the court had shifted from a conservative majority to a liberal majority which had proceeded to give judicial assent for the next five years to the legislative foundations of a reorganized American society.

Could this reform-minded court be depended upon to maintain what more than one legal authority described as the "legal fiction" that insurance was not commerce?

Anxious industry leaders thought they'd better play it safe by taking the matter out of the hands of the court. At the urging of the industry, identical bills were introduced in both houses of Congress. Both measures became known as the Bailey-Van Nuys bill, after the Senate sponsors. It declared the intent of Congress that regulation of insurance remain within the control of the states, and that none of the antitrust laws was applicable to the industry.

On June 22, 1944, the House passed the bill by a vote of 283 to 54, or better than a five-to-one margin. The lopsided vote reflected intense pressure on Representatives from insurance agents and companies in their constituencies, for the industry now was in a state of near-panic, and with good reason.

Two weeks earlier the Supreme Court had reversed the decision of the lower court and thus had overturned the precedent established in the previous century in *Paul v. Virginia*. Now the court, bowing to common sense, reality, and the twentieth century, acknowledged that insurance was indeed commerce.

"No commercial enterprise of any kind which conducts its activities across state lines has been held to be wholly beyond the regulatory power of Congress under the Commerce Clause [of the Constitution]," the court's majority opinion observed. "We cannot make an exception of the business of insurance."

The spokesman for the majority, Associate Justice Black,

said there was nothing in the Sherman Act to indicate that Congress did not intend the law to "exercise its power over the interstate insurance trade." Recalling that the law had been passed at a time when trusts and monopolies "were the terror" of the day, Black said that "combinations of insurance companies were not exempt from public hostility against the trusts," as demonstrated by the numerous anti-compact statutes of that period.

The minority opinion (the justices had divided four to three) argued that insurance had an effect on interstate commerce that would permit federal action, but Congress had never intended to apply the antitrust laws to an industry that was, by Supreme Court decree, not interstate commerce at all.

In the confusion that erupted after the decision was handed down, one of the few calm and practical comments came from an industry trade journal, *Best's Fire and Casualty News:*

"Insurance is now commerce, the rules have been changed, and it is up to the insurance business to adjust itself to the altered situation with as good grace and as great benefit to itself as it can. . . . The insurance business has always been able to adjust itself to changing conditions and we see no reason why it will not successfully meet the various contingencies of the present altered situation."

Most of the industry took quite a different attitude. After the first few days of stunned disbelief, the reaction was a stubborn refusal to accept the new political, social, and economic environment—the modern world—into which the insurance business had been unwillingly plunged.

A committee appointed by the National Board of Fire Underwriters saw in the decision not only a threat to "insurance specifically," but also to "our theory of government generally." Insisting that the ruling had to be nullified by enactment of the Bailey-Van Nuys bill, by reconsideration of the case by the Supreme Court, or even by Constitutional amendment if need be, the National Board's group said the aim of any action had to be "to return us . . . to the law which existed prior to the South-Eastern decision."

A similar committee of the Association of Casualty and Surety Executives also favored steps "to restore the *status quo ante* to the fullest extent possible." Warning of chaos and rate wars if the decision stood, the ACSE body conceded:

"Practically our whole structure of rates, uniform policies, and commissions is condemned by the antitrust laws."

Spurred by the industry, forty-one state insurance commissioners petitioned the Supreme Court for a rehearing of the case. The request was turned down.

On the legislative front, the industry suffered another defeat. The Senate, always harder to stampede than the House, let the Bailey-Van Nuys bill die without voting on it. Senate critics of the bill had asserted that it was class legislation designed to perpetuate "combinations of insurance companies to coerce, intimidate, and boycott competitors and consumers."

Nevertheless, all was not lost. That arch fiend (in the eyes of the industry), Attorney General Biddle, as it turned out, was the source of hope. Biddle said:

"I have not asked, nor has anybody in the Department of Justice considered, taking any action against any insurance company or group of insurance companies until the states have had an opportunity to consider to what extent they may wish to amend their laws, or until the Congress . . . has had a full opportunity [to decide if it] wishes to amend a federal statute." Biddle promised to give everybody ample time to "take such action as they might deem appropriate."

The result was federal legislation that did not restore the *status quo*, but did leave regulation of insurance in the hands of the states. The McCarran-Ferguson Act, usually called Public Law 15 (its number in the Seventy-ninth Congress), gave the states three years to pass laws to bring the industry under effective control. After that time the federal antitrust laws would apply to the insurance industry only "to the extent that such business is not regulated by state law."

However, one aspect of the Sherman Antitrust Act would continue to bear on the insurance business permanently —the prohibition of any "act of boycott, coercion, or intimidation."

In signing the act, President Roosevelt reiterated two points which had been made repeatedly during the Congressional debates that led to passage of the measure: that the state could not merely go through the motions of regulation, but would be required to control the industry "effectively," and that "Congress did not intend to permit private rate fixing."

One of the leaders of the Congressional group opposed to nullifying the Supreme Court's SEUA ruling was the widely respected Senator Joseph C. O'Mahoney of Wyoming. In a speech to the Insurance Federation of New York a few months later, he said: "The act . . . was an invitation to the insurance industry and to the states by the Congress to set up a formula of state regulation which will preserve a free economy in insurance by preserving competition and banishing the evils of monopolistic central control."

Congress, he said, wanted "to strengthen state regulation by closing the door to private regulation"—that is, regulation by industry organizations with inflexible rules. This concept should be welcomed, he suggested, "because it affords not only an opportunity to avoid all the dangers of central government control, but an opportunity also to make secure real freedom of opportunity in the industry itself."

To meet the requirements of Public Law 15, an "All-Industry Committee" drew up a model bill to be submitted to the legislatures. This AIC law, as it was called, was not what INA wanted. The company complained that the measure provided "for more stringent regulation than is necessary." Moreover, in practice it was likely that the law, through its interpretation and administration, would be used to "throttle competition, kill initiative, and thus deprive the public of the benefits of progressive underwriting." INA's criticisms had little effect, and the AIC Law was adopted in more than forty states.

The National Association of Insurance Commissioners defended the AIC bill as the best possible compromise.

"In drafting these bills," the NAIC said, "it was recognized that many companies desired to take independent action. It was recognized that uniformity, while authorized, should not be mandatory, thereby preserving freedom of action upon the part of those who desire to take action independently. . . .

"The purpose of this act is to promote the public welfare by regulating insurance rates to the end that they shall not be excessive, inadequate, or unfairly discriminatory, and to authorize and regulate cooperative action among insurers in rate-making and in other matters. . . . *Nothing in this act is intended (1) to prohibit or discourage reasonable competition, or (2) to prohibit, or encourage,* except to the extent necessary to accomplish [this] purpose, uniformity in insurance rates, rating systems, rating plans or practices." [Emphasis added.]

Lest anyone still remain in doubt about the intentions of the commissioners, they elaborated on this point to make it "abundantly plain" to all: "There should be ample room for initiative in the development of new ideas in the insurance business under rate regulatory statutes."

Although companies would have "the privilege of following the patterns set by others," they would be "by no means obligated to do so"—they would have "complete freedom to make patterns of their own within the framework of the law."

Now, with the SEUA case at an end, the criminal indictment having been dropped by the Department of Justice after the enactment of Public Law 15, it appeared that companies like INA that wanted to broaden their services to the public would have no difficulty.

But the millennium was not at hand. One year after Public Law 15 was passed, when many of the states still had not revised their insurance laws, Roger Kenney, a perceptive insurance commentator, wrote in the *United States Investor*: "[There] is a struggle—a terrific struggle—between two violently opposed factions in the stock fire insurance business.

"On one side is found what you might call the *status quo ante* group—a group of top executives dominated by a few choice mossbacks who believe that somehow or other a legal way back to conditions prevailing before the SEUA decision and Public Law 15 can be found.

"On the other side is a group—also of top executives—who recognize the momentous importance of recent events and are trying their level best to keep state regulation of insurance from becoming what we have termed . . . 'a state-blessed monopoly.' "

Kenney expressed the fear that rigid rules and laws regarding rates and rating procedures would give too much power to the state commissioners or "too much clique control" by standpatters in the industry.

"In either case," Kenney warned, "the result will be to kill initiative, to stifle competition, and to drift back into the old order whereby all decisions in regard to rates, rules, and practices—good, bad, and indifferent—were made within the [rating] bureaus, leaving individual underwriters to follow along like trained seals. All this to the disadvantage of the policy-buying public!"

By the time his words appeared in print, INA, one of the leaders among those favoring competitive freedom and change, was already at war with the power structure of the industry.

10: *Preaching Heresy*

THE CONFLICT between INA and "the club," the friendly clique of old-line stock insurance companies of which it had always been a congenial part, could be traced far back in the company's history, for the seeds of friction had long existed. As strongly and as often as it could, INA had taken an independent stand on issues on which it thought the rest of the industry was wrong. But it was not until John A. Diemand became president of the company that the cleavage in the industry was clarified and sharpened.

A love of liberty, even in business, had always characterized Benjamin Rush, who had been schooled in the unfettered tradition of marine underwriting and fretted under the restraints imposed by the insurance industry's bureaucracy. He was also willing for his company to go its own way when necessary, as he had shown by withdrawing from the national casualty organization in 1929 when that body refused to go along with an automobile coverage favored by INA. But Rush was an old man when he uttered his final call for reform in 1939, and battles must be fought by younger men.

Like Rush, Diemand was a product of a less restricted

field—casualty insurance—and the Indemnity, during the years he headed it, had been independent of the self-appointed organs of authority in that branch of the industry. So it was natural that one of Diemand's first acts upon assuming the presidency was to direct a re-examination of the company's practices and those of the industry as a whole.

"In 1941," Bradford Smith, Jr., disclosed, "we made a review of the fire insurance business, and some of the things that we saw we didn't like. Among them was the question of unfairly discriminatory commissions [paid to agents]. Other things included the rigid domination of the business by regulatory bodies and onerous state regulations. We were convinced that the policyholders' interests were being adversely affected."

The restiveness of INA under the tethers must have been clear to any close observer at that time, for the company's spokesmen made no secret of their feelings. Herbert P. Stellwagen made a detailed criticism in a speech to the North Carolina Association of Insurance Agents in 1941 in which, besides questioning price levels, he warned that "the large and medium-sized buyer of insurance believes that our methods are too inflexible, and that we insist on giving him what we have to offer rather than in giving him what he wants."

The industry's "self-made regulations" were described as "reprehensible" by Stellwagen. He pointed out that the Insurance section of the American Management Association had expressed the need for blanket liability insurance but only "within the last few months" had "the business of insurance sought to meet that need."

Calling for freedom from "bureaucratic regulation" and "hampering legislation," he said some insurance leaders wanted to eliminate competition through the industry's self-regulation. "Being unwilling to change themselves and having no taste for experimentation," he charged, "they try to see to it that no one else may change or experiment. . . . They wished to build a wall around their own business."

The next year was the company's 150th anniversary. On January 27 Diemand spoke to a gathering of INA's directors, officers, and executives, as well as fifteen insurance commissioners and other guests. Although every American was preoccupied by the war into which this country had been swept just seven weeks before, it's unlikely that any leader in the insurance industry missed the significance of Diemand's incisive remarks.

It would be "appropriate to the times and worthy of our heritage," he began, "to dedicate ourselves anew to the solution of certain problems" so that "the insuring public may enjoy in these difficult times an even higher degree of service and protection than it has in the past."

First he touched on three general problems which "adversely affected" the policyholders' interests. "Excess commissions and allowances" to agents had added to the costs of doing business, and thus inflated rates, without serving any useful function except to "draw premiums from one company to the other"—at the ultimate expense of the insurance buyer.

Then Diemand lamented the "arbitrary rulings" of the industry's self-policing "regulatory bodies," on which he blamed the inability of INA and other companies to serve the policyholders' needs adequately. He complained that the industry organizations lacked "a coordinated, uniform, and broad outlook."

Finally, there was the difficulty of "onerous state regulations" which permitted insurers "little freedom in rate-making and contractual dealing with individual risks."

In short, the insurance customer wasn't able to buy policies tailor-made for his needs, at minimum reasonable rates and with scarcely any red tape.

But Diemand was too forthright a man and felt too

strongly the need for reforms to stop with generalizations like these, so he listed a number of specific recommendations.

Charging that "the fire business has stagnated" because of self-imposed red tape, he scoffed that anyone who "approves of the number and character of company-made regulatory bodies under which the fire insurance business operates" should "forever hold his peace with respect to bureaucratic control of the business of government." The time had come "to take down the bars of [the industry's] regulation and restriction," so that every company could meet the requirements of any policyholder at any time "as long as there is no law or ruling of [a state] insurance department to prevent it."

Another recommended reform was the granting by the legislatures of all-risk insurance charters, under which one policy could be issued "to cover the entire exposure of any policyholder."

The next point was more of a pledge than a recommendation. It dealt with the "agents whose loyalty and friendship mean so much in the successful development of our company." Diemand said it was the company's intention to reduce the number of agents to "those who truly do act in a representative capacity" for INA and the policyholders.

Nevertheless, although there would be fewer agents, all who continued to represent the company would be treated equally. "We will not discriminate" among agents "by giving another improper advantages," he vowed. (This was a reference to the "Excepted Cities" problem, which will be explained later in this chapter.)

"At the risk of preaching heresy," Diemand concluded, candor compelled him to say that "the bane of the fire insurance business has been complacency, arising out of a glorious past." The industry had every reason to be proud of its history, but the customers were concerned with the present and the future. And so it followed that one of the duties of the industry was "to constantly keep pace with the policyholders' needs, even if these needs require frequent change" in insurance practices.

None of this sounds revolutionary or even remarkable to anyone familiar with other fields of endeavor, but to the senior executives of other fire insurance companies in 1942 "heresy" was too mild a word for it. To them almost every word he spoke was wild, reckless, irresponsible, impractical, and subversive of order and propriety.

The most conservative element in the industry, who controlled the Insurance Executives Association through the Committee of Fifteen, read Diemand's words with bitter disapproval. Then suddenly, it seemed as though he had opened a Pandora's box: for weeks, whenever one of them opened a newspaper, a trade journal, or a news magazine, a new challenge to his traditional ways confronted him. Of course, it was more than mere coincidence; Diemand was in tune with the times, and his opinions reflected the need for change in the industry.

For example, two weeks after Diemand's speech, the *Journal of Commerce* reported a speech by Ontario's Attorney General, C. D. Conant, in which he hit out at an evil which had plagued fire insurance ever since the latter part of the nineteenth century, when the industry's self-regulatory bodies virtually eliminated price competition. The stabilization of rates, he asserted, had been offset by "competition . . . directed too much at acquiring business from agents by the payment of excessive commissions."

"Such a situation," Conant warned, "invites investigation and encourages self-insurance by large corporations, government regulation, or the taking over of insurance by the state."

Next, the IEA and the rest of the industry were jolted by the news from Georgia that the federal government was investigating the business for possible anti-trust prosecution, having selected the South-Eastern Underwriters Association as the key target.

The federal inquiry gave *Time* magazine the idea of dusting off Diemand's speech, now two months old, and wrapping it into a package with the antitrust development in an article entitled "What Price Competition?" The first paragraph of the article said:

"Fire-insurance companies were caught in a cross fire last week: in front attacked by Thurman Arnold's trustbusters; in the rear by the oldest and third largest of their number, Insurance Company of North America. From both directions the charge was the same: that insurance rates are too high."

The article suggested "the attack" by INA might "well have greater results" than even the federal action, because "it represents the first crack to appear in many a year in the united front with which U. S. insurance companies have long gone about rate-making."

Many of the statements in the magazine's report were inaccurate, some apparently because of the difficulty of compressing complex technical matters into a brief, readable account for the general reader. (One or two of the statements which unintentionally misrepresented Diemand's position could only be explained by mysterious ways of the impish spirits who sometimes play tricks with time, fortune, and the affairs of men.)

The *Time* article was the last straw. A highly aroused IEA appointed a committee of four men, presidents of some of the largest companies, to meet with Diemand and lay down the law to him, not an easy thing to do to a man of Diemand's temperament. But they tried.

In a subsequent letter to the IEA, Diemand said:

"It soon became evident that the members of the committee first and foremost had in mind leveling accusations and making charges against the Insurance Company of North

America rather than hearing any presentation from me. . . . The members of the committee expressed the view that my [150th anniversary] address was not only untimely, but that I was guilty of washing our dirty linen in public."

To both complaints Diemand gave answer: "It is always the right time to do the right thing. In so far as public laundering is concerned, the comment made seems to me to be an admission of the existence of weakness."

Another criticism by the committee concerned INA's failure to force its casualty affiliate, the Indemnity company, to join the National Bureau of Casualty and Surety Underwriters. In replying to this, Diemand was something less than flattering. He said:

"Our feeling is that [the NBCSU] does not permit its members to meet the requirements of individual policyholders; that . . . by its inflexible rating methods the National Bureau imposes arbitrary and unreasonable restraints which adversely affect the interests of the policyholder. In so far as we are concerned, this question of joining the National Bureau will have merit only when that organization by its deeds and by its service to the public merits the confidence of the management of this company; then, and only then, shall we consider having the Indemnity company make application for membership in that organization."

As for the *Time* article, Diemand rejected any responsibility for it and pointed out that the magazine had printed a retraction of the inaccuracies in a later issue.

The bitterness of the other IEA leaders probably reflected a feeling that a member of "the club" had gone over to join the critics, for others had criticized the industry in sharper terms than Diemand. For example, one of the most respected authorities, Ralph H. Blanchard, president of the Casualty Actuarial Society, argued in favor of multiple-line underwriting; that is, the authorization of companies "to write

In Time of Disaster

The life of INA has been a history of the disasters that have
befallen the United States and the rest of the world. In this
group of illustrations are a few of the catastrophes, beginning
with the San Francisco earthquake and fire of 1906, which
killed upwards of 315 persons and destroyed 28,188
buildings. INA was one of the few insurance companies to
pay claims in full. BELOW: amid the ruins, only the tower
of the City Hall remained upright.

Flames that followed earth
tremor caused most of the
destruction in San Francisco,
as this photograph suggests.

Archives

Explosion of fertilizer aboard
ship at Texas City, Texas, in
1947, set off chain of blasts
and fires which virtually
destroyed the city and caused
at least 433 deaths, the worst
industrial disaster in INA
history.

A 1955 explosion, so powerful
that it caused damage three
miles away, started fires in
huge oil refinery at Whiting,
Indiana, that could not be
extinguished for eight days.

Wide World Photo

any sort of insurance, other than life, not contrary to public policy."

Of those, like the conservative group that ran the IEA, who opposed multiple-line and other concepts, Blanchard said:

"They are in the position of preferring limitation of powers—like old men who shun responsibility and new problems, preferring to cling to past successes rather than to pioneer. I venture to think that much adverse criticism of the insurance business would not arise if its practitioners were as interested in developing new methods as they are in defending what they already have—if they sought as diligently for what is worthy in new proposals as for reasons against their adoption."

If the IEA committee's confrontation with Diemand had any effect, it was probably to confirm that there was a good deal amiss in the insurance business, and that INA's only hope of bringing about the needed reforms lay in its own efforts, even if it meant fighting the entire power structure of the industry.

It was about that time that Diemand began serious discussions with his executives regarding the possibility of following an independent course in the future. Many of them were shocked at the idea. Having spent their whole business life in a rigid framework of regulations enforced by industry organizations, always with the justification that tight controls were necessary to prevent rate wars and chaos, their first reaction was that independence would be unethical.

As time passed, however, and most of the leaders in the industry made it clear that they would resist any attempt at the kind of change that INA men regarded as progressive, most of the company's executives were converted to the necessity, and even desirability, of independence.

In the spring of 1943 the company, following its usual practice, invited a representative group of agents from all over the country to come to Philadelphia, where their opinions were solicited on various aspects of the business. One question was on the subject of agents' commissions and the "Excepted Cities" pattern.

This pattern had grown out of the monopolistic, uniform-rate structure of the industry, which prevented companies from competing on a price basis. So many companies tried to get more business from agents by paying higher commissions. As the competition by excessive commissions grew hotter, the sums paid to agents spiraled upward, threatening ruin as rate-cutting had once done. Finally, the companies tried to bring some semblance of order to the scene by arriving at industry-wide agreements on what percentage of the premiums would be paid as commission.

However, the standard commission could not be enforced in some places, for various reasons. "There have been excepted territories as long as there have been associations with rules," William Hamlin Wandel found in his study of the industry. As early as 1849 there were "excepted" cities or territories, in which agents received more than the ordinary commission.

When INA asked its agent group how it felt about this matter, the agents agreed on a written reply: "We believe that excess commissions in the 'Excepted Cities' are not only inequitable but present an additional 'soft spot' in the industry which should be corrected within the business *before* the problem receives political attention."

The agents called for immediate action, but "to do much about the situation individually was extremely difficult in the light of the power of the various trade associations," as Bradford Smith, Jr., pointed out. Besides, the war was still on, and it was not easy for people to concentrate on radical changes in those tense times.

When and if the inequalities in commissions were abolished, it would have to be done against the opposition of a large part of the industry; that was obvious to everyone at INA.

In that same year, 1943, the insurance commissioner of Massachusetts, C. F. J. Harrington, who was then president of the National Association of Insurance Commissioners, appointed a committee to consider all aspects of the multiple-line insurance proposals. Diemand was named chairman of the group. (It is characteristic of the man that Diemand always referred to it as "the Harrington Committee," although insurance texts invariably call it "the Diemand Committee.")

It was a blue-ribbon committee, chosen to represent every part of the insurance business and the insurance-buying public. The members were Kenneth C. Bell of the Chase National Bank, S. Bruce Black of the Liberty Mutual Insurance Company, William H. LaBoyteaux of the insurance brokerage firm of Johnson and Higgins, Arthur F. Lafrentz of the American Surety Company of New York, J. Arthur Nelson of the New Amsterdam Casualty Company of New York, William D. O'Gorman of the O'Gorman and Young insurance agency, and William D. Winter of the Atlantic Mutual Insurance Company.

Multiple-line underwriting had existed for many years in Great Britain. A typical insurance charter there enabled the company "to carry on the business of insurance of all kinds in all parts of the world."

But in this country casualty and surety companies were permitted to write only certain classes of business, and fire and marine insurers were limited to different, equally specific kinds of coverage. For example, in 1940 fire and marine companies operating in New York state were authorized to issue only these policies: fire, miscellaneous property, water damage, collision, motor vehicle and aircraft, marine, and marine protection and indemnity.

Thus, full protection of a motorist meant that he had

to have two policies: a fire company cover for collision and motor vehicle, and a casualty company cover for liability, both personal (bodily) injury and property damage. The two forms of liability coverage could not be written by a fire company.

This nonsensical ossification of what should, in the nature of things, be one of the most adaptable of business enterprises had long been sanctified under the name "the American system." To be sure, there was some basis for the compartmentalization many years earlier, when American underwriters were less knowledgeable and the limitations forced insurers to specialize and become expert in their respective fields.

Diemand was a natural choice to head the NAIC study committee, for he had been discussing multiple-line underwriting for years with anyone who would listen. In the mid-1930's, when he was running the Indemnity company, he developed several broad-coverage policies which, although not truly multiple-line, were giant steps in that direction.

Of course, the idea did not originate with Diemand; others had looked to Europe before him. In 1914 Connecticut's insurance commissioner, Burton Mansfield, questioned whether the "American system" ought not to be abandoned in favor of multiple-line underwriting, and even then he was only reviving a topic discussed by the NAIC in 1871. And only fourteen years before the Diemand Committee was appointed, Colonel Howard P. Dunham, then NAIC president, told that body's 1929 convention:

"The principles of multiple line insurance and insurance companies are firmly established in the minds of the public and of insurance underwriters. Such principles are the natural outgrowth of public demand. Insurance retains its rightful place in the economic history of a country only as it meets the public needs. It should not be embarrassed in its development by statutory or other requirements which have not kept pace with the times."

The NAIC committee headed by Diemand met every Wednesday, beginning in October 1943, in the board room of the Johnson and Higgins brokerage house in New York. Before writing the final draft of their report, the members invited all interested parties to appear before the committee, which held open meetings for almost a week in the Hotel Biltmore in New York, and to comment on the group's conclusions.

In its final report, submitted to the NAIC at its convention in June 1944, the committee made five recommendations, all dealing with fire, marine, casualty, and surety companies—sometimes lumped together as "non-life" insurers. The first two recommendations would permit any non-life insurance company with sufficient financial resources to write any kind of policy outside the United States except life and annuities, and to accept reinsurance for the same lines within this country. The last three proposals would give underwriters the power to write comprehensive automobile policies, comprehensive aviation policies, and the personal property floater.

Moreover, the committee indicated in its report that most of its members also favored a comprehensive householders' policy, but the committee chose not to make this a recommendation, to avoid endangering acceptance of the report.

Because "the subject of multiple line underwriting is so involved," the committee said, there should be "a continuous open-minded and realistic study of the whole subject" after the recommended changes were put into effect. Undoubtedly reflecting Diemand's often expressed distaste for the red tape which tied the industry's hands, the committee report also urged that the definitions of the various kinds of insurance be standardized, and that "the numerous regulations and filing requirements now in effect be critically reviewed, so that those which no longer serve a useful purpose may be eliminated."

The report precipitated a hot fight, for most of the big fire and casualty companies were opposed to the multiple-line concept. Indeed, the Insurance Executives Association and the Association of Casualty and Surety Executives joined in a lengthy statement condemning the idea in whole and in all its parts.

They insisted that there was no real public demand for it, that it was unnecessary for any American company which wished to compete abroad against the British insurers, that it would be no more convenient for a policyholder than several policies, that commissions would be affected adversely, that it would not facilitate reinsurance in the United States, and that most companies would not be competent in terms of experience, funds, or personnel to deal with multiple-line underwriting.

In disputing the suggestion that any non-life company should be permitted to write personal property floaters, the opposition statement argued that the companies presently writing those policies "meet all demands," and that the Diemand Committee's proposal to let other fire, casualty, marine, and surety companies write such coverage "could result only in increasing the number of companies in the field." Showing their interest in limiting competition, they added: "There would seem to be no reason for disturbing the business of those companies now adequately meeting public demand."

One of those who supported the Diemand Committee's recommendations, C. C. Fraizer, the Nebraska director of insurance, described the *pro* and *con* groups as a cartoonist might see them. Of those who were fighting the multiple-line concept, he said: "The first cartoon would, like all cartoons should, exaggerate a pompous and pontifical insurance executive with steely eyes, a set and determined jaw, and portray an expression of standpatism and an attitude of maintaining the *status quo* at any cost."

The second cartoon, limning the advocates of the new plan, "would picture a keen, alert insurance executive, studious, progressive, cautious and careful and yet forward-looking, prudent and thrifty and yet showing a desire to render a higher public service."

"How better could the two attitudes in insurance thinking be contrasted?" he demanded.

At the NAIC convention, the lobbying of the old guard became so insistent that the commissioners finally declined to meet with its representatives, so one of them was sent to Diemand in one last attempt to dissuade him. "He got me out of bed at two o'clock in the morning," Diemand said, "and I nearly broke my skull, slipping in the bathtub while I was showering after he phoned to say he was coming to see me."

Diemand was in less of a conciliatory mood than ever when the envoy arrived.

Despite the vehement opposition of the men who had always been looked on as the industry leaders, the NAIC adopted the report of the Diemand Committee and referred it to the individual states for consideration.

In less than ten years, multiple-line underwriting had reached such proportions that John D. Phelan, writing in *The Annals of the Society of Chartered Property and Casualty Underwriters*, was able to refer to it as "the concept which is revolutionizing American insurance thinking." It was a monumental accomplishment for Diemand and the members of his committee.

But that was in the future. Before that time arrived, the entire industry would be plunged into a prolonged war that would test INA's resources, ingenuity—and determination.

11 : The Opening Battles

"IT IS THE MARK of a good action," Robert Louis Stevenson once remarked, "that it appears inevitable in retrospect," and INA's drastic move in opting for independence illustrates his point.

The march of events that led INA and, therefore, the industry, step by step to the final rupture was inexorable, as though the men and their companies had been caught up by fate in a process that could not be avoided. In a sense, this is more than an illusion; it is fact, for the relentless force engendered by economic and, to a lesser extent, political and social changes had finally created irresistible pressures compelling the insurance industry to accommodate itself to the twentieth century.

Within weeks of John Diemand's call for reforms in the industry, the South-Eastern Underwriters Association and its members were indicted for violating the Sherman Antitrust Act. Two years passed, and then, in the same month in which the Diemand Committee urged the insurance commissioners to authorize multiple-line underwriting, the Supreme Court handed down its SEUA decision, bringing the insurance industry within the embrace of the federal antitrust laws. Then came the passage of Public Law 15.

Besides leaving insurance regulation in the hands of the states, this law outlawed the use of boycotts, coercion, or intimidation to keep in line those companies that preferred to follow an independent course.

A few days after Public Law 15 took effect, John Diemand resigned from the Insurance Executives Association, the organization of fire insurance presidents. He had long been disenchanted with the IEA, which had attempted to chastise him after his 1942 speech and had actively opposed the multiple-line proposals of his NAIC committee.

Diemand's resignation served notice on the industry that his company, hitherto one of the most powerful supporters of the complex structure of organizations controlling the insurance business, was striking out on its own whenever it believed its freedom of competition was being limited.

If the significance of the withdrawal from the IEA escaped anyone, other developments that year 1945 underlined the meanings of INA's action.

In the spring, the Eastern Tornado Insurance Association (which we shall call, for brevity's sake, the ETIA), to which the company still belonged, began studying the question of providing "wave wash" insurance; that is, protection against damage caused by flowing water, including tidal waves. Although wave wash is rarely, if ever, associated with tornadoes, the ETIA had jurisdiction, probably because storms usually are responsible for wave damage. The state insurance commissioner of New Jersey had been urging the industry to write this kind of policy, because owners of ocean-front properties suffered heavy losses whenever a severe storm caused high tides and battering waves.

Learning that the IEA had been in communication

with the ETIA's manager regarding wave wash coverage, H. Richard Heilman of INA wrote to the ETIA:

"Obviously, we are not now in a position to sit on a committee whose actions are subject to the review or jurisdiction of the Insurance Executives Association. Since it is our understanding that the Wave Wash Committee [of the ETIA] is destined to take this course, we will be compelled to reserve the right of independent action."

That appears to be the first time that INA explicitly asserted its "right of independent action," a phrase that would be used hundreds of times in the coming years.

Replying to Heilman's letter, the ETIA assured him that the findings of its own committee would not be "submitted for review or decision" to the IEA, so INA continued its participation in the ETIA talks. In the end, the ETIA did nothing to provide wave wash coverage to the public, so INA did begin writing this policy independently, without objection from any of the industry organizations. But the company's insistence on its rights was not lost on the rest of the industry.

In October of the same year the insurance superintendent for the District of Columbia reduced rates five per cent, and the industry, including INA, objected because of the superintendent's method. However, when hearings were held on the matter, INA refused to delegate authority to the industry committee; instead, it was represented by its own counsel.

At the end of the hearings, the superintendent reaffirmed his order. The company agreed to comply, but the rest of the industry took the dispute to the federal court, asking, among other things, that INA be restrained from obeying the superintendent's order. Eventually the superintendent achieved the rate reduction he had sought.

To many insurance men, the most meaningful aspect of the affair was INA's independence.

But the most important of the company's deeds that year occurred in September, just before the District of Columbia case. This was the introduction of the Installment Premium Endorsement (IPE).

Fire insurance could be purchased on an annual basis, or for a three- or five-year term, but any fire policy had to be paid in advance. The yearly cost of the term policies was much less than the premium for an annual contract, of course; on the other hand, prepayment of the entire premium on a term policy required a much larger initial expenditure. Many insurance buyers simply could not afford a payment of that size.

"It is no argument to say that such a person can buy an annual policy," INA said. "That simply means that the poor man must pay more for his insurance."

Clearly, what many buyers of fire insurance needed was a plan under which they could buy protection for a term of three or five years, paying for it in installments. For years installment payment of premiums had been a matter of course in other forms of insurance, including life, casualty, and inland marine. Even fire insurance companies had permitted installment payments for policies covering farm property, but not for any other fire protection.

As a result, a customer who could not afford to pay the full premium in advance but wanted to enjoy the saving on a term policy was forced to borrow from a bank to make his payment. INA felt that it could use a small part of its own funds available for this, at a lower cost to buyers.

Nevertheless, when INA tried to persuade the industry organizations to adopt the Installment Premium Endorsement, the idea was rejected out of hand. There were those who said that *no* companies should permit installment payments because *some* companies didn't want to. It was alleged that installment payments would give big companies an advantage over the small ones; but others complained that, if such a plan were permitted, "you could let a company go out and write a terrific amount of business with practically no capital."

After the proposal was turned down by the regional groups—the SEUA, the Eastern Underwriters Association (EUA), the Western Underwriters Asociation (WUA), and the Pacific Board of Fire Underwriters (PBFU)—INA filed the form independently in every state. Within a year the plan had been approved in a majority of states.

The independent action caused an uproar that continued for years.

"No doubt many of the opponents of the endorsement were sincerely outraged," an INA review of the controversy said in 1951. "But at what were they outraged?

"Simply this: the successful effort of a single company to act independently, to compete without first securing the agreement of a majority of its competitors. Nothing like it had occurred before in the fire insurance business.

"When [INA] opened the door and stepped out of the room, a draft of fresh air shocked those remaining in the room into action. The shock deepened into injury when the competitive effect of the endorsement was felt. This combination of motives stimulated the opposition."

To block the IPE, the industry put the rating laws newly enacted by the states to a use for which they had never been intended. The harassing tactics included registering objections, which resulted in prolonged hearings, almost all of which ended with a finding in INA's favor.

The innumerable hearings, however, consumed a great deal of time and energy on the part of Bradford Smith and other INA officers, who went from one state capital to the next, testifying on and refuting complaints.

"During this period," the 1951 INA review said in a rare display of sarcasm, "it was heart-warming to realize that so many of [the company's] competitors were concerned lest it violate the new laws. It is a tribute to many executives and agents that they were not only able to supervise their own businesses, but had time to help prevent so many insurance commissioners from making errors in applying the rating laws to the installment problem."

In litigation, an issue once ruled upon is not reopened, but this legal principle, *res judicata*, does not apply to administrative proceedings. So the appointment of a new state commissioner sometimes resulted in a review of the IPE, and in a few instances even the commissioner who originally approved the endorsement ordered a new hearing. As many as four hearings were held in some states.

Vexing as all these impediments were, they were not entirely bad, for they did attract more attention to the company's willingness to accept installment payments on fire insurance.

"[INA] could not have advertised the installment endorsement as successfully as its opponents did for it," the company later observed, with somewhat malicious pleasure. "It was the company's invariable experience that its volume [sales] increased markedly after each hearing. Many agents came to hearings as opponents and left as advocates."

As one might expect, the company sometimes engaged in protracted filings, hearings, negotiations, and lawsuits, only to lose out in the end. In Mississippi, for example, the commissioner disapproved the installment plan four times, so INA took the matter to Chancery Court, which, after a complete trial of the issues from the beginning, overruled the commissioner and approved IPE. The commissioner appealed the ruling to the state Supreme Court, which reversed the lower court's ruling on a technicality. So the company lost, although the only court to consider the installment endorsement on its merits decided in INA's favor.

In Virginia, another protracted series of administrative and judicial proceedings ended adversely for INA when the state Supreme Court ruled that a state law barred installment payments. The statute, the only one of its kind in the country, called for payment of the entire premium within a "reasonable time." Unfortunately, Virginia's highest court didn't regard yearly payments as meeting the requirement of the law. However, in 1958 the legislature changed the law to permit installment payments.

Despite setbacks, the company's plan had been approved in 39 states by May 1951, and in several areas around the country the very rating bureaus which had attempted to prevent its approval were filing installment plans of their own. One of the best statements, if not the last word, on the issue came when the Arkansas Supreme Court, on April 30, 1951, in deciding the first appellate case on the merits of the endorsement, affirmed the commissioner's finding:

". . . The installment premium plan enables the fire insurance industry to serve its policyholders in the same way that many other businesses have been doing for years. [It] reduces the occasion for resorting to outside agencies to perform functions which the fire insurance industry itself is capable of doing.

"Indeed, it is the commissioner's findings that the insuring public is better served by the installment premium plan, which plan is less complex and less expensive than facilities offered by other agencies."

The court agreed with the commissioner that he had no authority to reject the IPE, and if it were disapproved, insurance buyers would still indirectly (that is, through bank loans) pay their premiums by installments. But the net result, in that event, would be an "increase [in] the cost to the policyholder."

About the same time that the fight for the Installment Premium Endorsement began in 1945, the first shots were fired in what developed into another full scale war between INA and the rest of the industry. This dispute involved the four regional underwriters' associations (EUA, SEUA, WUA, and PBFU), plus thirty-three other organizations which operated as "rating bureaus."

In the insurance business, a rating bureau compiles statistical data, inspects and classifies "risks" (*i.e.*, the property covered by the policy), and sets the rates which are quoted by its member companies. These regional associations and the bureaus, before the Supreme Court's epochal 1944 decision, had been the instruments through which the insurance companies muffled competition and imposed uniform rates and forms.

The high court's decision and the enactment of Public Law 15 made it necessary for most of these groups to reorganize and formulate new constitutions and bylaws. As these were drafted and submitted to the members, INA's legal department examined them meticulously to make sure they conformed to the new position in which the industry found itself, particularly with regard to the antitrust laws.

One organization whose basic law was believed to be in accord with the spirit of competition was the Middle Department Association of Fire Underwriters, a rating bureau covering Pennsylvania and Delaware. From 1946 to 1949 INA vice president Bradford Smith, Jr., was chairman of the board of governors.

The "Middle Department," as it was usually called, made its services available to every kind of company, stock, mutual, and reciprocal (a distinctive variety of mutual), on, either a membership or a subscribership basis. Deviations from its rates were permitted on the part of members and non-members alike.

(At least, that was the intent of the constitution. In practice, the Middle Department, within weeks after Smith's term as its chairman had ended, opposed one of INA's earliest competitive efforts in what became known as "the Pennsylvania Rate Deviation Case," as we shall see in Chapter 17.)

Flaws were found in most of the other drafts. The SEUA's, for example, denied members the right to deviate from the organization's rates, even though state law might permit deviations; the company thought that this was coercive, despite the provision that a deviating insurer could be a subscriber without voting privileges.

The proposed constitution of the Maryland Rating Bureau required member companies to employ only the rates, forms, and rules established by the bureau. Robert B. Ely III, of INA's legal department, told vice president Bradford Smith, Jr.: "This would appear to constitute a concert of action which would deprive the public of the benefit of the resourcefulness of particular members or subscribers. As such it appears contrary to the spirit of Public Law 15 . . . [and] of doubtful legality."

Moreover, the sanctions provided for departing from the bureau's rates—expulsion of the company or refusal of membership to it—amounted to an "instrument of coercion."

Smith notified the chairman of the appropriate committee that INA objected to those features of the drafts. Suggesting certain liberalizing changes to bring the constitution and bylaws into compliance with the antitrust laws, he said that if the changes were not made, the company could not accept the drafts because the bureau "would tend to restraint of trade and would result in interfering with the exercise by a member company of rights given it under the laws."

The company did sign the constitution and bylaws, at the same time transmitting a letter to the bureau saying that it reserved all of its rights under the federal and state laws, including the "principle of initiative and innovation" (the latter a word that would one day become a motto of the company, and with good reason).

However, the bureau's governing committee decided

that INA's qualified assent was unacceptable, so it rejected the company's application for membership.

At that point INA requested the state insurance commissioner to hold a hearing on the matter. At the hearing the company's representatives emphasized their determination to open up new fields, experiment with novel forms of protection, and pioneer in broader underwriting practices.

The threat to the company's freedom inherent in the Maryland Rating Bureau's constitution and bylaws was more than theoretical, as the evidence set forth at the hearing proved. Another bureau, the Association of Fire Underwriters in Baltimore, was already stamping INA's installment premium policies as violations of the association's rules even though the state insurance commissioner had approved the Installment Premium Endorsement! Obviously the old guard which controlled the bureaus still regarded itself, and not the state governments, as the ultimate authority, as it had been before the Supreme Court decision.

At the conclusion of the hearing, the commissioner ruled in INA's favor, declaring that under the state's rating law he alone had the supervisory jurisdiction over rates, classifications, rating methods, schedules, underwriting rules, and bylaws or regulations of rating organizations.

Reviewing the case in the *United States Investor*, Roger Kenney wrote:

"All state associations organized under [rating] laws are subject to the state, and the latter assumes a very definite responsibility to see that nothing even remotely resembling coercion prevails therein. For the diehards in the industry to believe, therefore, that under any and all conditions they can use the bureaus to perpetuate their control of the rating formula is very short-sighted indeed."

INA's attempts to persuade all the industry organizations to liberalize their constitutions and, failing that, to make clear its own reservations with regard to any coercive provisions, continued through 1946. Because of the leading role the company's executives had always played in the industry, these efforts often had their ironic side. Thus, when G. Brinton Lucas, INA vice president, addressed a letter of protest to the Inland Marine Insurance Bureau, the communication was put on the agenda for the next meeting of the IMIB's executive committee, of which the chairman was G. Brinton Lucas.

The basic issues, in INA's view, as the company stated in one of a series of letters sent to the industry organizations, were these:

"We recognize the authority of the state as controlling.

"Any attempt to restrict a company's legal rights of initiative and innovation in the public interest . . . is coercive and in conflict with Public Law 15.

"The association has not the power to force a member to forego its charter rights."

Acknowledging the value of the industry groups, INA tried to make clear that it was merely trying to obey the law as it was understood by the company, but most of the other companies took a quite different view of its stand. At the SEUA's annual convention in May 1946, at Myrtle Beach, Virginia, one man reflected the general attitude when he charged that INA's stand "could be so construed as to permit a member to enjoy all the benefits of a voluntary organization without assuming important responsibilities which look to the public interest."

Bradford Smith, Jr., took the floor to explain his company's reasoning. He said that "initiative and innovation" must be encouraged so that new and extended coverages could be developed for the public, but this might not be possible if a majority vote of the members of an association, and not the authority of the state, exercised control.

Reiterating the company's willingness to cooperate with other members in any lawful way, he pleaded with his colleagues to meet the responsibilities imposed by Public Law 15 "by conceding that the duly constituted public supervisory officials are invested with supervisory powers . . . as the final arbiter." And he insisted that no private organization had the "power to intervene in the relationship between the legislature of a state and a company."

On the following evening the SEUA's executive committee, of which Smith was a member, opened its meeting to the entire membership of the association. Only one speaker other than Smith spoke up for INA. The tenor of the meeting was set by the first speaker, the executive committee chairman. Describing INA's position as "a totally unjustified reflection upon the association and its members . . . without any foundation," he said the association's officers recommended that the company be requested to either withdraw its letter of objections or resign from the group.

After hearing a torrent of accusatory speeches, Smith rose. "It seems incomprehensible," he said, "that a member, seeking to place before the association a fundamental principle, is to be treated in this manner, indicating an attitude of defense, rather than being granted the courtesy of a full discussion in an effort to make an area of common understanding. . . . I cannot stand here and listen to you impugn the faith of the North America."

And with that Smith walked out, assuming the outcome of the meeting a foregone conclusion. However, his indignant remarks apparently affected some of the men, for the motion against INA carried by only one vote.

In the following weeks, both sides took a somewhat more conciliatory attitude. The SEUA said it would be satisfied if INA agreed simply to be bound by the constitution, bylaws, and rules, and John Diemand wrote a letter meeting those requirements but repeating his company's determination to adhere to the principles it had previously set forth.

In the meantime, the Maryland Rating Bureau case had been won by INA, and optimism grew in Philadelphia. In a memorandum to Diemand on June 10, general counsel Edward M. Biddle said:

"I am convinced that there is more misunderstanding of our position, resulting from a failure to grasp the points involved, than we have been willing to acknowledge. The opposition in a large measure, I firmly believe, comes from such misunderstanding and not from a perverse attitude.

"In my opinion there will be no refusal by a rating bureau to rate such new or additional coverage as we may wish to write. . . ."

He was wrong. Later that year INA began to run into opposition from the rating bureaus on the Installment Premium Endorsement, and from that time on, matters went from bad to worse.

By the spring of 1947 the attitude of INA's critics had hardened so much that the company's membership in the WUA, the Western Underwriters Association, which covered the states from the Alleghenies to the Rockies, was terminated March 18. Fourteen months later the company changed its relationship with the SEUA from member to subscriber, and later in 1948 it withdrew from the EUA and from the National Board of Fire Underwriters.

It was not until 1950 that it withdrew from the last of the regional organizations, the Pacific Board of Fire Underwriters, and in that same year INA resigned its membership in all the fire rating bureaus throughout the country, except in a few states where the laws made membership mandatory, becoming merely a subscriber instead.

Its independence was complete in 1952 after the company severed connections with the Inland Marine Insurance Bureau and the Inland Marine Underwriters Association.

Predictably, the company's break with the industry organizations only sharpened the old guard's hostility to the company's new independent course.

12: *Bitterness and Broken Friendships*

DURING THE TENSE 1946 SEUA convention at Myrtle Beach, Bradford Smith, Jr., strolled into a reception crowded with insurance men, all of whom got up and walked out. Of perhaps 600 insurance men at the convention, scarcely any would so much as nod a greeting in the hotel corridors.

The next evening, when Smith spoke at the executive committee meeting to the entire angry membership of the association, he began his defense of INA on a personal note.

"I am looking down," he said movingly, "into the faces of men I have looked upon as friends for many years. . . ."

The gratuitous insults were only the beginning of years of affronts and vituperation to which not only Smith, but scores of other INA men, were subjected in the following years, a painful period of more than a decade when many old friendships were torn apart, as the controversy that divided the industry sank to the level of bitter personalities.

It was probably inevitable, for in few other industries were business and fellowship as intermingled as in insurance; indeed, the legion of insurance industry organizations was equaled only by the multitude of fraternal groups.

Perils: Named and Unnamed

Throughout the United States and Canada, fire insurance men belonged to the Honorable Order of the Blue Goose. Locally there were other bodies at every level of business; for example, the top twelve company representatives in Chicago, including INA's man, belonged to the Round Table Society, which met socially at the Union League Club. There was a similar top-level brotherhood in Iowa called the Ashkota Society, and Nebraska executives lifted their cups of cheer together as members of the Ak-Sar-Ben group, irreverently dubbed "the Horsecollar Club" by their subordinates.

"This fraternalism comes up through your whole life in the fire insurance business," Russell H. Petefish said. "It's pretty deep-rooted with these people."

H. Richard Heilman described the mixture of work and play that was the life of a fire insurance company's field man:

"There were fieldmen's clubs, social groups which served to build the feeling of unity. By using the same rates and by sharing the same social life, you had the feeling that you stood shoulder-to-shoulder with the men of the other companies. It was like the labor slogan: solidarity.

"When I was a special agent [i.e., a field representative] in the 1920's and 1930's, many, many special agents would ride around their territory on trips together, although they worked for competing companies. They would call on agents together and it was thought ungentlemanly to take business from one company to another.

"For many company field men, their only real friends were their competitors. These people were moving around too much to form other friendships outside the business. Typically, you were in a town which was a center, usually a state capital —Columbus, Ohio, had 500 special agents or state agents. All the friends you had were the men in the business, the men you met through the industry organizations and the clubs. And

[174]

their wives were the women your wife played bridge with. That was your whole social structure.

"But after INA decided to follow an independent course, then it was another matter. Now you were cast out. This was very difficult for men in a very gregarious business. It wasn't a question of whether you were right or not—it was a matter of the social environment in which you were brought up."

The bitterness of the split would have been unthinkable in other industries which had known and relished competition for years. In the South, a field man for another company was so upset by INA's action that he broke off a close friendship of many years with a man who worked for it. A year later the man died, and his old friend, the INA man, went to pay his last respects, only to have one of the many insurance men at the wake say to him, "Well, you put him in his grave."

In San Francisco, one insurance executive tried to embarrass INA's resident vice president, Francis F. Owen, in the staid and genteel precincts of the Pacific Union Club. Even on the streets of that financial capital of the West, there were silent displays of hostility: other insurance men would cross to the other side to avoid Robert W. Wilson, who shrugged it off as "childish."

Despite the excesses of INA's opponents, it must be remembered that they were truly outraged by what they regarded as the willingness of the industry's oldest company to adopt a program that the industry had long considered worse than improper. Stability was in the public interest, they thought, and competition could lead only to company failures, with disastrous results to the people who had paid premiums for protection against various perils. So cooperation was "the moral, ethical, and correct way to do business," as Heilman recalled.

[175]

"Those who did business on a competitive basis," he said, "were price cutters in the eyes of the industry. The belief had been deeply held for many years that this was an evil thing, that these people were beneath contempt. I was taught this myself, when I first went to work for INA in 1925. I was brought up in the school that believed rate-cutters were not fit to associate with, and no honorable man would buy insurance from them."

A number of men resigned from the company because of the dispute. Many left because they could not endure ostracism. But there were others who felt, as one man in Cincinnati said in his letter of resignation, "I can't work for a company which is not friendly to its competitors and wants to be independent of the rest of the industry."

For the substantial number of INA men who had previously worked for rating bureaus before coming to the company, the inner struggle was especially confusing. Russell Petefish, for one, had spent seven years with a bureau in St. Louis, and he, like the others, was troubled by the widening chasm between his employer and the bureau companies.

"It left you with a very mixed feeling, this new movement," he said. "Many of us in the field wondered: Were we right? Where would it lead us? Could we be the only company out of step with everyone else?"

Understanding what his men would have to go through, Diemand had begun the process of indoctrination, beginning with his senior executives, about 1942. Three years later, when Petefish was transferred to the home office in Philadelphia, he was drawn into the discussions. There were innumerable staff meetings at the time, so that everyone could be kept informed of developments, the staff then being much smaller than it grew to be in the following years.

"The point that sold me," Petefish said, "came in a meeting I'll never forget. Mr. Diemand stated unequivocally,

'Make no mistake about it, our true competitors are not the old-line companies in Hartford and New York, not the bureau companies. Our real rivals in the insurance business are the new companies that are using a different merchandising technique—the direct writers, the companies that sell directly to the public, and not through agents. We are determined to remain a part of the American Agency System—we are not going to become direct writers—but we have got to be able to compete with the direct writers. If we recognize them as our true competitors, then we jolly well better get with it and not just wait hopefully for an end to the lethargy that afflicts the bureaucrats that run this business.'

"Then I began to see that this was the only thing that could be done if the company was to survive and prosper, that we had to be competitive. It got to me; I could see very definitely that this was exactly what had to happen."

During the ensuing period of unpleasantness, the pleasure of discomfiting a disagreeable critic of the company fell to Petefish. It happened as a result of the $50,000,000 fire that destroyed General Motors' auto transmission plant at Livonia, Michigan, in 1953. Then as now INA had a six and a half per cent share in the Factory Insurance Association, a syndicate composed of many fire insurance companies. The FIA had covered the Livonia plant, and INA's share of the loss was $1,660,000.

In the aftermath of that catastrophe, Petefish went to Hartford for two weeks to work with the FIA in devising a reinsurance program for similar risks. After two lonely weeks in Hartford, as a pariah in an insurance-centered city, Petefish was asked by Ludwig C. Lewis to submit the plan to the FIA's executive committee in New York.

The chairman introduced Petefish in rather caustic fashion, and he then passed out copies of his report and commented on it. After he had finished, a fire insurance company president, without deigning to look at Petefish, asked the chairman, "Who is this young man? I presume he is from INA, but I didn't get his name."

"I've always had fun with my name," Petefish recalled years later. "It's been a lot of fun to live with.

"So this man asked me if I would spell it. Now that was just carrying it a little bit too far. So I told him a story.

"I told him that he reminded me of an agent that I called on out in Iowa one time on my first trip in that territory. I went in and introduced myself, and this gentleman said to me, 'Would you pronounce that again?' I did; I repeated it three times. Then he asked me to spell it, and I did. Finally he said, 'Young man, I don't get it. You'll have to come nearer and speak louder. It keeps sounding to me as though you are saying 'Petefish.' "

The laughter that greeted the story put the heckler in his place.

If Diemand's role was that of theoretician of INA's revolution, Ludwig Lewis was the fiery commander of the rebel forces, and Bradford Smith led them into combat.

"Wig" Lewis had a remarkable ability to arouse the enthusiasm of his men. At meetings of the company's field men all over the country, he kept pounding away at the fundamental issues, relating them to the long history of the company and its significance in the development of the nation.

Recalling that the Insurance Company of North America was founded immediately after the thirteen states had achieved independence from Great Britain, Lewis would remind his listeners that "the country's credit structure, the lifeblood of commerce, was weak." Politically, the nation had won its liberty; economically, it was still dependent on England.

"Creation of the insurance corporation," Lewis said, "aided the process of uniting the states, and represented a great step toward making independence secure."

Bitterness and Broken Friendships

The original charter pledged the company to do business so that "advantages would result therefrom to the community in general, and to the mercantile interest in particular." This meant, said Lewis, that "a venture for profit was established in the public interest" when INA was established. Whenever a business forgot the public interest, it risked governmental intervention, control, or even seizure, he argued, for responsibility is an inseparable part of our free enterprise heritage.

"What is this public interest?" Lewis asked rhetorically. "We believe it involves these principles: The insurance-buying public is entitled to protection against insurance losses with the broadest forms possible, at reasonable rates, backed by unquestioned financial strength.

"This public interest is best served when there is flexibility in underwriting practices. A company cannot be wedded to tradition and serve the public interest. Change is the nature of the universe. We must change to keep pace with the economic growth of the country. We must look ahead. And this job must be accomplished on the basis of true private enterprise."

In the fight for freedom from the industry organizations, which we will lump together as the "bureaus" from this point on, the basic conflict was over whether the company should "subject our right of action to the voting power of our competitors." Lewis said, "That's the antithesis of the free enterprise system. It's as simple as that."

If a bureau majority could dictate the forms of protection, the prices, and the other services that the company could make available to its customers, the bureaus would be in a position to prevent the company from acting "in the public interest." The public's need for new coverages could be blocked by a majority which was unready or unwilling to offer them, thus blocking progress.

[179]

"There would be no automobiles on the roads today," Lewis said, "if the pioneer auto-makers had submitted their ideas to the 'voting power' of the wagon makers."

Moreover, there was a philosophical difference between the company and its competitors. "Few, if any," of the other companies agreed with INA's "theory of policyholders' interests coming first," he asserted.

Many years later, Lewis characterized Bradford Smith's handling of the independence fight as "superb." It was to Smith and his assistants, including Heilman, that the bulk of "the actual dirty work," as someone put it, fell.

The legal brains who helped to develop strategy and joined with Smith's group in the endless filings, hearings, and trials were the men of INA's own Legal Department, assisted by local counsel in several states. The company group of lawyers who concentrated on the problems of independent action varied from time to time. William B. Pugh, Jr., took part in the war from the beginning. At that time Edward M. Biddle was general counsel. Biddle, who died in March 1950, was not altogether enthusiastic about the company's breaking free from the industry pattern.

In 1949 John C. Phillips joined the Legal Department to assist in the fight. When Phillips moved to the Claim and Loss Department in 1953 (he later became the first head of the Policyholders Service Division), W. Perry Epes replaced him. The choice of Epes indicated the increased burden of battle being borne by the Legal Department, for he had been a trial attorney in the Antitrust Division of the United States Department of Justice for several years. Another federal antitrust lawyer, Bertram C. Dedman, was invited to join the Legal Department in 1957; he became associate counsel after Epe's death in 1962, and general counsel when Robert Ely retired in 1966.

To the lawyers, the long years of war held the same

interest and challenge that military combat does for an army officer. It was quite another matter for their associates in the fire insurance branch.

"Here you'd be," Heilman said, "in a room with forty people who were really sneering at you and making all kinds of remarks about you—'blackguard,' 'pirate,' and so on. They got quite emotional. It was a severe strain on our people. You felt completely drawn out, thoroughly exhausted, after you had been through one of these ordeals. You felt just like Luther, more or less."

The sharpest attacks were leveled at Smith, who was subjected to offensive, anonymous telephone calls and vilified in slanderous rumors. At a meeting of one bureau, he was left to cool his heels outside the room for ninety minutes. After he was admitted to make his statement, which was heard in utter silence, the chairman invited him to leave. As he strode from the room, he could hear one of the men inside saying, "That will teach those so-and-so's."

There were many critics of INA's position who never stooped to personalities, of course. For example, J. Victor Herd, one of the most vehement opponents, often was the chief spokesman for the other side in lengthy, heated hearings before state insurance commissioners, and usually he was confronted by Smith, who had been a close friend for years. But neither man let his business disagreements affect their relationship. Unfortunately, their friendship was the exception, not the rule.

In a sense, the very fury of the opposition helped INA. Most of its field staff stayed with the company, and they were drawn together, as any beleaguered group is likely to be. After the initial confusion over the attacks on the company, they rallied to its defense with heightened loyalty, feeling somewhat like crusaders.

"It was very easy to develop the enthusiasm for the

point of view of our company," Francis F. Owen said. "It must have been hell to fight the other side of the battle. I wouldn't want to have been on the other side, to attempt to hold to an impossible line, to defend a restrictive practice. I consider myself very fortunate that I was on the side that had something to fight for—and was willing to fight for it."

13: The Saga of Petersen

 IN 1932, when INA's fight for independence was far in the future, V. I. G. Petersen and his wife arrived in the United States on home leave after four years in China, where Petersen represented the American Foreign Insurance Association.

When they headed back to Asia later that year, Petersen had accepted an invitation to join INA, which had opened a Shanghai office in 1929. He was happy with his new business affiliation, having known a number of INA men from 1921 to 1927, the years when he served in the marine department of a fire insurance company in Hartford.

It was in Hartford that he met and married Madge Shepard in 1926. When the AFIA first offered Petersen the opportunity to work for it in China, he talked it over with his wife and then accepted because, as Mrs. Petersen put it, "we decided it would be a much more romantic and interesting and exciting life."

It was all of that—and more. Before it was over, both would have come very close to a terrible death, and "Petey," as he was called, would have completed a hazardous odyssey unparalleled in the annals of the company.

The Petersens returned to a China that was not at war—not in the formal sense—but was far from peace. Japan had begun fourteen years of aggression by invading and conquering the Chinese province of Manchuria, and the fighting had spread to the environs of Shanghai. Before leaving for home, the Petersens had bought a house just outside the city, but they were unable to go to it for weeks because of the fighting in that district, although the house was within the International Settlement, a foreign enclave which was not subject to Chinese law or government.

For the next eight years, like all the other foreigners in China, the Petersens had the sense of living on the edge of an active volcano that might erupt at any time. "It was always uncertain," Madge Petersen recalled years afterward. "You never knew what was going to happen."

Despite the unsettled conditions, it was a good life. "We played a great deal," said Arthur Sullivan, who also represented INA in China at the time, "although we always worked very hard, as hard as I worked anywhere."

Foreigners in China were untaxed; labor was cheap; servants were plentiful; and the social life was as cosmopolitan as one could find anywhere in the world, with Americans, British, French, Germans, Russians, and almost every other nationality living together. There were country clubs and fine restaurants and shops, and the night life of Shanghai was world famous.

A good deal of insurance was written in China during the 1930's. The way it was done would have horrified the people in Philadelphia, for an insurance man couldn't do business by the book in Asia. The rates were high, but the broker always negotiated for a discount, which might run as high as eighty per cent.

"What the broker did with the discount we didn't care," Sullivan said. "We knew that many people got a piece of it, right down to the coolie who swept the floor."

Mid-air collision of two
airliners over New York in
1960 sent this wreckage
hurtling down onto Brooklyn
streets and buildings, killing
128 aboard the planes and
five others on the ground.

Recurrent floods in many
parts of country, like this
Midwestern inundation,
caused widespread hardship.
INA pioneered in attempt to
provide insurance protection
against such losses.

Perils of the sea have gripped man's imagination throughout history. When the "unsinkable" liner TITANIC *(*LOWER LEFT*) went to the bottom in 1912 after striking iceberg (*UPPER LEFT*, still showing marks of ship's scraping), only 705 of the 2,200 were saved. Part of its insurance was with* INA.

U.S. Coast Guard

Another marine loss was suffered by the company
in 1951 when the FLYING ENTERPRISE sank despite
valiant efforts of its captain, Henrik Kurt Carlsen,
who remained aboard for two weeks after passengers
and crew had been taken off by rescue ships.

Mute victim of sinking of oil tanker TORREY
CANYON off southern England in 1967 was this
bird, its feathers glued together by spilled oil.
Costliest single disaster at sea in peacetime
caused death of hundreds of thousands of sea
fowl and fish, vast damage to British beaches.
Catastrophe was entered as a loss in records
of INA, which writes more marine insurance
than any other American company.

Everything about insurance in China was different from
the business as it was known in Philadelphia. Pirates were so
common that all the coastal ships were armed and carried
guards, usually Indian. From time to time an INA-insured ship
would be captured by the pirates. Late in the 1930's one of
Sullivan's closest friends was captured when pirates seized
the ship he was on, and he was their prisoner for months
before being ransomed.

One day a Chinese broker entered Sullivan's office with
a stack of insurance policies.

"Mr. Sullivan," he said, "I want you to cancel all these
policies."

"But why, Mr. Lee?" Sullivan inquired.

"I happened to be in Kongmoon last week," the broker
replied, with the usual flowery Chinese indirection, "and I
saw the Fire Demons walking in the street."

The Fire Demons, in Chinese mythology, presaged a
serious conflagration. As Sullivan interpreted Lee's story, the
broker knew that business was bad in Kongmoon and a number
of merchants were going to burn their buildings in order to
collect the insurance money.

"I understand, Mr. Lee," Sullivan said. "I'm very ap-
preciative of this. And of course I'll cancel the policies immediately."

About a week later Sullivan read in the local Chinese
newspaper that a conflagration in Kongmoon had burned a
large part of the business district there. When he next saw
Lee, Sullivan said, "I certainly appreciate how you saved us
a great deal of money."

"Oh," Lee beamed, "you my very good friend."

"Tell me," asked Sullivan, "What happened to all your
clients in Kongmoon? No insurance?"

The broker leaned back and gazed impassively at the
wall over Sullivan's head.

"Well, not exactly," he said blandly. "Mr. Hepburn,

of the Commercial Union insurance company, he *not* my very good friend. . . ."

Another incident that could have occurred only in China involved a rice mill in Paoshan. Half of the insurance on it was written by INA, the rest by a Japanese insurance company. (Throughout the undeclared war between Japan and China, the Japanese continued to write more insurance business in China than all the other foreign companies together.)

When the mill was destroyed by fire, Sullivan suspected that it had contained not nearly as much rice as the owner had claimed. And he also thought the owner might have set the fire.

A few days after Sullivan inspected the ruins, he received a visit from the Japanese insurance man, a fellow named Watanabi.

"The owner of the rice mill has been arrested for arson," Watanabi told him, "and will soon be tried before the local Chinese magistrate."

"Indeed," murmured Sullivan, remembering that the penalty for arson in China was death.

"I hear from my friends in Paoshan," Watanabi continued, "that the relatives of the accused are paying the magistrate $25,000 to bring in a judgment of not guilty. If he is acquitted, your company and mine will have to pay the claim, even though we are sure it is fraudulent."

Sullivan nodded.

"My suggestion," said Watanabi, "is that each of us put up $25,000, so that together we can pay the magistrate a bribe of $50,000, twice the amount he has been offered by the relatives of the accused, and then the magistrate will bring in a verdict of guilty, thus saving our companies $200,000."

"Mr. Watanabi, I understand your idea perfectly," Sullivan responded, "and I think it is an excellent plan. There is just one difficulty."

"What is that?"

"Unfortunately," said Sullivan, "I have no place in my books to put '$25,000—for killing one assured.' "

In 1938 Sullivan and his wife went to the United States on home leave, and they never returned to the Orient. Because the climate of Shanghai was bad for his wife's health, although she had been born there, the company transferred him to Toronto and later to Los Angeles.

A year earlier the Petersens had taken their home leave. While they were in the United States, the Japanese, who had been nibbling away at China's territory for more than five years, used a brief clash between Japanese and Chinese soldiers at the Marco Polo Bridge near Peking as an excuse to widen their aggression into a full-scale war against the Chinese.

On their way back to China, the Petersens had to mark time for a month in Japan because the fighting in and around Shanghai was so fierce that no ships were able to enter the harbor. Finally they made their way into the embattled city aboard a French cruiser. Unable to reach their home because of gunfire, they lived for a few weeks in a hotel in the heart of the International Settlement, going up to the roof from time to time to watch the fighting in the distance.

The Japanese advance continued for more than two years. By 1939 Japan controlled the coast, all the major cities (except the enclaves of Shanghai, Hong Kong, and Macao), the rail lines, and most of the lowlands and the lower reaches of China's great river systems.

In the winter of 1938 INA transferred Petersen to Hong Kong and appointed him resident manager for the Far East. Nine months later war broke out in Europe, and Britain became a belligerent. Because of the known pro-German attitude of most of the Japanese military and government leaders, it was obvious that Hong Kong was in great danger, especially since the Japanese occupation of nearby Canton and the rest of the adjacent mainland made the British colony militarily indefensible.

Nevertheless, the Westerners in Hong Kong enjoyed a gay life. The Petersens had a house on the elegant south side of the island, high on the mountainside overlooking Repulse Bay, six miles from the city of Victoria.

"We had a yacht built by Americans," Mrs. Petersen said, "and we sailed a great deal. It's the world's most perfect sailing spot. We would sail for miles and miles, and then anchor off one of the lovely islands in the surrounding areas for lunch.

"Of course, we were inclined to worry, but we pushed the thought of danger away. The mood in Hong Kong at the time was to make the most of life while you have got it. We always felt we had lived such a wonderful life that—all right, if it's going to end here—well, let it."

Afterward Petersen said, "Like everyone else in the Far East, we in Hong Kong had heard the cry of 'Wolf! Wolf!' so often and for so many years that we had grown almost completely indifferent to such alarms. Through the years we had seen wars all around us, from the perfect safety of grandstand seats in the Foreign Concessions and the colony. We were a favored people, protected by treaties and foreign arms. . . ."

Meanwhile the European war was going badly for the anti-fascist alliance. Germany overran all of the Continent except for Spain (its non-belligerent ally), Portugal, Sweden, Finland, and the British Isles (which appeared in imminent danger of invasion). In September 1940, Japan joined the Axis by signing the German-Italian Anti-Communist Pact, and the shadow of war over Hong Kong darkened.

Many of the women, especially those with children, left for home or sanctuary in neutral countries. As Japan tightened the pressure by sending planes over the island, the

British sent up fighters of the Royal Air Force to practice aerial maneuvers. Troops poured into Hong Kong from India, Canada, and other parts of the Empire. Guns were set up, all pointing out to sea.

"The British always maintained that Hong Kong was a fortress that could never be taken," Mrs. Petersen said.

Like almost everyone else in the colony, her husband had volunteered for duty, as a non-combatant, of course, because the United States was neutral. Actually, Petersen was a Dane, but the German occupation of Denmark make the citizens of that country "friendly," at least in Japanese eyes. Petersen was assigned to the Auxiliary Fire Service.

Sunday, December 7, 1941, in the United States, was Monday, December 8, in Hong Kong because of the International Date Line. The evening before, the Petersens went sailing, returning about nine o'clock. As usual, all was quiet, and they drove through the darkness—a blackout had been in effect after 9:00 P.M. for some time—to their home.

At six o'clock in the morning the telephone rang.

"They were screaming for Petey to come at once," Mrs. Petersen said. "The airport had been bombed, and the Japanese had landed in Kowloon across the harbor. They expected fighting. We were only six miles from the airport, but we couldn't hear the bombs.

"So Petey got dressed quickly and told me to pack up the silver and we'd get it out of the house. He told me not to be too worried. Then he went off to town and left me, and I started packing."

Dressed in a uniform consisting of a fatigue suit and a beret, Petersen must have been a strange sight indeed to his friends, for he was a rather formal person, a meticulous dresser who always wore a Homburg in the city.

Despite his official duties, Petersen didn't forget his company's interests. He found that the first Japanese aerial attack on Hong Kong had also brought INA its first loss. Later it turned out that this was the first war risk loss suffered by an American insurance company in the Pacific.

Pan American Airways' China Clipper was floating in the harbor, ready to take on passengers, when it was bombed. It caught fire and sank. Destroyed aboard it were mail bags which contained, among other things, a registered package, insured by INA, containing bank notes valued at 6,600 pesos ($3,300 U.S.). The package was being sent by the Chase National Bank in Hong Kong to the Philippine National Bank in Manila.

Petersen got a message out to the United States about the loss, and INA paid the claim in full to the Chase National Bank in New York.

Sitting high on a ridge with four other houses, the Petersens' home made an excellent observation post for the British, who billeted five officers in the house.

"Of course," Mrs. Petersen said, "the Japanese were flying over constantly and noticed all this commotion around our place, and it wasn't long before they started shelling from across Kowloon, trying to hit the ships that were anchored below us in Repulse Bay. The shells would come zooming over, and the planes came shrieking above us, dropping bombs.

"The British threw together a bomb shelter of sand bags and steel plate, just big enough for six of us. I packed three trunks, but I had no opportunity to do anything else, because we were bombed constantly, and there I was, crouching in that damned shelter every day."

One day Petersen stopped by with a truck and carried off two of the trunks, which he put in the office for safe keeping.

Every morning, when Petersen left for his duties in Victoria, Madge, kissing him goodbye, wondered if they would ever see each other again. And her husband, aware of the atrocities committed elsewhere by the Japanese troops, tried not to think of the ordeal that might lie ahead for his handsome wife.

Vulnerable as it was, Hong Kong held out for sixteen days. The Westerners kept hoping that British and American forces would come to their rescue. "You don't have to worry," the British soldiers would say. "Help is coming." At one time rumors flew across the island that the Chinese Nationalist Army was on the offensive, trying to break through to the relief of Hong Kong.

But help never came. Instead, the bombs kept falling; one killed a neighbor in a nearby home.

One day the Japanese asked for a temporary cease-fire and sent a peace party to the British to urge a surrender. Everyone on the island hoped that the British would refuse; it was feared that a surrender would mean an end to any hope of survival. And the British did reject the proposal.

That night the Petersens huddled around their radio with the British officers. The news was disheartening: the British Far Eastern fleet had been crippled by the loss of the battleship *Prince of Wales* and the battle cruiser *Repulse*, both sunk by Japanese aircraft, and an enemy land force was moving down the Malay Peninsula toward Britain's key colony, Singapore. The American Navy had withdrawn from the Philippines to Australia, and our troops in the Philippines were retreating toward Bataan. The mid-Pacific islands of Wake and Guam, American possessions, had been overrun by the enemy.

In a despondent frame of mind, the Petersens went to bed fully clothed, as always in those days. About 5:00 A.M. one of the officers knocked on the door. He said the Japanese had landed on the island and the Petersens had better leave the house quickly.

"Petey went into the kitchen to make some tea," his wife said, "and as he looked out the doorway he saw the

Japanese troops climbing the hill and entering near the garden. He spoke to the British about it, and then the firing started around our ridge. The Japanese were in the hills all around us. More British troops came in and crouched back of the stone wall that led all the way down to the road, along the driveway, and they kept firing."

Because of the heavy fighting, the Petersens dared not leave the house. As British soldiers were wounded, Mrs. Petersen brought out bedding and did what she could for them. By now the house was entirely surrounded except on the downhill side, toward Repulse Bay.

About five o'clock a British major slipped into the house and said, "This is hopeless, Mr. Petersen. You had better try and get away. We don't expect to hold out here the night."

At the suggestion of the major, the Petersens made their way to the garage, where their little Austin was parked. (Their Packard, parked outside the front door, was so riddled with bullets that it couldn't be used.)

"After dreadful maneuvering," Mrs. Petersen said, "Petey got the Austin out of the garage, and we made a beeline down the long, long driveway, with the Japanese firing at us all the time. The car was hit by bullets several times—one struck the radiator—but we escaped unscathed and arrived at the Repulse Bay Hotel."

Telephone communications had not been cut, so they called their house. They were told that a shell had entered the house and it was only a matter of minutes before the British would have to evacuate it. Regretfully, the Petersens asked the soldiers to shoot their two pet dogs, chows, to spare them unnecessary pain.

The hotel was full of soldiers, including a Canadian regiment, and refugees of all nationalities. Two days later the Japanese raised their flag over the hotel's garage, about a thousand yards from the main building, and shellfire began to strike the hotel. Snipers in the hills overlooking the building poured fire into the windows and doorways.

The women and children took shelter in a large storm drainage tunnel, about seven feet in diameter, during the day; there was no fighting at night. Later the Japanese began to direct their fire toward the tunnel, so it could no longer be used. Then a huge storeroom under the hotel was employed as a shelter.

After the Japanese gained control of the beach, the shellfire grew heavy, smashing holes in the walls and ceilings as everyone lay on the floor. That night the military decided to slip out and try to break through the Japanese lines in order to spare the civilians the enemy's wrath for having helped the troops.

After the soldiers crept out, the civilians sat in the lobby, which was lit by one candle. Petersen and a half dozen other men went down to the cellar and destroyed the liquor supply, to avoid trouble from drunken Japanese soldiers. About midnight, sitting in the darkness, with white sheets as flags of surrender at every window, they heard the Japanese moving through the hotel corridors, firing from time to time.

"That was one of the most tense moments I have ever suffered through," Mrs. Petersen said. "We were all terribly jittery."

Two of the civilians spoke Japanese. They called out that there were no soldiers, just civilians. Petersen and the others who had served as non-combatant volunteers with the British had long since destroyed their uniforms.

The Japanese soldiers, "a terrible-looking lot, filthy and ragged," moved cautiously into the lobby, their rifles aimed at the frightened civilians, who were forced to stand with hands up. As others, spreading out through the building, sent back word that the British soldiers were indeed gone, the Japanese relaxed somewhat. Moving among their prisoners, they took watches from the men, but ignored the small jewelry box in which Mrs. Petersen carried her jewelry and money.

At daybreak—it was Christmas Day—they marched the entire group to "the Chinese castle," a fantastic structure built by a rich Chinese. All the civilians were lined up against a wall, with machine guns pointing at them. They were sure they would be slaughtered.

They were wrong. The Japanese treated them quite decently. Civilians of enemy nationality were marched into Victoria, a long seven or eight miles for women and children. The neutrals and those of "friendly" countries (including the Nazi-occupied countries of Europe) were kept in the hotel. Mrs. Petersen, although an American, also had a Danish passport, but she would have been kept with her Danish husband anyhow, because the Japanese made a point of not separating families.

Nevertheless, the civilian prisoners felt that they were living from day to day. Mrs. Petersen kept a diary "because I was afraid I was never going to see home again and I thought, well, in some way maybe I can wangle someone to take it back to the States so my family will know whatever became of us."

After three weeks, the civilians were set free to go into Victoria. All along the road there were dead bodies; the Japanese, who were still executing British soldiers at the "castle" within earshot of the civilians, had not begun to clean up the island. The Petersens lived first at the Danish Consulate and later in the home of a Danish couple halfway up the Peak.

Now having papers issued by the Japanese, they were able to move about the city. The behavior of the occupation troops depended on the individual soldiers, as one might expect: one lieutenant went out of his way to be courteous and helpful, but twice soldiers slapped Petersen in the face sharply, in his wife's presence, because he didn't whip out his papers fast enough to suit them.

There were atrocities, mostly against the British soldiers and nurses. Foreign civilians generally were treated not too unkindly, and so were the wealthier Chinese, although the coolie class suffered greatly.

The spirits of the Westerners were buoyed up in February 1942 when a Swedish family who had hidden a radio heard the news of the American bombing of Tokyo by General James Doolittle's raiders. There was a surreptitious celebration that night by all the foreigners.

In the spring of 1942 plans were announced for repatriating Americans and some others, as part of an exchange of Westerners for Japanese who had been caught by the war in Western countries. Mrs. Petersen objected to going without her husband, but he insisted that she leave, because he had worked out an escape plan. The homeward-bound group was carried on a Japanese ship to Mozambique, a possession of neutral Portugal, and there they went from the Japanese ship to the Swedish liner *Gripsholm*, as the Japanese who were being repatriated passed them on the gangplank.

Mrs. Petersen spent the rest of the war with her relatives in Hartford, waiting anxiously for word of her husband.

Petersen's first act after getting back to Victoria had been to go to the INA offices in room 609 of the East Asia Building. Outside the building he found some of the Chinese office staff, who had given him up for dead. Upstairs they found that, although there had been some petty looting, all the records were intact. Under the very noses of the Japanese, Petersen and his assistant sneaked all of the important records out and hid them in the small branch office in the Chinese shipping district.

Everything that bore the name "Insurance Company of North America" was destroyed or hidden. Petersen also had represented a Swiss company, in a sort of pool arrangement with INA, and so he went to Swiss consul Harry A. Keller and received from him an official notice, bearing a hand-lettered Swiss flag, which said: "I, the undersigned . . . hereby certify that the contents of this office . . . are also the property of the Switzerland General Insurance Company, Limited, of Zurich, Switzerland, whose manager is Mr. V. I. G. Petersen."

The notice, posted on the door of the office, was effective; the Japanese never bothered the place.

A few weeks later, after receiving a Japanese license to occupy the premises, Petersen and his aides brought the hidden records back to the main office. There they wound up the business by bringing all the accounts up to date, just as if they were working in normal times. When that was done, the records were wrapped in protective materials, carried out secretly, and hidden in holes dug in the mountainside. After the war, the records were all exhumed and found to be in perfect order.

As a precaution, the painstaking Petersen had copies made of all the vital records, and they were smuggled, a few at a time, into the neutral Portuguese colony of Macao, forty miles from Hong Kong.

As a final service to INA, Petersen stored much of the office furniture and equipment and rented the rest, along with the office, to a Chinese-Japanese firm.

All in all, Petersen's work spoke well not only for the man, but for the insurance business, which had trained him to deal calmly, carefully, prudently, and thoroughly with emergencies, which are part of the insurance way of life.

After Petersen had done everything he could in Hong Kong, he prepared to depart from the island as inconspicuously as possible. His Chinese chief clerk, at risk of his life, volunteered to help him.

People in Hong Kong were permitted to visit Macao for a maximum of three days, so Petersen boarded the Macao boat with his assistant, disguised as a coolie, carrying a bag, so that it would not seem that the Dane intended to overstay the allotted time.

From Macao, Petersen sent a cable to his wife in America. All it said was: "Have landed in Macao." But she knew it meant that he had begun his attempt to escape.

Then he went to the British consulate to get certain documents he would need to show Chinese guerrillas and Nationalist troops as he made his way into the interior. To facilitate the preparation of the papers, he left his passport and re-entry permit with the consul, who assured Petersen that he'd put him in touch with a guide who could help him get to freedom through China.

Unfortunately, however, Japanese police agents in Macao began to follow him as soon as he landed from Hong Kong. They had somehow conceived the notion that he was one of the American fliers from the Doolittle mission who had been shot down and were trying to escape across China.

Learning that Petersen was being shadowed, the British advised him to lie low for awhile, so he managed to lose his "tail" and proceeded to check into a disreputable Chinese hotel in the worst quarter of Macao, which was then, and is still, considered possibly the most evil city in the world. It seems likely that Petersen was in greater danger from his fellow lodgers in the hotel than from the Japanese.

It was July 29, 1943, more than a year after his wife's departure from Hong Kong, when Petersen arrived in Macao. For three weeks he remained in hiding before he was able to slip away. He had to turn back the first time because a Japanese patrol boat had anchored near the sampan on which he was to be smuggled out. Two or three nights later he was able to begin his journey, hidden in a secret two-and-a-half-foot-high compartment in the fish hold of the sampan.

Perils: Named and Unnamed

After a close shave when the sampan inadvertently drifted close to a Japanese naval station, Petersen was put ashore near a guerrilla post up the Pearl River.

For more than two months he traveled through Japanese-occupied territory by junk, sedan chair, and on foot. He never knew whom he could trust: besides the Japanese and their spies, the countryside was overrun with pirates and bandits. When he had to take to the rivers, there were Japanese patrol boats, and always overhead Japanese airplanes cruised on reconnaissance. At night he slept in dirty, verminous hovels that passed as inns (this the fastidious Petersen!).

When he left Hong Kong, he weighed about 168 pounds. When he reached freedom, his weight was down to 123 pounds, and the inadequate diet on which he had subsisted had made him ill with beri-beri.

At Kueilin, Petersen finally was sufficiently far from Japanese patrols to be able to rest for a week. But he had difficulties there with British officials, for he had no identification papers. While he had been in hiding in Macao, the British consul heard a rumor one day that the Japanese were about to take over the Portuguese colony suddenly, so the consul burned all the documents in his possession, including Petersen's passport and other papers. (The rumor, of course, was untrue.)

By a stroke of luck, Petersen came across an old friend, a former Shanghai bank official who was then in the American consulate in Kueilin. The American vouched for Petersen and helped him to get his papers in order again.

Finally Petersen was able to travel by railroad, but this was a Chinese provincial railroad in time of war. Traveling at a snail's pace, the train stopped whenever Japanese planes approached, and the passengers had to scramble out and lie in ditches or pressed against the side of cliffs while the enemy planes dropped their bombs and swooped low in strafing runs.

There was delay after delay, and Petersen was getting sicker all the time.

Part of the trip to Kunming was made with a British military convoy over the Burma Road. Sitting in the back of a truck that lurched like a punch-drunk fighter around the hairpin turns that occurred every half-mile along the Burma Road, Petersen braced himself one day as the driver slammed on the brakes. The truck collided with another vehicle, and the load of oil drums tumbled down on Petersen. He was in agony with a broken nose, broken shoulder, and dislocated vertebrae, and there was no doctor available.

And so, in intense pain, he was lifted back aboard the truck, and he resumed the slow, tortuous journey to Kunming, an expedition interrupted several times each day by Japanese aircraft that left shattered trucks and lifeless bodies in their wake.

At Kunming, Petersen received medical care, but without waiting to recover fully he boarded an RAF flight going over "the Hump" of the Himalayas to India, his teeth chattering from the cold at 22,000 feet. The plane set him down at Calcutta, whence he made his way by train to Bombay.

There he was able to board an American cruiser bound for Australia, where he was put aboard another Navy vessel that delivered him in San Francisco, forty days after leaving Bombay.

It had taken him seven and a half months to travel from Hong Kong to San Francisco.

After a long period of rest in Arizona and Mexico, Petersen resumed his work for the company, but not in the Far East. He specialized in international insurance, devoting most of his attention to Latin America, until his death in 1961.

In 1960 the Petersens went out to the Far East again on a long trip. Their first stop was Japan, and Mrs. Petersen wondered, "Can I ever face the Japanese again, hating them so?" But she and her husband spent four months in Japan, and "made very close friends" there. All the old hostility, on both sides, was gone.

In Hong Kong, where they had once planned to spend their years in retirement, they found their old house repaired and turned into a two-family dwelling. They stayed at the Repulse Bay Hotel, in the very room where the Japanese had incarcerated them.

"But Hong Kong had changed," Madge Petersen sighed. "It just didn't seem the same place. I didn't like it at all."

14: 'A Shooting War . . . Right Now'

T. LEAMING SMITH took a trip to England in March 1938, because INA, in his words, "saw the handwriting on the wall." The writing spelled War.

In retrospect it seems that the message should have been clear to anyone. In 1932 Japan had begun her aggression against China. Three years later Mussolini invaded Ethiopia, one of the oldest Christian nations in the world, and the League of Nations did nothing, although the Ethiopian emperor, Haile Selassie, warned the members "of the deadly peril which threatens them," concluding prophetically, "God and history will remember your judgment."

Early in 1936 Adolf Hitler's storm troopers marched into the Rhineland, with no real opposition, and later that year the Spanish Civil War broke out when a Spanish general, Francisco Franco, with the encouragement and aid of Germany and Italy, rebelled against the Madrid government. As Germany got ready to occupy Austria, which it did on March 12, 1938, the shape of things to come was so apparent to some people that INA decided it was time to prepare for the war that seemed almost inevitable now.

From a business point of view, the company's primary

concern was over the ocean marine war risk rates. Of course, when and if war began, the war risk rates would be raised, but those ships which had left port before the opening of hostilities would be exposed to enemy action, and low peacetime war risk rates would not provide a sufficient cushion against the losses to be expected in the first few weeks, for the peacetime rates were one-twentieth of one per cent, "a nominal charge," in Leaming Smith's opinion.

In London he discussed with British underwriters the necessity of raising war risk rates. The British were not concerned.

"None of the British to whom I talked had any idea there was going to be a war," he recalled.

That was, it must be borne in mind, the year of Munich: in September Prime Minister Neville Chamberlain returned from negotiations with Hitler to declare to cheering crowds, "I believe it is peace for our time"—at the expense of dismembered Czechoslovakia.

But we Americans have no right to be smug, for "American public opinion," in Frederick Lewis Allen's words, "was perhaps more isolationist than at any time since before the [first] World War." The country had rejected several opportunities to take a stand against the march of the dictators. There were many Americans who recognized the peril, but there were similarly prescient Britons, exemplified by the Cassandra of the House of Commons, Winston Churchill.

Although the London underwriters did not hike their war risk rates (which meant that American insurers, for competitive reasons, also would be unable to boost the charge), they did offer to reinsure in full the war risk coverages of INA and other American companies at the going rates. "So we jumped at that," Leaming Smith said.

When war did break out, little more than a year later,

his company saved about $60,000 in losses as a result of the deal.

Again, as in World War I, there was no question of impartiality in Philadelphia. It was clear that the ultimate confrontation would be Britain against Germany, and never for a moment did anyone in the company dream that INA would not favor the British forces.

When Mussolini made it clear that Italy was irrevocably on Hitler's side, Benjamin Rush issued a directive: INA would write no marine insurance for trade with Italy. According to Ludwig Lewis, Rush was asked by the renowned New York underwriter, Hendon Chubb, "Is this a matter of principle or business?"

"There is no difference," Rush replied tersely.

Whereupon Chubb told him that he would go along with the boycott on commerce with Mussolini's dictatorship.

The 1939 Davis Cup matches for the international lawn tennis team championship, bringing together the top tennis stars from every part of the world, were to be held at the Merion Cricket Club at Haverford, on the Main Line outside Philadelphia. The club's insurance broker asked Bradford Smith, Jr., if INA would write what was, in a sense, an all-risk policy. The coverage would provide for the company to reimburse the club for all its expenses if the tournament, for any reason, could not be held. The club was investing a good deal of money in special work on the grass courts, erection of grandstands, printing of tickets and advertisements, and other preparations, so it wanted a policy of about $50,000.

Such a request would not raise eyebrows today, but in those prewar days it was very unusual for an American underwriter to handle that sort of thing; Lloyd's was the place where a broker usually placed it. But INA, already stirring impatiently under the restraints of the business as it was then conducted in this country, found the idea intriguing, and after some negotiation Smith wrote the policy.

Shortly afterward, he went off with his wife, a woman witty as well as attractive, for a vacation in Central America. The beginning of September found the Smiths in Chichicastenango, a colorful market town of less than 2,000 souls, more than a mile high in Guatemala's western mountain range. (Chichicastenango, which is not even listed in many atlases, enjoyed brief fame in the 1930's when its name was used in a popular American song.)

The only electricity in the town was provided by a diesel generator which was turned on only when darkness fell; there was no power at all during the day.

One day Smith heard an extraordinary hubbub in the village square. There he found an animated crowd that seemed to include every inhabitant of the place, all of them straining to listen to a radio voice coming through loudspeakers mounted in the plaza. The voice was screaming excitedly in very rapid Spanish.

"I could hardly catch a word," Smith said. "But it sounded as though he were announcing something about war."

Smith tugged at the sleeve of the man next to him and asked, "What is it? What's he saying?"

The man shrugged, "*No inglés.*"

The next man didn't speak English, either. Nor the man beside him.

Finally Smith found someone who could manage a bit of English. It was war. Germany had invaded Poland; London and Paris had presented Berlin with an ultimatum; they were expected to be at war in a matter of hours.

The next day the Smiths made their way to Guatemala City, where they saw big black headlines in the newspapers: "¡La Guerra!"

That night they had dinner in a restaurant run by an

Englishwoman. She told them about the torpedoing of the SS *Athenia* 250 miles off the northwest coast of Ireland, the first ship to be sunk in the war. With 1,102 passengers, most of them Canadian and American, and a crew of 315, the ship had been en route to Quebec and Montreal with refugees from the war zone. Fortunately, other ships had been close enough to rush to the rescue, so only 112 persons, including 69 women and 16 children, perished. Later the Smiths learned that a Philadelphia neighbor and her baby had been aboard the *Athenia*.

On the narrow gauge railroad down to Puerto Barrios on the Gulf of Honduras the next day, Smith remembered the Davis Cup policy. Had all the tennis stars been able to get to Philadelphia before the war started? Would they be permitted to compete, or would their governments call them home at once?

After some difficulty, the Smiths managed to secure passage to the United States on a United Fruit ship. When they got home, they found that all of the tennis players had received permission from their governments to remain in Philadelphia until the tournament was over. For the first time in twenty years, the Australian team won the Davis Cup. And, apart from the blow to the national pride of INA's tennis enthusiasts, the company suffered no loss.

The initial impact of the war on the American insurance market was bound to be felt by the marine branch. More than four months before the outbreak of hostilities, the American Institute of Marine Underwriters had appointed a five-man committee, including Henry C. Thorn, INA's marine manager in New York, to find a solution to the potential reinsurance problem. As a result of the committee's work, the American Cargo War Risk Reinsurance Exchange came into being and began operations on June 10, 1939.

Thus, the American marine underwriters were not

caught off balance in September. Their machinery for coping with the new conditions "was not only set up but had actually been functioning for several months," as Thorn later pointed out.

About 150 companies were members of the Exchange. Each member ceded to the Exchange all of its war risk coverage, and each company accepted a fixed percentage of the total risk, according to its size and inclinations. As the largest American marine insurer, INA accepted the largest share, ten per cent.

T. Leaming Smith explained how the company decided on its subscription to the pool. In World War I, when every company was on its own, INA had a limit on trans-Atlantic war risks of $75,000. Smith figured the relation between $75,000 and the company's resources during World War I.

"Then I applied the same ratio to the company's resources as of 1939," he said. "I found our resources at the beginning of World War II were such that we could have taken something like $600,000 or $700,000 as our share. That seemed a little too much so we settled on $250,000, or ten per cent of the total pool capacity."

The day the Nazis invaded Poland, September 1, 1939, the Exchange's rate committee tripled war risk rates throughout the world, except for shipments confined to the Western hemisphere or carried by American-flag vessels "not touching European ports or not via the Mediterranean." The rates kept fluctuating rapidly, of course; the rate committee often met several times in one day. Two weeks after war began, rates went up, but by the end of the month they had declined somewhat; United Kingdom rates then were five per cent for belligerent shops, one and a half per cent for Americans, and three and three-quarters per cent for other neutrals.

That was during the early period of the war, however,

when Hitler paused to complete his conquest of Poland and prepare for the next phase, a time when there was so little combat that some Americans called it a "phony war" and the English dubbed it the "bore war." Soon everyone would look back nostalgically to those days.

After the lull was ruptured by Germany's victorious offensive in the spring of 1940, striking first at Denmark and Norway and then, about a month later, at Western Europe, rates soared. The occupied countries were dropped altogether; many other high-risk areas had no listed rates; they were marked "quoted on application."

After Italy, as President Roosevelt put it, stabbed France in the back by invading it from the South while the French were trying to stop the Germans in the North, rates for Mediterranean shipping went to twenty-five per cent. During the intense air war, later to be called the Battle of Britain, rates for London reach fifteen per cent.

In the United States, still a neutral although most Americans sympathized with the British cause, the first two years of the war witnessed the transition within INA from Rush to Platt to Diemand. On March 20, 1941, Diemand was elected president, and soon afterward the company started preparing for a big celebration of its 150th anniversary, beginning with publication of a history of the company, *Biography of a Business*, by Marquis James, who had won two Pulitzer Prizes (for biographies of Sam Houston in 1929 and Andrew Jackson in 1937).

American neutrality was being increasingly threatened by Germany's successes. In response to them, war supply shipments to Japan were belatedly cut off; the President arranged a deal by which Britain acquired fifty old but badly needed destroyers in exchange for military bases on British soil in the New World; the Lend-Lease Act made it easier for

the British to buy munitions in the United States; and Roosevelt sent American troops to occupy Iceland to prevent the
Germans from seizing that island.

(Long after the war was over, a bell from one of the
ships in the destroyers-for-bases deal hung in the study of
Bradford Smith, Jr., who had received it from H. C. Mills,
INA's Canadian general manager and later vice president. The
bell had been presented to Mills by a prominent citizen of
Halifax.)

On May 21 an American merchantman, the *Robin
Moor*, had the unhappy distinction of being the first vessel
flying the American flag to be sent to the bottom by a Nazi
submarine. An American destroyer, the USS *Greer*, was unsuccessfully attacked by a sub off Iceland in September, and
Washington issued a "shoot-on-sight" order to the Navy. A
month later another of our destroyers, the *Kearny*, was damaged by a German torpedo that took the lives of eleven American sailors, and a fortnight after that the destroyer *Reuben
James* was sunk by a sub, with a loss of about 100 lives.

"It may not be possible to maintain [the] differential
[between belligerent and American war risk rates] much
longer," Henry Thorn wrote in the New York *Journal of
Commerce* on November 24. "We are engaged in a shooting
naval war with Germany right now . . . [and are] faced with
more than the possibility of becoming an all-out belligerent
in two more or less separate wars."

During that same month an INA advertisement appearing in national magazines was headed "Meet Me on the Moon
Next Tuesday." The text of the ad said in part:

"A giant passenger rocket, hurtling through blank space
on a plume of flame, bound for the moon.

"That would have sounded utterly fantastic only yesterday—but today we're not so sure it is impossible, because fuel
for such a trip is available here and now! Scientists have learned

how to develop and control almost unlimited power . . . by splitting the atom of an isotope of the metal uranium (called U–235).

"If this newly found power is harnessed for general use, this is what it will mean to you! With a tiny lump of U–235, the size of a pin head, you will heat your home for two years, or drive your car 200,000 miles! Everyone will enjoy undreamed comforts and luxuries, when U–235 is made cheap and plentiful! . . ."

On the very day that advertisement was being published, a secret committee of the National Academy of Sciences was reporting to the White House that a "fission bomb of superlatively destructive power" could be developed using U–235. Of course, nobody at INA had any knowledge that the ad was, by the wildest coincidence, drawing attention to the scientific discovery that made possible the manufacture of the atomic bomb.

On December 7 the Japanese struck at Pearl Harbor, and the United States was at war.

Nothing was ever quite the same again—for any American, for any business, for American society itself.

INA immediately called off all its plans for the 150th anniversary celebration, limiting its observance to John Diemand's vigorous speech for independence from restrictive industry practices.

Male employees of draft age began enlisting or preparing to answer the call to duty when it might come, and some of the women joined the armed forces too. The board of directors authorized payment of one year's salary to the dependents of any employee who was killed while on active duty, and Christmas gifts to employees in the services, usually eight and one-third per cent of one year's civilian pay but not less than $50, were voted to be given annually as the holiday season approached.

[209]

Perils: Named and Unnamed

With insurance classified, as someone put it, "down around artificial flowers in importance" with regard to draft deferments, women had to be asked to carry an increasing responsibility for the company's business. By the end of 1944, women constituted sixty per cent of the company's personnel, compared with forty-six per cent before the war.

For the first time in the company's history, women were used even in what the industry calls "judgment-level" jobs. "Many of them did marvelous jobs for us," Frank Owen, in charge of West Coast operations, said.

Like all other companies, INA also turned perforce to the vast numbers of women who in those unsettled times followed their husbands from one Army post, airfield, or Navy base to the next as long as they were stationed in the United States, a gallant, loyal band of wives who wryly called themselves "camp followers," giving a new, respectable, and honored meaning to that ancient term of opprobrium. Understandably, and properly, their first and overwhelming concern was for their husbands, and there was not, could not be, the slightest permanence in their residence or employment.

All of this created considerable problems for those who employed them in order to carry on the business. Continual turnover, incessant training of new employees, uncertainty about when the remaining men might be conscripted—that was the life of INA managers and supervisors all over the continent during the war.

The company bought war bonds up to the statutory limit, and the employees, too, purchased so many bonds that they, as well as INA, received citations from the government. They also contributed to the Red Cross and other war-related appeals, donated blood for the wounded, and provided companionship for GI's at the USO facilities and the employees' lounge of the home office. None could forget that in 1943, on an average, one man left the company every day to go into military service.

[210]

'A Shooting War . . . Right Now'

In the early days of the war, the only part of the continental United States that believed itself to be in serious danger from enemy action was the West Coast. The worst result of that fear, the decision to take action against all Japanese-Americans west of the Rockies, affected the company, too, for many of these people were policyholders and respected, stable customers.

There were only 110,000 Americans of Japanese ancestry on the West Coast, two-thirds of them in their late teens and early twenties, but hysteria exaggerated their numbers and maligned their loyalty. According to Captain Allan R. Bosworth, who was assigned to Navy Intelligence in San Francisco, not a single Japanese spy was convicted during the war and fewer than 2,000 were regarded as security risks who had to be interned until war's end.

Thirty-three thousand Japanese-Americans served in the Pacific theater of war and in Western Europe, and one outfit composed entirely of these men, the 442nd Regimental Combat Team, suffered the heaviest casualties of any American unit in the entire war and became the most decorated outfit in the long history of the United States Army, one of its men even receiving the Congressional Medal of Honor.

Despite this record of loyalty, 70,000 persons of Japanese ancestry, including American citizens born in this country, were forcibly removed in the spring of 1942 from their homes on the West Coast with only the possessions they could carry (no pets allowed) and immured behind barbed wire at several "relocation centers," which Bosworth described in a book on the subject, *America's Concentration Camps*.

One of the Army officers reluctantly supervising this evacuation was INA's Robert W. Wilson, who, as an Infantry reservist, was called to duty about a month after Pearl Harbor and assigned to the Military Police.

"It was a very distasteful duty to perform," Wilson recalled. "It bothered my conscience. Regardless of the rationalizations, the fact remains that we put them in concentration camps and guarded them with live ammunition. The whole thing was disgraceful."

When an opportunity arose for Wilson, who had a private pilot's license, to become a glider pilot, he leaped at the chance, and eventually saw perhaps more combat than any other INA man.

"The Japanese-American evacuation involved a considerable amount of our business," Owen said, "because a number of our agents and producers had substantial Japanese business."

Unable to draw on their frozen bank accounts, compelled to abandon their homes and businesses, most Japanese got only about ten per cent of what their properties were worth, and they didn't get that until war's end. But some Japanese found a way to protect most of the gains they had laboriously earned over the years. "They transferred all their properties to people in whom they had confidence, who then retained those properties in the names of the Japanese owners until the end of the war," Owen recalled.

One such man was Theo Thomas, an INA agent in Stockton, California, who returned "tremendous amounts of money" to his Japanese-American friends and business acquaintances upon their release from the camps.

Admittedly the West Coast had reason to be jumpy, for it was the only American territory in this hemisphere to be the object of enemy action apart from the U-boat depredations along the Atlantic and Gulf coasts. A Japanese submarine, I-17, surfaced and shelled oil tanks near Santa Barbara on February 23, 1942. Bomb-carrying balloons released in Japan set some small fires in the Pacific Northwest and killed six Oregonians. And there was a moment of near-panic in June 1942, when the Japanese occupied two islands in the Aleutians, stepping stones to Alaska (losing them to an American counter-offensive a year later).

The most long-lasting effect of the war in the Western states, however, was the incredible increase in population and industry. For half a century or more the West had been growing in population faster than any other part of the country, but the change during the war years was sharply increased: in the decade from 1940 to 1950 the population of the West soared 40.4 per cent, while the Northeast was growing a mere 9.7 per cent, the North Central states 10.8 per cent, and even the South only 13.3 per cent. Boeing, Lockheed, Douglas, Kaiser, and hundreds of other major manufacturing organizations brought a new dimension to the economic development of the West, which would have considerable significance to INA in the future.

"I remember one trip that Bradford Smith, Jr., took out here during the war," Owen said. "We went out to the Santa Monica plant of the Douglas Aircraft Company at night and walked around the perimeter of the operation. Brad Smith made the line [*i.e.*, determined the terms of the policy] that night, or maybe it was the next day, that made it possible for the brokers and our agents to place the risk."

At that time Owen obtained for the company two of the largest surety (performance-of-contract) bonds, both for Douglas, one for $250,000,000 and the other for $150,000,000, although the rating bureau companies were sure that only they could handle such a massive undertaking.

War damage had always been excluded from ordinary fire policies, but it was obvious from the events abroad that insurance protection had to be provided to American plants which might be subjected to enemy air raids, shelling from hostile warships, or other perils inherent in our state of belligerence. Because of the unprecedented size of the risk, only the government could offer such protection, so Congress established a federal institution, the War Damage Corporation, in which 546 insurance companies joined with the government.

The member companies subscribed for ten per cent of the total profits or losses to a maximum of $20,000,000. INA's twenty-eight service offices were authorized to act as fiduciary agents for the WDC.

Before American entry into the war, the British underwriters had transferred a large part of their money and securities to this country as a precaution, but they themselves remained in their besieged island. Since Lloyd's continued to play an important role in reinsuring American risks, there were some problems. For example, all cables had to be in code, because the facts needed for underwriting can tell an enemy a great deal about strategic industrial production. (In fact, certain officers of the company to this day must be cleared for security by the federal government, and even members of the board of directors are not permitted to see the files on risks that include classified information.)

But even in code INA could not transmit some information to the London reinsurers.

"We had complete freedom to negotiate coverage," H. Richard Heilman said. "All we didn't have freedom on was to name places or what a risk was doing. We were proscribed from saying that in this plant they were making this or that. This was classified."

Sabotage was a major worry, of course, for there had been several successful attempts to hamper war production in this country in World War I. During the second global conflict, INA bought reinsurance from Lloyd's for a sabotage cover, but it ran into an unexpected problem in negotiating the contract.

"We were fearful," Heilman said, "that perhaps all the plants of a certain kind would be attacked simultaneously by saboteurs—all of Alpha Corporation's ball bearing plants, let's say. One of the interesting things about that cover was the debate of limits.

"The problem was to define an event—what is a single

event, what is a series of events. This was essential to the contract, because if you are going to pay losses up to a certain sum, and recover from the reinsurer for losses above that level, the key to it is this: if two plants suffer a loss of $100,000 each (assuming that you bear a loss up to $100,000 and the reinsurer pays losses in excess of $100,000 up to $1,000,000), is the damage to these two plants one event, in which case your total loss would be $100,000, or is it two events, which would cost you $200,000?

"We finally agreed two or more related losses in a single metropolitan area would be adjudged one event, but if they occurred in different metropolitan areas, the burden of proof would be on us to show that more than coincidence was involved."

It was in the course of charting each metropolitan area that the men at INA first recognized "the so-called corridor, that these metropolitan areas ran together to form a single band from Norfolk up to Boston," Heilman recalled. "It was an interesting by-product."

No sabotage of consequence was ever proved.

"We often suspected sabotage," Heilman said, "but because of the great secrecy we couldn't get enough facts to pin any loss down to that cause."

In the first year of American participation in the war, net written fire premiums rose 21.6 per cent over the previous year, but the business was beset with problems. There was no new construction except of war plants; non-essential inventories were dwindling. The draft and the difficulty of replacing outdated and defective equipment hurt the efficiency of fire departments. The immense shifting of population, in addition to the usual breakdown of standards of conduct to be expected in wartime, increased the "moral hazard." Finally, new manufacturing processes came into being, and it took time before they could be evaluated accurately for insurance.

Auto insurance fell off in 1942 because of rationing

and the lack of new civilian cars, and the reduced exposure, because there were fewer cars on the roads, impelled the industry to lower rates. In 1943, on the other hand, INA's casualty affiliate, the Indemnity, wrote more auto insurance than it had the year before. The explanation for this lay in the financial responsibility laws that several states had passed.

Until the end of 1943, when the construction of war plants and military bases had been largely completed, the Indemnity wrote workmen's compensation and liability policies on a scale unprecedented in the company's history. It also began insuring risks which had hitherto been regarded as too hazardous—munitions plants and the like.

These high-risk policies produced some unusual claims. An explosion in one plant blew a workman out of the building and through a barbed wire fence. Because he shot through the air with his body horizontal to the ground, however, he happened to pass between the strands of barbed wire, and he picked himself up with nothing worse than a few scratches and bruises and a bad case of nerves.

In another munitions plant, INA's safety engineers believed they had eliminated almost everything that could set off an explosion. But one day there was an explosion in the factory in a room where three women had been working. Two of the women were injured. It was the third woman who had inadvertently been the cause of the blast, according to subsequent investigation. The blonde in question had worn silk panties under her overalls, and a charge of static electricity, built up in the silk, had provided the spark that did the damage. Which only proved that there were limits to the hazard-investigating efforts of the safety engineers.

About 1944 a brokerage firm approached the Indemnity and a large Chicago insurance company at the same time with a suggestion that the companies begin writing group accident and health insurance to cover civilians who were exposed to unusual hazards in support of the war effort.

"This type of insurance, until then, had been placed in London," explained Edwin H. Marshall, who was given the responsibility for underwriting this new coverage. "No American company had been writing this, until we and the other company entered the field on the same day.

"Starting with accidental death insurance on war correspondents and photographers, including Ernie Pyle, Raymond Clapper, and all *Time, Life*, and Scripps-Howard personnel, we soon added insurance for the test pilots of many major aircraft manufacturers. [However, Pyle was not covered by the Indemnity when he finally was killed on April 18, 1945, on Ie Shima, near Iwo Jima.]

"Our market soon came to the attention of the government, which also was in need of such a facility. We were asked to devise a trip accident policy for civilians and military personnel while traveling worldwide on the Army Air Transport Command and the Naval Air Transport Service [planes] in support of the war. This we did successfully."

This coverage, drawn up at the request of the government, led to the company's being asked to write accident and health insurance for the Manhattan District's thirty unnamed men, the scientists working on the development of the atomic bomb.

The new field of activity took five per cent of Marshall's time at the start, but within six months he was spending all his working day on it.

Obviously, such war risk coverage was difficult to underwrite, especially at the beginning, when nobody at INA or the Indemnity had any experience in this specialty.

"We were pulling rates out of the air," Marshall said. "They were nothing but educated guesses. Our philosophy was that we had self-preservation working for us. We felt that when a war correspondent or even a test pilot personally thought that the odds were too much against him, that he had only one chance in five of coming out of a hazardous spot alive, he just wouldn't expose himself to it. These were reasonable people, and we figured that very few men would deliberately expose themselves to death when the odds got much greater than one out of ten."

By a curious turn of circumstances, the casualty underwriters of the Indemnity even found themselves writing marine insurance in one of those rivalries between branches of the INA family that occurred from time to time before Bradford Smith reorganized the operations in the 1960's. This is the way it happened:

The government needed insurance protection to cover the trial runs of the Liberty ships, oil-burning freighters, that were being produced in great numbers by American shipyards to meet the war needs. When the marine underwriters of the hull syndicate, to which INA belonged, submitted their bid, the government thought it too high. Just about that time Herbert P. Stellwagen happened to drop into the office of an official in Washington.

"This fellow began to berate the insurance companies generally," Stellwagen said. "He didn't tell me what the bid was, but he bellowed that the government certainly wasn't going to do business on that basis. Then he demanded to know whether I could do anything about it.

"Well, under the general heading of Bodily Injury and Property Damage we were privileged to write marine insurance, for those were the two things that could happen. So, in sheer ignorance, we made a price and wrote the cover. Then all hell broke loose with the marine people, including our own, who wanted us to rescind and get out, which we refused to do.

"I think we got about $300,000 in premiums out of that and no losses.

"It was a good risk because at that time they were testing the Liberty ships about two hours. There was no relationship between that kind of trial run and the sort of shakedown cruise you'd give to a ship like the *Queen Elizabeth*. They'd take the ship out to see if it would run, and then the government would take it over, and that was it. We were just insuring for those two hours of trial run."

One of the Liberty ships, incidentally, was the *Benjamin Rush*, named for the great-grandfather of INA's board chairman. Launched at Baltimore in 1942, the ship made fifteen trans-Atlantic crossings in convoy, carried supplies to two beachheads during the invasion of North Africa, and was the second merchant ship to enter the harbor at Toulon when the Allied forces made their landing in the South of France in 1944.

In 1941, during which the country was a neutral until the last three weeks, INA's ocean marine business was, as the somewhat complacent annual report put it, "satisfactory."

"There seemed then," the following year's annual report said, "no reason to anticipate that 1942 would not conform to the pattern of the previous two years. The first sinking in mid-January by a submarine off the Atlantic coast, and the one or two which followed, did not cause undue concern, as they seemed to represent a logical consequence of our entry into the war, and there was confidence that the government had foreseen this eventuality and had taken or would take proper steps to deal with the problem.

"However, the situation steadily deteriorated, and the heavy rate advances which were successively imposed were insufficient to compensate for the steadily increasing risk.

"The marine insurance market underestimated the extent of the submarine attack upon our shipping and overestimated the government's ability immediately to cope with it.

"Further to aggravate the position, war risk insurance on American hulls of which the company had a share and on which severe losses had been incurred was taken over by the War Shipping Administration at rates lower than those ac-

[219]

ceptable to the American commercial market, thus removing the opportunity of recovering the loss already sustained on this class."

The havoc wrought by German submarines on American coastal shipping in the first half-year or so after Pearl Harbor was "calamitous" and, "to a great extent, unnecessary," in the view of a British naval historian, Captain Donald Macintyre. In his book, *The Battle of the Atlantic*, he wrote: "Though war with Germany had for some time been inevitable and foreseen, no steps whatever had been taken to prepare for the institution of a convoy system on the American East Coast, along which ran the densest and most valuable stream of shipping in the world at that date, carrying cargoes of cotton, sugar, oil, iron, steel, and bauxite."

The enemy submarine commanders found a happy hunting ground off our Atlantic and Gulf Coasts. Ships streamed placidly along with their navigation lights pinpointing their position at night. Lighthouses, beacons, and buoys were still flashing their signals.

"There was still no evidence," wrote Wolfgang Frank in *The Sea Wolves*, "that the Americans were switching over to wartime conditions. . . . Their captains stopped close to torpedoed ships and asked for information over the loud hailer: should a ship be hit but remain capable of steaming, the captain never bothered to zig-zag or vary his speed so as to impede the U-boat in dealing the *coup de grâce*.

"And they had no idea of security; they chattered about everything under the sun over the 600-meter wave band—and as if that were not enough, the coastal defense stations sent out over the air a regular program of information, giving details of rescue work in progress, of where and when aircraft would be patrolling, and the schedules of anti-submarine vessels."

As a result of this carelessness, 40 ships were sunk off the Atlantic seaboard in January 1942, 65 in February, 86 in

March, 69 in April, 111 in May, and 121 in June, after which the institution of a convoy system along the Coast cut our losses sharply. (It had not been until April that the first U-boat was sunk off the United States coast.)

But ships were still not convoyed in the Gulf of Mexico and in the Caribbean, so in May 41 vessels, more than half of them tankers, were sent to the bottom of the Gulf, and another 38 ships were destroyed in Caribbean waters. In May and June 148 ships were sunk in those areas, before destroyers, shepherding the freighters in convoy, put an end to the open season on American shipping.

T. Leaming Smith still remembers the first six months of 1942 as "a frightful time" because of the enemy onslaught. Some of the companies which had subscribed to the American Cargo War Risk Reinsurance Exchange got cold feet and wanted to withdraw. Although INA was already the biggest single member of the pool, it agreed to pick up the shares of the defectors, bringing its total participation to twelve and a half per cent.

Benjamin Rush personally insisted that INA could not withdraw because of its leadership as the No. 1 marine insurer and its history of serving the public interest. Besides, Rush added, if private enterprise failed to rise to the occasion, it would be an open invitation for the government to inject itself into the business of insurance.

To those who lived through those breathtaking months, INA's display of confidence by accepting the extra shares was one of the "high spots" of the company's history, one of the sources of the pride that is one of the hallmarks of people who work for the company.

Of course rates went up. The coastwise rate between New Orleans and New York skyrocketed 1,000 per cent above the original rate of fifteen cents per $100. At one point the rate from Brazil reached twenty-five per cent, "and we thought that ought to be adequate," said Leaming Smith, "because if it wasn't, this country was blockaded and we'd lost the war."

The company's faith and courage paid off in a material way before the end of 1942. When the U-boat offensive was finally beaten that summer (although there were sinkings from time to time afterwards), INA's increased participation in the Exchange gave it a larger return of the profits, thus helping it to recover part of the losses sustained in the first half of the year.

By 1944 matters had improved to the point that the government permitted an end to the "brown-out" which had dimmed the lights of cities on the coast.

When the conflict came to a close the following year, INA was able to tell its stockholders that it was stronger than ever, "fortified by the experience of war."

Most of the 574 men and women who had gone off to serve in the armed forces of the United States or its allies were beginning to return to the company. But fourteen of the men would never come back. For them, the supreme challenge of their life had also been the last.

15: *Arsenal for a Different War*

BY THE END OF WORLD WAR II, INA's fight for independence had barely begun, but the magnitude of that incipient conflict could already be perceived, if only dimly. And it was clear that the company could not expect to win unless it were strengthened internally.

Fortunately, the temperament of John Diemand caused the necessary changes to occur naturally. In the days of that great patrician, Benjamin Rush, the presidency had an aura of grandeur and hauteur. When Rush stepped into an elevator in the morning, it became an express to the twelfth floor, the eyrie of top management. And somehow it seemed appropriate in those days, a fit setting for a man like Rush, who was viewed by his subordinates with respect, admiration, and a good deal of awe.

Everything changed when Diemand became head of the company. The elevator was a local, whether Diemand was aboard or not. The president was a familiar figure to almost everyone in the company, especially those in the home office. His door was open to all. His was a paternalistic administration; some of the employees tagged him privately "Big Daddy," but they applied the label with genuine affection.

[223]

"There was the feeling that Diemand would always take care of you," one veteran of those days explained. "And remarkable care was taken of a lot of people. It was a pretty soft-hearted organization."

There was nothing deliberate about this; Diemand could not have behaved otherwise. But the paternalism helped bolster morale at a time when the struggle for independence was making life more difficult for a good many employees. They knew that the company was doing as much as possible to recognize their contribution.

For example, World War II had been over only a few weeks when Diemand began negotiating for the purchase from the defunct Roxborough Country Club of its property in Whitemarsh Township, Montgomery County, about twelve miles from the home office. The price of the property, including a clubhouse, golf course, tennis courts, and other facilities, was $130,000.

One member of the board of directors objected vehemently to the very idea of the company's providing a country club for the people who worked for it. But Diemand, who had never forgotten what it was like to be without much money, told him:

"Most of our people live in row houses, many of them no wider than fifteen feet. You don't know—but I do—what it's like to live in a house like that, with a tin roof, on a hot Fourth of July. It can get pretty hot in Philadelphia. You don't know what it's like in the city then, because you get out of the city at a time like that, and so does everybody else who can.

"But what about those people who live in those steaming hot row houses? Suppose they've got a car and they want to get away? Where are they going to go? If they camp alongside some farmer's place, they get chased by a dog or by the farmer himself.

"It seems to me that this company, in a real spirit of

humility, could do something for its employees by giving them a nice place where they can take their families for recreation."

Eagle Lodge, as the company renamed the property, has been a great success. A decade after it was acquired, the company was able to report that "the estimated attendance at picnics, dances, and athletic events" there was "over 31,000" a year.

Today the club is open to all members of the Employees Association and their guests. An individual membership in the association costs $3 a year, a family membership only $6, merely nominal fees.

There are three family events each year, at Christmas, Memorial Day, and Labor Day, and each draws as many as 900 people to Eagle Lodge. In addition, there are eleven dances a year, each built around a motif like "Riverboat Night."

For many years before the country club was purchased there had been employee social activities, of course. Frank Kelly, who retired in 1966 after more than forty-eight years as an INA employee, was especially active in sports—soccer, bowling, and ice hockey. He was goalie on the hockey team, which also included some of the officers, among them Henry Farnum and Weir Sargent, both of whom had played hockey at school. They played in the arena at 46th and Market Streets, and tried valiantly to ignore the professional hockey players who, on their nights off, enjoyed sitting beside the rink, watching the amateurs.

"They went into hysterics," Kelly recalled ruefully. "Absolutely into hysterics."

Other insurance men got so interested that an insurance league was organized.

"But there were so many injuries," Kelly said, "that the company insisted that we give it up. Dave McIlvain broke his leg, and Phil Meakim had something like twenty stitches in his leg, and there were a number of other injuries. The company decided we knew so little about hockey that we were really poor risks, from an insurance man's point of view. We were spending too much time in the hospital."

Bowling was a more successful venture. Before long the company had sixteen teams of men, and somebody thought the women might like to organize a league, too, so it was suggested that Kelly take the initiative in this. When he began making inquiries, he heard that an employee named Helen Corrigan was the girl to whom he should broach the idea.

In time, Miss Corrigan became Mrs. Kelly. A good many other marriages have resulted from employee social and athletic activities since then.

Originally employee activities were spontaneous, but about 1935, at Diemand's suggestion, the North American Companies' Association was organized with the hope of breaking down some of the barriers between the fire, casualty, and marine people through recreational contacts. Charles Arthur was appointed the first president of NACA, but thereafter the members of the association elected their own officers.

About ten years later NACA became the INA Employees Association, with Margaret Woolley as permanent secretary. A library and ping-pong tables were provided in the employee's lounge at the home office, and the association maintained a discount store, selling merchandise at cost. According to Vernon J. Schumacher, association president in 1966, activities sponsored by the association then included softball, basketball, bridge, pinochle, chess, a flower show, a doll contest, a camera club, a stamp and coin collecting group, golf, table tennis, a chorus, and movies shown every Saturday night at Eagle Lodge.

More significant than the establishment of Eagle Lodge was the organization by the company of a training school. Of course the company had trained its personnel since the earliest days, but for many years this training was little more than an apprenticeship—a new man was entrusted to the care of an experienced employee, who was expected to show him how things were done.

In 1925 the company took a slightly more formal approach to the training problem. A few young men were selected, one of the first being a Haverford College graduate named H. Richard Heilman, who rose in the course of time to the presidency of INA. It is unlikely that the officers foresaw such a bright future for him at the time, for he was "a sorry-looking sight" when he showed up for work the first day. Accidentally burned in a fire at the beach the day before, he had to wear carpet slippers to the office, and his face was blistered and raw.

These youths worked in each of the departments, listened to talks by the officers, and in the evening took courses at the Insurance Institute, an independent school.

Toward the end of the 1930's, top management considered the desirability of improving the quality of training, but the outbreak of hostilities in 1939, with the likelihood of eventual American involvement, meant that any such plan had to be shelved. However, as it became apparent that peace was not far distant, the idea was dusted off.

At that opportune moment Ludwig Lewis happened to be introduced to H. Paul Abbott, who had been headmaster of Newark Academy before going into service as a flight instructor in the Naval Air Corps. A few weeks later Abbott was invited to join the company as director of education.

When he reported for work on November 26, 1945, Abbott was faced with a staggering task. Although he had no knowledge of the insurance business, he was expected to be ready to start the first class on January 8, 1946, just six weeks later, and those weeks included the holiday season.

"It was a mad scramble," he later recalled, but somehow he managed to organize a curriculum and find officers to teach the class. On the scheduled date the school opened, with fourteen students and forty-eight part-time instructors. One of the students was Charles K. Cox, who later rose to senior vice president.

"Officers, department heads, supervising examiners, and examiners all pitched in as the demands of the course required," Abbott said. "They delivered lectures, conducted discussions, prepared quizzes and examinations, and corrected and graded them. Men busy with normal administrative and underwriting responsibilities carried home briefcases bulging with school work."

This state of affairs could not continue indefinitely, nor had it been intended to. From the first it had been agreed that this school would not be operated like the training programs of other companies. This would be a *school* in the fullest sense of the word. Other company-run programs used experienced insurance men who were expected to pass on their skills. The flaw in that system, as Abbott expressed it, was this:

"A good insurance man, particularly a good insurance salesman, would make a very good teacher, but you can never spare that fellow. So the tendency is to give you the fellow who can't sell, but—well, he knows the business. The trouble with that approach is that if a man can't sell, he can't teach. The enthusiasm isn't there. He doesn't get the message across."

INA's solution to this problem was to recruit "qualified and seasoned educators" who would learn insurance and then transmit their knowledge, using the most modern educational methods.

Thus, the second class, starting in March 1946, included four educators, two of them still with the Education Department in 1967. One was Acis Jenkinson III, CLU, who had earned his M.A. in economics at the University of Pennsylvania and was then working toward his doctorate. The other was Charles Henderson, from Penn's English faculty.

In its first twenty years, the department conducted courses lasting four to six months for more than 1,800 men and women employees, sixteen of whom subsequently became officers of the company. Correspondence courses proved a great success; 12,108 certificates were awarded. A year after the department came into being, Abbott launched a School for Agents; through classes in Philadelphia and regional seminars it reached 3,000 agents.

As time went on, the company also instituted a program of tuition aid to employees who wanted to continue their education. At first this was limited to courses directly related to the employee's work. Later it was expanded to include studies leading toward college degrees. Half the tuition was refunded at the outset, and the rest was paid at the successful completion of the college program (or, in the case of clerical employees, six months later). So it became possible for an employee with a high school diploma to go on and obtain a bachelor's degree or even a graduate degree from an accredited college or university entirely at INA's expense.

Still another testament to the company's belief in the importance of education and the necessity for learning to be made available to all, regardless of means, who could profit by it was the establishment in 1963 of an INA Foundation program. Each year a panel of judges, none of them employed by the company, selected six young men and women to be given four-year, all-expense (up to $2,000 a year) scholarships. The only qualification was that the college chosen by the student must offer courses related to insurance although the recipients were not required to take those courses.

Although any qualified youth was eligible, preference was given to the offspring of INA employees, and the judges found no dearth of ability among that large group. Among the 1966 winners was a brilliant young man whose mother was a cleaning woman in the home office.

By 1967 INA's Education Department had a staff of fifteen, "bigger than the insurance faculty of any college or university," according to Jenkinson, who became head of the department in 1955 when Abbott was assigned to plan and run the company's first really modern Personnel Department, of which the Education Department later became a part.

The Education Department assured the company of a continuing supply of high-grade manpower in the demanding days of the postwar period that lay ahead. But there were other steps that the company could also take to mobilize its forces.

One move was to take advantage of the company's financial strength. In its annual report for 1946, the first full year of peace, the company quoted from the minutes of its stockholders' meeting held in 1866, after the Civil War:

"The return of peace finds the [company] in a much stronger position than at the start of the war. . . . The future of the company, as far as can be foreseen, promises well. . . . The large business now transacted is well distributed and management is in competent hands. . . . The age and standing of the company give great advantages in the competition for business . . . and it is not unreasonable to look for still further healthy growth."

To that somewhat self-satisfied statement, eighty years old, INA now added: "Truly, history repeats itself. Today, following World War II, the Insurance Company of North America and its affiliates find themselves in an enviable financial position, stronger than ever, fully equipped and ready to meet the growing demand for every type of fire, marine, and casualty insurance."

The financial power of INA was to be put to use to

work another fundamental change in American insurance. Part of it would be allotted to the development of the company as a major factor in reinsurance.

Reinsurance is a method for distributing risks among insurance companies, following essentially the same procedure that a bookmaker employs when, having accepted a bet larger than he can afford to handle, he "lays off" part of the wager with bookies in other parts of the country. (Insurance men detest comparisons with gambling, maintaining—with good reason—that insurance is based on actuarial probabilities, the desire to protect legitimate economic interests, responsibility, and good faith, while gambling is based simply on naked greed, the urge to get rich quick.)

Although there are many intricate variations to reinsurance, the basic transaction goes like this: Company A insures Manufacturer X for $1,000,000. However, in order to minimize the possible loss, Company A retains only $100,000 of the cover, placing the remaining $900,000 with company B (or sometimes with Companies B, C, and D). Company A is said to *cede* $900,000 to Company B, which *assumes* that portion of the risk.

Without reinsurance, small insurance companies probably could not survive, and they certainly would be unable to grow. But even the largest companies have always ceded a good deal of their risks to diminish the chances of a catastrophic loss.

Although many of the larger American companies, including INA, occasionally assumed some reinsurance before the war, none had a department devoted to reinsurance. In this country there were about a half dozen "professional" reinsurers; that is, companies which only assumed reinsurance, never writing direct business. The biggest reinsurance market was in London, although there were also major reinsurers on the Continent.

Perils: Named and Unnamed

In 1946 INA became the first general insurance company in the United States to set up a department to handle nothing but reinsurance. The man assigned to head this new operation was John A. Diemand, Jr., better known as "Buzz" Diemand.

One of the innumerable INA men who belie the popular caricature of the insurance man as a pompous prig, "Buzz" Diemand graduated from college in 1936 and immediately went to sea as a deck hand on a series of freighters. After a couple of years as a seaman, he reluctantly gave up the sea and took a job as a claims man with the company in Philadelphia and New York. But he had joined the Naval Reserve, and in 1940, as war loomed, he volunteered for active duty and was sent to officers' training school.

During five and a half years of service he was assigned to a destroyer in the North Atlantic, then to the armed guard aboard various merchantmen carrying war supplies, and finally to the blimps that maintained an anti-submarine patrol along the East Coast. After the war he maintained his interest in aviation as a private pilot.

When young Diemand returned to INA in 1946, Ludwig Lewis told him, "We are going into the reinsurance business. I want you to find out all about it and get started."

"For years Wig had been watching American money going to reinsurers abroad," Diemand said, "and he felt we ought to build a domestic reinsurance industry to try to catch it here, for our account. Then, too, we were loaded with surplus. There were very few companies in the business, if any, that had as much surplus for the amount of volume they did. So the reasoning was: here's one way to put the surplus to work with a minimum of overhead."

Other companies quickly followed INA's example. Between 1946 and 1961, forty-one American companies plunged into this field as "professional" reinsurers (the term now having been expanded to include insurance companies which had reinsurance departments). But a study by Warren E. Taylor, then reinsurance secretary for INA but later an independent reinsurance broker in Seattle, showed in 1961 that forty per cent of the total reinsurance assumed by American companies was ceded to INA and two other large companies.

"If INA's Treaty [Reinsurance] Department were an independent professional reinsurance company," the *International Insurance Monitor* reported in April 1962, "it would take fourth place among the world's leading professional re-insurers."

At the same time that INA was assuming reinsurance, it was also ceding part of its own risks to other reinsurers, especially in London. On April 16, 1947, Bradford Smith, Jr., was in England, negotiating a new and, INA hoped, more favorable reinsurance agreement with Lloyd's.

On that day in Texas City, Texas—a Gulf port packed with chemical plants, oil refineries, and tin smelters—a fire was discovered about 8:00 A.M. in the hold of the French freighter *Grandcamp*, which had been loaded with ammonium nitrate fertilizer. At 9:12, as a crowd of 200 watched crewmen, long-shoremen, and firemen battle the blaze, the ship exploded with such devastating force that hundreds of people, many of them far from the docks, were killed, and most of the buildings in the town were knocked down or badly damaged, starting scores of fires.

Sixteen hours later, while rescue workers were digging the injured and dead out of the ruins of Texas City, a second ship full of the same chemical fertilizer blew up, completing the destruction. The ultimate toll was set at 576 dead, 3,000 injured, and more than $90,000,000 in property damage, with more than ninety per cent of the town demolished. It was the worst industrial disaster in America's history.

As INA's officers in Philadelphia rapidly dispatched

claims men to the scene of the catastrophe, Ludwig Lewis remembered Brad Smith's mission to Lloyd's. This was no time to be dickering for better reinsurance terms, for reinsurers were certain to be hit with very heavy losses. So Lewis fired off a cable to Smith: "Think it best you get out of London. Go anywhere you like."

In a matter of hours, Smith was on his way to the Continent, after sending a reply to Lewis. All Smith said in his cable was: "Just like turning rabbit loose in cabbage patch."

So many claims men from scores of insurance companies arrived in Texas City that one observer said it looked "like an adjusters' convention." One of the first to get there was INA's state manager, L. F. Dakin, who began settling claims immediately. He remained several weeks, working closely with the company's agency there, owned by Carl A. Rust and J. C. Trahan, who was then mayor of Texas City.

"Following the disaster," Rust remembered twenty years later, "company after company withdrew from the area. Only INA remained in the agency."

"Largely with Mr. Dakin's efforts over a period of several months," in Rust's words, other insurance companies, heartened by INA's example, gradually returned to Texas City to write policies. Without insurance to protect the new buildings arising from the ruins, Texas City could not have recovered.

But come back it did; by 1967 its population was three times what it had been before the disaster, and Texas City was enjoying a prosperous new life.

Rust, now a partner of the Rust, Ewing, Jordan and Smith agency, said, "The insurance industry, as a whole, should be proud of men like L. F. Dakin and privileged to have his representation."

Another major policy decision by INA's top management at the close of the war was to expand the company's operations in other countries. In 1956 the international efforts were made part of a combined International-Reinsurance Department, which was headed in 1967 by "Buzz" Diemand, with L. O. Thames assistant vice president in charge of the foreign efforts.

Canada was not regarded as a foreign area. In 1873 INA wrote its first business there, in the form of two ocean marine policies handled through a Canadian agency. Fire insurance was written through the same agency, Robert Hampson and Son, Limited, beginning in 1889.

It was not until 1928 that INA opened its own office in Canada, with H. C. Mills in charge. A fourth-generation Canadian, "Cliff" Mills had joined the company as a field representative in 1919, working through the Hampson agency. When the first INA office was opened, in Winnipeg, the Western provinces of Manitoba, Saskatchewan, and Alberta were his jurisdiction.

In 1931 operations were extended to Ontario, and a head office for the dominion was established at Toronto, with Mills as general manager. In 1967 there were, in addition to Toronto, INA offices in Moncton, Montreal, Vancouver, and Winnipeg.

The first truly foreign office of INA was opened in 1930 in London, but its activities were limited largely to settling marine claims in the Old World. In 1932 INA moved into Shanghai, and its base there was a complete service office, supplemented later by offices in Hong Kong and Tientsin.

Next came Mexico, where the company opened an office at a time when all other foreign companies were withdrawing from that country because of political developments. A decade later INA was the only United States insurance company having a branch office in Mexico.

The flight of foreign insurers had created a severe problem for the Mexican economy in 1936. Instead of abandoning its efforts there, INA decided to help a group of Mexicans who had organized their own national company, "La Azteca," Compania Mexicana de Seguros, S.A. Although INA could have bought a large interest in "La Azteca," Benjamin Rush chose to provide financial assistance in other ways. The Philadelphia company deposited with the Mexican government securities to meet the legal requirements for the Mexican company's assets and reserves. INA also handled reinsurance for "La Azteca" and trained and advised the officers and employees on underwriting, claims handling, and other insurance matters.

In 1956 the general manager of "La Azteca," Manuel Alonso de Florida, wrote to INA to announce the dedication of the Mexican company's new head office building.

"I can do nothing else but remember, with respect and affection, the great Benjamin Rush," he wrote, "[and how] we obtained from your company and from your president the understanding and affection necessary to support a small Mexican insurance company which had just started its activities. I want to ask you that, in our name . . . your secretary takes a flower bough to Benjamin Rush's grave."

Before the war, private American investments in other countries amounted to a mere $12,000,000,000. But within ten years of the war's end, that figure had more than doubled, to over $29,000,000,000, and in 1964 a government estimate put those investments at close to $75,500,000,000. In other words, American commerce and industry had boosted their financial stake in other countries by *seven hundred per cent in* a quarter-century.

At first, American corporations, in their foreign expansion, tended to buy their insurance in the country they were entering. As time passed, this proved unsatisfactory for many organizations.

"Most often glaring inadequacies have been uncovered in the insurance programs provided locally, both as to policy amounts and scope of coverages afforded," Thames explained. "To protect the enormous overseas assets of American business adequately, concerted effort is being directed today toward development of insurance coverages commensurate with those [customarily purchased] by corporate management for its United States properties."

As American industry spread across the seas and continents, it was accompanied by INA. Within a few days of the end of hostilities with Japan, the Hong Kong office was reopened, and soon afterward the company returned to Shanghai.

On the other side of the world, the London office had been active all through the war. As the combat forces in Germany were replaced by occupation troops settling down for a long stay, the company opened an office at Frankfurt, primarily to write automobile and other coverages for the GI's and their families.

During 1947 the company extended its offices to Singapore, and to Sydney, Australia, and in the years that followed a web of offices was spun around the globe: the Philippines, Japan, New Zealand, South Africa, Kenya, Rhodesia, Italy, Spain, the Netherlands, Brazil, Venezuela, Colombia, Puerto Rico, and Cuba. Regional head offices were established at The Hague (for Europe), San Juan (for the Caribbean), Hong Kong (for the Far East), Sydney (for Australia), and Johannesburg (for Southern Africa).

Over the postwar years, for business or political reasons, INA found it desirable to buy into some foreign insurance companies. The only majority interest purchased by the company was in France, where it bought almost complete ownership of the Compagnie Nouvelle d'Assurances, popularly known as "La Nouvelle." In Mexico, nineteen per cent of the shares of INA's old protégé, "La Azteca," were acquired, and the company purchased interests ranging from nine to about twenty-nine per cent in La Venezolana de Seguros in Venezuela, La Pazateva in Peru, Las Amazonas in Ecuador, and a Chilean company with the charming, if startling, name of La Philadelphia Consolidada.

By the end of 1953 INA was able to assert that it was the only American company "operating independently, worldwide (except behind the Iron Curtain), in all classes of insurance except life."

Twelve years later Thames said, "INA finds itself in an enviable position today from a competitive standpoint. No other American insurance company has international facilities established throughout the world, with offices staffed by its own personnel. INA retains an ability to operate free of tariff control in a number of important countries abroad and is unusually responsive to the insurance requirements of American industry."

Of course the company's offices abroad were not limited to the demands of American corporations. In 1967 Thames said that only one-third of the income from INA's foreign operations came from American business. The rest of the business was generated locally, from firms native to each country.

The expansion of the company's foreign activities made it more acutely sensitive to international political developments, in a changing world disturbed by tensions between the East and the West and between the underdeveloped countries and the industrialized nations, as well as by the instability of the emerging countries as they felt their way along the new and untried paths of independence.

In this uncertain environment, INA, now a mighty corporation with global interests (reflected in the designation of the home office as "World Headquarters"), mirrored events around the world.

The conquest of mainland China by the Communists closed the company's profitable Shanghai office. Although the Hong Kong office was still able to function in that British colony, it was sharply curtailed in the business it could write after the United States, in 1950, imposed an embargo on trade with China because of the entry of the Red Chinese into the Korean war.

Similarly, the success of Fidel Castro's revolution in Cuba and his subsequent hostility toward the United States resulted in the confiscation of INA's assets there, for a very substantial loss.

In a number of countries nationalist sentiment stimulated the enactment of restrictive insurance laws. One country set a very low limit on the size of the risk that a foreign company could accept. Another required foreign companies to relinquish to a government bureau thirty per cent of the cover for every risk. Still a third nation prohibited any company from writing insurance unless at least fifty-one per cent of the ownership was in the hands of citizens of that country; for this impediment, the only solution for an outside company like INA was the purchase of a minority interest in a native company.

Some unusual claims were handled by INA because of its foreign operations. In one African country the company insured a corporation that operated a plantation. One day the native workers who lived on the plantation were on their way by truck to see a movie when a man fell off the vehicle and was killed.

"The workmen's compensation law there isn't at all like our laws," said assistant vice president C. Sumner Katz, "but under the law, in addition to paying benefits to the widow, we do pay the burial expenses. Well, this man belonged to a tribe in the hinterlands which didn't bury its dead; it burned them, with ceremonies that seemed fitting to those people. So we got a bill for funeral expenses that included forty-five dollars for a case of whisky for the chief and the other mourners."

In Germany an engineering corporation insured by INA prepared the plans and specifications for a catalytic cracking tower. After it was built, the American corporation sent over four engineers to teach the local people how to operate the equipment. During the instruction period, one of the trainees, sitting at a control console, saw a red light and thought that it indicated a stack fire when it actually pointed to a fire in another component.

"Before the error was discovered," Katz said, "we had

a leaning tower that could stand comparison with Pisa's. The incident put the plant out of commission, and under the German law they had to continue payments to their employees even though they were't working. And the German company lost profits, too. We negotiated a settlement that cost us well over $1,000,000."

A complicated claim arose in Monrovia, Liberia, when a hotel owned by Israeli citizens who lived in Switzerland was destroyed by fire. Lloyd's had written the insurance on the hotel during its construction, and INA's coverage was to take effect when it was occupied. The fire occurred before construction was completed, but a number of tenants had already moved in, mostly diplomats, including the Russians. This posed a problem: which insurance was in effect at the time of the fire, Lloyd's or INA's?

After prolonged negotiations in Geneva, it was agreed that INA would pay part, but the bulk of the loss would be accepted by the London underwriters.

When the United States became involved in the long, complex war in Vietnam, INA, too, found itself there through travel insurance, workmen's compensation policies covering men building barracks, administrative buildings, and other facilities, and a number of other coverages. The company had resigned itself to the likelihood that some of the men covered by its policies would be shot by Viet Cong terrorists, but the first loss resulting from a fatality occurred when a government official slipped and fell in his bathroom in Saigon.

The first fatality from gunfire that produced a loss for INA occurred when one American shot and killed another in a row over a Vietnamese woman. The unexpected is only to be expected in insurance.

16: Flying Solo

 AT THE ANNUAL company Christmas luncheon for officers in 1953, John A. Diemand drew INA's chief actuary, L. H. Longley-Cook, aside and asked him if he could predict the probability of two airliners' colliding in mid-air.

Longley-Cook wasn't altogether happy to be asked the question at that time. ("I really don't like those things mixed with martinis.") But the idea rather intrigued him, and he told Diemand that he thought he could come up with a forecast, given enough time to study the data.

Actuaries are a very special breed, both academic and commercial, always dealing with statistics, higher mathematics, and the law of probabilities, but tempering the brittle facts with the intangible, immeasurable ingredients of judgment and intuition. Actuarial work is as much art as science, frustratingly personalized in the eyes of classic mathematicians and mysteriously abstruse to laymen, including insurance executives who have dealt with actuarial conclusions for years.

So the processes by which Longley-Cook set about solving the problem before him must remain a sealed book —except to actuaries. However, on January 6, 1954, he wrote a memorandum to Charles A. Sanford, then assistant vice president in charge of aviation insurance.

Concluding that the available data on airline accidents was sufficient to reach a prediction, Longley-Cook said that although there had been no mid-air collision of airliners causing fatalities or serious damage up to then, "it is possible to envisage an accident, involving the collision of two fully loaded passenger liners, where the total possible liability and property damage would be very great."

This need not discourage INA from insuring airliners, he added. "In the insurance business we may be prepared to accept exposures of this astronomical size if the probability of loss is sufficiently remote. For example, we are continuously exposed to such possible losses by windstorm."

Nevertheless, the basic question remained: "What is the real risk of a mid-air collision involving catastrophic damage and liability?"

After touching briefly on the mathematical foundation for his solution, Longley-Cook stated the chances:

"Other conditions remaining equal, we may reasonably expect anything from 0 to 4 air carrier-to-air carrier collisions over the next ten years, and the possibility of one such catastrophe involving [immense] damage is not so remote that it can be ignored. In considering the adequacy of premium rates for air carrier business, the probability of losses on this scale should be taken into account. Further, the protection of such an account by reinsurance . . . seems essential. . . .

"The introduction of higher speeds with jet air carriers may well increase the probability of catastrophic losses and improved techniques in traffic handling may take some years to catch up."

Although the government and the air transport industry had been insisting that air traffic control procedures made even one mid-air collision of airliners almost impossible, Diemand

and Sanford gave Longley-Cook's prediction serious consideration in charting the company's course in aviation insurance.

The memo had said that in ten years there were likely to be 0 to 4 such collisions, which the average layman could translate as two collisions.

Two years later, on June 30, 1956, two airliners, operated by different companies, took off from Los Angeles three minutes apart. One was a DC–7 and the other a Constellation. Although both planes were flying at altitudes prescribed by ATC (the federal Air Traffic Control system) and were operating under orders from controllers on the ground, they both reached a point at 21,000 feet over the Grand Canyon at 10:31 A.M. Pacific Standard Time. After the collision, the wreckage of the two planes fell into the Grand Canyon. It was the worst disaster in commercial aviation up to that date, 128 persons having lost their lives.

Score one grim point for the law of probabilities over the "foolproof" system.

Four years after that, on December 16, 1960, a DC–8 jet smashed into a Constellation in the skies over Staten Island in New York harbor and staggered on for three or four miles before plunging into a crowded Brooklyn apartment house district, damaging buildings and causing fires. All the passengers and crewmen of the two aircraft, 128 persons in all, perished, as did five persons on the ground.

As INA began paying off its share of the losses, its executives acknowledged that Longley-Cook's unhappy forecast had come true.

The company first began writing aviation insurance in 1927. That was the year that changed the nature of aviation. A year earlier the Air Commerce Act had been passed, and the first licenses to planes and pilots were issued by the new federal Bureau of Aeronautics in 1927. Later in the year Charles A. Lindbergh crossed the Atlantic by air, a flight that "acted like adrenalin in the blood stream of American aviation," as Arthur Gordon has put it.

He points out: "In a single year after Lindbergh's flight, applications for pilot licenses in the United States jumped from 1,800 to 5,500. In 1928 the nation's airline operators doubled their mileage, trebled their mail load, and quadrupled the number of passengers they had carried in 1927."

From 1927 to 1930 the first three transcontinental airlines, United, TWA, and American, emerged from amalgamations of smaller lines.

There were three great aviation insurance syndicates in the decade before World War II, and INA was a member of one of them. But all the rest of the industry took note of a three-sentence statement that appeared in the company's 1944 annual report:

"The sum of $2,500,000 has been set aside out of the General Voluntary Reserve earmarked for the development of aviation business. Because private aviation is new and can be expected to grow very considerably in the years following the war, it will present many new hazards. Accordingly, it seems prudent to set up a reserve fund which will absorb the abnormal expenses and losses which can be expected during the period of development."

The impetus for this action came from several sources, both personal and general. John Diemand's son "Buzz" was a flying enthusiast; after the war he and his wife, who was also a pilot, would fly about the country in their Beechcraft Bonanza. Another and perhaps more impressive spokesman for aviation was William A. Patterson, then president of United Air Lines, who accepted an invitation to become a director of INA in 1943.

Then, too, the war itself had fostered the progress of flying and stimulated wide interest and participation in it. Out of the bombers would flow the designs for the postwar airliners, but even during the war, because of the stepped-up tempo of life, many Americans who had never flown before discovered for the first time the convenience and beauty of air travel, some of them on civilian airliners, many more on air transports. And great numbers of young men trained to fly in the war might be expected to maintain their activities as pilots when peace came.

Finally, INA's growing determination to break loose from industry restrictions was a factor. In the aviation insurance pool to which INA belonged, all decisions had to be unanimous. "I knew that my thinking would never make me say 'Yes' to something I didn't believe in," Diemand said. "So I decided we'd go it alone."

In 1945 he told the pool that his company was going to operate as an independent in aviation insurance but added that INA would like to remain a participant in the pool's airline business. The pool rejected this, insisting that the company had to be all the way in or all the way out, so Diemand chose the latter.

To head the new aviation effort, INA recruited Charles A. Sanford, who ultimately became vice president in charge of Personal Lines before his retirement in 1967. His experience in that specialized field was almost as long as the company's, for he had gone to work in July 1929 for the aviation underwriting group of Barber and Baldwin, which had been founded by a "very gifted, somewhat eccentric" Englishman, Horatio Barber.

The stock market crash of October 1929, just three months after Sanford joined Barber and Baldwin, had an even more devastating effect on aviation than on most other industries, for there had not yet been enough time to demonstrate how important flying could be to the economy, and most people regarded it as a sport, a form of suicide, and a luxury, a point of view still held by a few, including some of the professional skeptics in the Internal Revenue Service.

Hard hit by the Depression, Barber and Baldwin went

through several metamorphoses until it took final form as Aero Insurance Underwriters. Sanford remained with Aero until the war, when he went into the Air Force, serving in Central Africa and later North Africa in cryptography, communications, and administration. On his return to civilian life in 1945, he settled down in Philadelphia as an INA man.

From the outset the company delegated much more underwriting authority to its local service offices than other aviation insurers customarily did. This was a calculated risk; it was recognized that fieldmen unused to writing aviation insurance probably would accept some undesirable risks, but it was hoped that they would quickly learn from experience and provide the company with a nationwide reservoir of knowledgeable representatives. Both the fear and the hope came true over the first few years.

Several underwriting principles were adopted before INA wrote a single policy as an independent aviation insurer, and they proved so sound that most of them were still being followed more than a quarter-century later. For example, the company would not try to become a major *primary* insurer of airlines, on the ground that the possible losses were so great that they might better be handled by one of the syndicates. Although the company insured some of the "feeder," or regional, airlines, it only accepted a portion of trunk lines' insurance as a secondary insurer.

In other words, Syndicate A might insure a transcontinental airline for $20,000,000, but the airline wanted $30,000,-000—$10,000,000 more than the syndicate would accept. INA would take perhaps $1,000,000 of that additional cover. But it would not be required to pay anything until the total loss exceeded the syndicate's basic cover of $20,000,000.

Because one of the company's major reasons for going into aviation insurance independently was "to extend a facility to its local agents," as Sanford pointed out, INA chose to concentrate its efforts on two groups of potential customers: the private pilots and the corporations that maintained their own aircraft for business purposes. Before long the company insured more corporate aircraft than any of its competitors.

As Sanford had warned, the company was buffeted by heavy losses for the first couple of years, but top management "backed me up all along the line," Sanford said. Many other companies had plunged into aviation underwriting, and in their eagerness for business precipitated price wars that drove rates down to untenable levels. After two or three years of unthinkable losses, many of the newcomers, and even a few of the old-timers, including Sanford's old outfit, Aero, withdrew from the aviation field or went out of business altogether.

With aviation in a completely new phase of incredible expansion after the war, everyone had to operate by trial and error, even experienced aviation underwriters like Sanford and his new assistant, another Aero alumnus named Robert A. Morrison.

The phenomenal growth of aeronautics brought into civil aviation thousands of men who had been trained during the war to fly in the Air Force. Although many of them went to work as pilots for the scheduled airlines, there were even more involved in the air freight concerns and the non-scheduled airlines that proliferated at the end of the war. With inadequate financial backing, too few were able to maintain their aircraft properly, and the resulting crashes took lives, damaged property, and inflicted big losses on the insurers.

"Management here felt we shouldn't run from this," Sanford said. "So we had every one of these risks very carefully inspected by really competent flying people.

"If they reported the operation was not good, was not a safe one, we laid down the rules that we felt they had to comply with. If they objected to complying with our rules, we gave them a month in which to locate other insurance.

If they agreed to comply, we reinspected them in a couple of months to see if they were really doing it. Those who were going along with us, we stayed with; the others we cancelled. It worked out all right. We kept about half of them and we had a reasonably good experience."

The process of weeding out the undesirable risks exemplified the role that the insurance industry plays in making life safer for everyone—to be sure, not for disinterested, altruistic reasons (although the insurance man is likely to be at least as responsible as his next door neighbor), but in order to protect the industry's legitimate business interests.

One of the earliest unusual claims involving aviation during the postwar period had nothing to do with INA's Aviation Department, oddly enough, but it did touch Edwin H. Marshall, who would, by coincidence, take Sanford's place as vice president in charge of Personal Lines after the latter's retirement eighteen years later. In 1949, however, Marshall was still in the New York office promoting the company's group accident and sickness coverage, including travel insurance.

On September 9 of that year an airliner on a routine flight from Montreal to the northeastern reaches of the province of Quebec, with intermediate stops at Quebec City and Baie Comeau, exploded in the air forty miles north of the city of Quebec. There were twenty-three persons aboard, and all perished, including three top officers of one of the largest metals corporations in the world—its president, president-elect, and a vice president.

The metals corporation was covered by one of the INA group policies, and when the news was headlined in the New York newspapers, Marshall reacted at once.

"I said, 'We are going to have to pay $80,000 for each of those three men, $240,000 in all, but let's make a stir about this. Let's make a name for ourselves by paying that claim im-

'Any Risk Can Be Underwritten'

The philosophy that "any risk can be underwritten for a price" has resulted in an extraordinary diversity of risks and coverages by INA. The range is from the ridiculous to the visionary: on the one hand, the company will insure a golfer against the hazard of having to foot the bill for drinks for everybody at a country club, if he happens to get a hole-in-one; on the other hand, the company that is making the first American SST (supersonic transport plane, of which a model is shown here) is one of INA's insureds.

dated February 11th 1794 @ 6. Mos.
11 Insur.

John Collet Dr. To Insuran
for Premium on his Person again
Algerines & other Barbary Corsairs
a Voyage from hence Philadelphia
London in the Ship George & Bar
himself Master — valueing himself
Drs 5000 — @ 2 ρ Ct . . . . 100.
Policy

1 Received of John Collet by the ha
of his Wife Ann Collet his Note to
Francis Bailey endorsed by him
dated Feby 8. 1794 @ 90 days f
Premium on the above Insurance

Cash received for the Policy —

Received of Alexander Foster h
note to John Swanwick endorsed
him dated 11th Feby. 1794 for —
@ 6 Months

First life policy written by INA (FACING PAGE) was for a sea captain, John Collet, who wanted protection "on his person against Algerines and other Barbary corsairs." After 1817, life insurance was not offered by INA until World War II, when travel and accidental death policies were written for certain groups. Among them were thirty men identified only by number who were working for the "Manhattan District."

Los Alamos Laboratories

In 1945 INA discovered that the men were scientists— like Nobel Prize winners Enrico Fermi and J. Robert Oppenheimer (ABOVE, LEFT AND RIGHT)—who had been making the atomic bomb shown here.

Technological progress in every form is reflected in INA's
long list of insureds. Construction of Mackinac Bridge,
longest suspension bridge in the world, was insured by INA.
General Dynamics, builder of first nuclear-powered
submarine, NAUTILUS, became INA insured when no other
company was willing to assume such a risk.

mediately, this very day.' So we contacted the Claims Department, and we rushed around and gathered all the documents we could get. We did it: we got the check out to the broker and the insured that day, a check for $240,000."

Marshall and his associates congratulated themselves on a job well done, and with good reason.

Their triumph was short-lived.

A few days later INA's Canadian office passed along some information from Quebec. The plane blast had not been an accident. It was murder. A bomb had been planted on the plane. Later it was proved that twenty-two others on the plane had been killed so that Joseph Albert Guay could get rid of his wife, Rita, who was one of the passengers. Guay and two accomplices were hanged for their crime.

Shocking as the disclosure was to everyone, it had a special impact on Ed Marshall.

"We had just paid out $240,000," he groaned, "and we weren't sure now that our policy covered such an event. The question was: is it an *accident* if a bomb placed aboard a plane destroys it?

"You should have seen the confusion in our office. We pulled ourselves together and held a conference. It was decided that, regardless of whether or not the policy covered that situation, certainly the purchasers of our insurance had understood the protection covered a death like this, even though they hadn't thought of such a thing. Therefore, the company concluded, our insured had a right to expect that the policy did cover, and, regardless of any technical interpretation of the language of the contract, it was a loss that we should and would pay.

"I heaved a sigh of relief."

Incidentally, that act of sabotage turned out to be only one in a series of attempted bombings of airliners, many of them successful. It is believed that this was the cause of at least fourteen accidents, not all of them fatal, between 1949 and 1967. A number of those accidents resulted in losses for INA.

A unique accident to an airliner on which the company was the primary insurer (the plane was operated by a regional airline) occurred May 7, 1964, when a Fairchild turboprop aircraft crashed near San Ramon, California. Evidence collected by the Civil Aeronautics Board indicated that one of the forty-one passengers had brushed past the stewardess, forced his way into the cockpit, and shot the captain and the co-pilot. All forty-four persons aboard the plane were killed in the crash.

All manner of unusual aviation risks were insured by INA, like a helicopter carrying a steeple to the church on which it was placed. In addition to insuring flights for crop-dusting, mosquito control, power line inspection, geophysical surveys, and fighting forest fires, the company issued policies covering air meets, sky-diving, and even model airplane competition.

It is a field of insurance that produces many strange claims. A goodly number of fabric-covered aircraft, imprudently tied down in pastures, had big chunks chewed out of them by cows, who seem to find the fabric uncommonly appetizing.

Several pilots of light planes, finding themselves in trouble over densely forested land, managed to set their planes down *on top* of a thick stand of trees, without a great deal of damage to the aircraft.

"Once or twice a year," Bob Morrison said, "we get word that a pilot we've insured has made an emergency landing on a highway. Recently we had a case like this that had an unusual twist.

"It seems that some people were driving along a highway when they heard a loud noise—bang! Apparently they thought another car had hit them in the rear, although they couldn't see anything in the rear-view mirror. They stopped the car and got out to look.

"What they found was a light plane, flown by one of our insureds, who had landed it on top of the car. At the moment the pilot flared out [*i.e.,* dropped his airspeed down flying speed] the plane was flying over the ground at just about the same speed as the car. The pilot brought it down so lightly that there was very little damage done to the plane, no one was injured, and even the car wasn't badly damaged—the plane just ripped the roof in the back."

Occasionally aviation claims have a comic quality about them. The most remarkable of this type of claim was submitted by a parachutist. He was floating down toward the ground when a small plane, which happened to be insured by INA, passed under him.

The sky-diver landed astride the plane near the tail, creating a severe problem for the pilot, who couldn't see the 'chutist and had no idea why he was having so much trouble controlling the aircraft.

Equipped with a second, emergency chute, the sky-diver managed to get off the plane and float safely to the ground. A few minutes later the plane landed without trouble, too.

"The parachutist had the nerve to turn around and sue the pilot," Morrison said. "He was relying on the fact that if our insured's plane had run into him, the pilot would have been at fault, because the sky-diver was in free flight, which gave him the right of way. However he fell on our man's plane, and that's quite a different matter. The courts threw out the case.

"As a matter of fact, the only injured party was the pilot. He ended up with a small dent on the top of his fuselage, back near the tail."

17: A Cowpath Full of Chuckholes

INSURANCE CIRCLES THROUGHOUT the country were
startled in the fall of 1947 by a dispatch from
Chicago in a trade journal, *The National Underwriter*, about a rate increase announced by the Cook
County Inspection Bureau, to which INA then belonged. The
front-page news story said:

"Much bewilderment exists in Chicago . . . as a result
of North America [as INA was then called] in advising its
agents that the rate increases . . . would not be applicable to
North America. . . .

"This created a great hubbub in the city. It was something new in fire insurance to have an important market
[company] writing at a deviation [from the bureau rates], and
company men and agents alike were seeking to divine the
significance and possible consequences of the situation. . . .

"North America's rate action and the Excepted City
commission situation are bracketed in all the excited discussion
that is going on. . . ."

A month later the same periodical carried a headline
that read: "Much Turmoil in Chicago Fire Insurance Arena—

North America's Rate Deviation Has Profound Effect on Business." The article said:

"All elements of the business are intently seeking to evaluate the situation created by the action of North America in deviating ten per cent on dwelling business in Chicago and Cook County. The atmosphere was clouded with all sorts of unfounded rumors and fantastic speculation. . . .

"Some observers believe that agents will be under increasing pressure from their assureds and brokers to utilize North America. Already, it is reported, certain mortgage houses and building and loan associations have directed that their business be placed in North America. . . .

"North America's independent action as to rates has pretty well settled the commission issue in Chicago, it is believed, and perhaps in the other Excepted Cities. The agents realize that under a condition of rate competition and with a situation existing in which a rate war could flare up, there will not be margins for commission scales as of yore. This does not mean that the agents are happy about the new commission setup. . . ."

What lay behind this uproar was a simple fact: The industry had expected to give lip service to the concept of competition while quietly restoring the state of affairs existing before the Supreme Court's SEUA decision, and most of the men in the insurance business had assumed that INA's frequent calls for true competition were also merely the expression of pious hopes, not the statement of a determination to compete.

The Cook County deviation made clear to all that INA meant what it had been saying. The deviation grew out of the discriminatory system of agency commissions, the "Excepted Cities" arrangement, which, as we saw in Chapter 10, was condemned by INA's advisory group of agents in 1943.

The Excepted Cities developed out of the industry's effective structure for preventing price competition. Unable to increase their share of the business by lowering rates, almost all companies had tried to induce agents to place more clients with them by offering the agents excessive commissions, until this competition by commissions became as ruinous as the early price war had been.

To put a ceiling on agents' commissions, industry-wide agreements were arrived at. But the power of agents' associations and other problems made it impossible for the agreements to be applied to certain cities and areas. These, then, were exceptions to the agreements, and they became known as the Excepted Cities.

For years INA had taken a dim view of the Excepted Cities. If the policyholders' interests were to come first, as the company believed they should, then competition should take the form of lower rates and better service, for these would benefit the buyers of insurance. But competition by the payment of higher commissions necessarily added to the cost of insurance, and thus injured the policyholders.

When the Chicago Board of Underwriters was wrestling with the problem of inordinately high commissions in March 1942, INA expressed its philosophy in a letter to that body, in which it said that "whenever special privileges are extended to offices [selected agents], an offsetting reduction in rate is to be made to the benefit of the insured."

In 1947, as Simon N. Whitney observed in his Twentieth Century Fund study, *Antitrust Policies*, agents' commissions were "tending to move upward, and the North America Companies [INA] decided to hold them at twenty per cent— or fifteen or twenty-five per cent where the agent performed less or more than the customary services." According to Whitney, "Rates offered by competitors ranged as high as thirty-five per cent in [the] 'Excepted Cities' "—and it was the buyer of insurance, of course, who bore the cost of those excessive commissions in higher prices for protection. It was because of the higher commissions that the other companies needed the rate increase in Chicago and Cook County.

Before the SEUA ruling, "the penalties of individual action"—because of "the rules and the power of the trade associations"—made corrective action by INA virtually impossible, a company statement pointed out. But the changed legal status of the industry after the war opened the door for unilateral moves.

About the time that INA declined to raise its rates in Chicago, several industry organizations began to study the problem of the Excepted Cities. Believing that such discussions were improper under the new laws, INA refused to participate, although it agreed to cooperate "in principle" with the rest of the industry.

In fact, the company had already formulated its own plan for dealing with this matter. During the last two months of 1947, INA executives discussed the new plan with agents in all of the affected areas except Detroit and the New York suburbs. The plan was effective on the first day of 1948.

Briefly, the plan was based on what an agent did, on the services he rendered, and not on where he was located. Three categories of agents were established. The *standard policy-writing agent* was allowed a commission of twenty per cent; most of the agents were in this group.

Next came a small number of large agencies that "rendered greater services for the company by relieving it of some work effort," as Bradford Smith, Jr., pointed out. The staff of these agencies included experts in various lines, engineers, and rate men.

These agencies would be entitled to the standard twenty per cent, plus a five per cent expense allowance and a ten per cent contingent commission, but only if they were willing and able to become a *contract agent*. They were required to sign a contract which bound them to furnish adequate technical service (thus relieving the company of that expense), to guarantee the company a specified volume of business with a balanced spread of risks, and to pay premium balances to the company within forty-five days. In 1955 only 414 out of more than 17,000 agencies were on a contract basis.

The third category consisted of agents who did not write policies or perform other standard services, depending wholly on the company for these. They were classed as *non-policy-writing agents* and received the same commission as brokers, fifteen per cent.

In the month before INA's plan went into effect (over the protests of agents in the Excepted Cities, as one might expect), one of the industry organizations, the Eastern Underwriters Association, unveiled its own scheme. The EUA also adopted twenty per cent as "the maximum reasonable rate of commission" for most agents.

But the geographic differential was retained by the EUA under another name. Now the agents in Excepted Cities were designated "Metropolitan Agents," and they got twenty-five per cent on policies covering property in the city. The Boston agents were given an even fancier title, "Supervising Metropolitan Agent," and they got an extra two and a half per cent, for a total commission of twenty-seven and a half per cent.

As matters turned out, it didn't really matter who was called what. Only a few of the EUA companies put the plan into effect in the first half of 1948, but they were apprehensive of the agents' reaction. Unwilling to make a stand, they soon began to retreat from their position, and before long they were in full flight. The Excepted Cities still stood apart, only INA treating them the same as the rest of the country.

At that point the controversy subsequently known as the

"Pennsylvania Rate Deviation Case" arose. Under the Excepted Cities arrangements agents in Philadelphia received up to thirty-five per cent, plus seven and a half per cent contingent commission, for a total of forty-two and a half per cent. Excessive commissions were also the rule in Philadelphia's four suburban counties and in Allegheny County, which includes Pittsburgh.

However, INA, because of its new scale of commissions, found that it cut down markedly on its expenses by eliminating the concept of the Excepted Cities and their excessive commissions.

"Rather than retain this saving in expense for its own enrichment," a company statement said, "and in order that the company be placed on an equality of competition for business with other companies who continued to pay a higher rate of commission to agents, the company decided to resolve the saving in expense in favor of the policyholders through the medium of a deviation in rate."

The theory was that INA's agents could make more money by selling more insurance in an expanding market created by lower rates than by getting higher commissions from a diminishing volume of business. And the public interest would be better served by less expensive policies.

On December 21, 1948, INA filed a deviation of fifteen per cent below bureau rates. After a hearing in February, the state insurance commission ruled in May that the deviation would be allowed.

But now the opposition joined ranks to fight INA. An appeal for a review of the decision was filed with the commissioner in July 1949 by 140 companies.

Prolonged hearings were held in Harrisburg. One day Bradford Smith, Jr., was on the witness stand from mid-morning until midnight, sparring with a battery of hostile lawyers. As Smith slumped, exhausted, in the back seat of his car that night while riding back to Philadelphia, his driver, an ex-Navy man, asked solicitously, "That guy giving you a hard time? If you want me to deck him, just give me the sign."

Before the commissioner could rule on the appeal, the rating bureau, representing the opposition, announced a reduction of rates to meet INA's deviation. This meant that its "competitors were once more in a position to buy our business with commissions which they themselves had found to be above the maximum reasonable rate" (that is, more than twenty per cent), Bradford Smith, Jr., lamented.

The concerted action to block INA was a portent of the unyielding hostility with which the company would be confronted for many years to come. The Pennsylvania Rate Deviation Case also taught the company how painfully expensive it might find the path to independence. The opposition had spent more than $100,000 on legal fees, an insignificant total when divided among so many companies. On the other hand, INA had to pay all of its legal costs itself.

Moreover, the company suffered a substantial loss of business because of its action. Within a forty-eight hour period, INA lost $400,000 in premiums, according to Smith, as agents turned to other companies.

Of course it was to be expected the Excepted Cities agents would be unhappy when INA ended their privileged status. Besides, the agents, as Whitney's study found, were "strongly opposed to company price cutting." Since their commissions were, and are, a percentage of the premiums, lower premiums must result in lower commissions.

Many of the more farsighted agents, nevertheless, did realize that their total income would grow, despite lower commissions, if less costly insurance enabled them to sell more policies.

While the INA deviation was being fought in Pennsylvania, its Cook County deviation was renewed in Illinois.

A Cowpath Full of Chuckholes

Under the All-Industry Committee laws which had been passed by most of the states, deviations had to be filed again and approved every year. A number of commentators had warned that this provision would enable the bureaus to hamstring competition, and they were excellent prophets. As two antitrust experts, Joel B. Dirlam and Irwin M. Stelzer, said with some degree of understatement in 1958, "There can be no denying . . . that the path of the independent or the deviator is not an easy one."

The vice president of a Midwestern insurance company made the same point with a good deal more heat: "The company finds that the rating law in some states is not a road or a highway, but a winding cowpath lined with a forest of pressures and paved with the chuckholes of discouragement, stifling imagination, vision, logic, and common sense."

In January 1951, INA stumbled over one of the chuckholes: the Cook County Inspection Bureau challenged the company's deviation there and requested the state to call a hearing. A series of fatiguing hearings in May and September ended when the state director of insurance approved the deviation for one year. The bureau appealed to the courts; the Circuit Court upheld the approval, and so did the Appellate Court. When the bureau tried to carry its appeal to the Illinois Supreme Court, that bench dismissed the appeal on the ground that the one-year deviation had now expired.

Undeterred by the bureau's obstructive tactics, INA filed a new deviation, to which the bureau promptly announced its intention to object.

Now the opposition got its first taste of how tough the affable Bradford Smith, Jr., could be.

"I went to Chicago," he said, "and visited the managers of a number of companies. I informed them that if they insisted upon having a hearing, we would be compelled to subpoena them to testify as to the commissions they were paying to Cook County agents. They persisted in their course of refusing to waive a hearing, so the subpoenas were issued. Shortly after receiving the subpoenas our opponents waived a hearing."

None of them wanted public disclosure of the inordinate commissions they were paying. Besides, the facts about the commissions would have proved INA's contention that its lower commissions had cut its expenses so much that it could well afford to sell insurance at a lower rate than the bureau's.

But the pattern of opposition was beginning to emerge. The fight in Illinois had taken two and a half years, had consumed the time of Smith and other executives, and had cost the company a good deal of money for legal expenses.

In 1950 INA took the lead in an effort to write catastrophe excess-of-loss coverage. Some other companies took INA's side, and at its December meeting the National Association of Insurance Commissioners approved the plan. Despite a letter from the head of the Insurance Executives Association to all of the commissioners asking them to disapprove any policies of this kind, all but four states authorized it within eighteen months.

Previously only the London underwriters wrote this kind of policy, under which the owner of a business undertakes to absorb a substantial first loss himself, the insurance company being called upon to pay only if the loss is unusually large, and then only for a specified amount in excess of an agreed figure. Thus this coverage is similar to the $50 deductible collision policy that many motorists buy.

It says something about the inertia of the industry hierarchy that, despite the urging of two big insurance companies that belonged to the bureaus and the pleas of steel and electric power trade associations, the industry organizations continued to reject this coverage. In 1959—*nine years after INA and a few other companies began soliciting catastrophe ex-cess-of-loss business*—the Senate Subcommittee on Antitrust and Monopoly found that the bureau companies "were firmly agreed upon a course of non-action."

In the period between 1948 and 1951 INA made independent filings through most of the country for fire and extended coverage of multiple-location risks. These are manufacturing concerns, chain stores, and other corporations that have property in several states and wish to have them all protected by an overall policy. It was the first wholly independent move by the company, which by now had changed its status from member to subscriber in all the bureaus except those to which it was required by law to belong.

While all these battles were being waged, as well as a few other fights, including the campaign for acceptance of the Installment Premium Endorsement (discussed in Chapter 11), John Diemand's great idea was coming to fruition under rather ironic circumstances.

"The most significant landmark in [the] growing urge to permit multiple line insurance," as Dr. David L. Bickelhaupt, Associate Professor of Insurance at Ohio State University, has written, "was the work of the Diemand Committee of the National Association of Insurance Commissioners."

For years Diemand had been espousing the cause of multiple-line underwriting with a fervor that was downright evangelistic.

"We're almost ready," he liked to tell anyone who would listen, "to start with a blank sheet of paper and write a policy for a man's complete insurance needs."

Although the National Association of Insurance Commissioners had approved the multiple-line principle in 1944, it was not until five years later, because of technicalities that need not concern us here, that the multiple-line era really began. By 1951 laws permitting multiple-line underwriting were on the books of all but four states, and four years later it had been authorized in every state.

But the distinction of introducing the first multiple-line policy was not Diemand's. In the fall of 1948 a well-known Hartford fire insurance company opened discussions with the New York Insurance Department regarding a multiple-line coverage especially designed to meet the needs of automobile manufacturers. The company called it an Automobile Manufacturers' Output policy. (Since then "manufacturers' output" has become a generic label for such policies.) The policy combined several kinds of protection: fire and extended coverage, riot, vandalism and malicious mischief, water damage and flood, burglary and theft, and various types of inland marine insurance—transportation, tools and dies, and the like.

Because the company in question had been a stalwart supporter of the industry organizations—*Fortune* called it "the pride of the fire insurance lodge"—its action shocked the old guard. The company was "invited" to appear before a subcommittee of the Joint Committee on Interpretation and Complaint, set up in 1933 to police the Nation-wide Definition, that instrument for keeping insurance divided into watertight compartments. Obviously, the very existence of the Joint Committee after the enactment of the state multiple-line laws represented an attempt to hold back progress.

The company declined to appear before the subcommittee, but it did appear when the full committee met in February 1950. The committee's remarkable logic has been summarized tartly by one interested observer, INA's assistant general counsel, William B. Pugh, Jr.: "The committee [concluded] that the policy was inland marine in nature and therefore could only be written under that power, if at all; and, further, that since it did not come within the Definition, it could not be written at all."

To proponents of the multiple-line principle, the committee's report sounded like something out of *Alice in Wonderland*.

("There's no use trying," Alice said; "one *can't* believe impossible things.")

A Cowpath Full of Chuckholes

("I daresay you haven't had much practice," said the Queen. "When I was your age, I always did it for half an hour a day. Why, sometimes I've believed as many as six impossible things before breakfast.")

The New York state superintendent of insurance, Robert E. Dineen, expressed his own interpretation of the committee's report in a gentle but slightly incredulous manner: "In effect, the committee held that in spite of the fact that the [company was] a multiple line group with the broadest of charter powers, they could not write this particular policy because it was at war with a definition adopted long before the advent of multiple line underwriting."

With that, Dineen approved the policy. He added a comment that should have been borne in mind by the industry in the years ahead, but wasn't:

"Without in any way challenging the good faith of the Joint Committee, which, we repeat, was interpreting a definition of the pre–multiple-line era, we must make equally sure that departmental and legislative roadblocks are not replaced by roadblocks erected by companies which are unable or unwilling to write all-risk coverages themselves and do not wish to see their competitors do it."

INA's first multiple-line policy was an all-inclusive automobile contract, first issued in 1949. John Diemand bought the first policy himself, with pride.

But his greatest hope, from the first, had been to make available a policy for householders. When he mentioned this during a meeting of his committee in 1944, he had said: "I am not thinking of it from the standpoint of the rich man. In my own territory I am thinking of the 400,000 individually owned homes around Philadelphia. . . . I think this form can be made to appeal to that particular fellow."

Early in September 1950, H. Richard Heilman and John Etchberger, both of INA, were attending the annual convention of the Pennsylvania Association of Insurance Agents at Bedford Springs, Pennsylvania. They had barely seated themselves to hear a speech by the state insurance commissioner, Artemis Leslie, when they heard Leslie say, "I have this day approved a filing by the Insurance Company of North America to write a so-called Homeowners policy."

"Let's call Philadelphia," Heilman whispered to Etchberger.

As unobtrusively as possible the two men left the hall and went to Etchberger's hotel room. Heilman called the home office from there, and a few hours later, that same day, a mailing went out to all agents announcing the introduction of the new policy.

"John," said Heilman to Etchberger, "you've been present at the making of insurance history today."

It was no exaggeration. *Business Week* heralded INA's announcement as "revolutionary."

In one package policy INA combined at least nine different coverages, including fire and extended coverage (*i.e.,* lightning, hail, windstorm, explosion, riot and civil commotion, aircraft, land vehicles, smoke or smudge) on the home and its contents, residence theft insurance, legal liability for accidents on the premises, and medical care for injuries to guests and others. And the package cost twenty per cent less than the total value of all the policies that had been woven into it.

Because it met a need long felt by the public but hitherto unrecognized by most of the industry, the Homeowners policy caught on immediately. A number of competitors quickly prepared similar policies to cash in on the popularity. One company moved a bit too fast; it was so eager to market a policy that it simply reprinted INA's policy form by photo-offset, and then found, to its embarrassment, that it had forgotten to blot out the words "Insurance Company of North America" in one place.

It is unlikely that any other insurance policy ever was

welcomed as enthusiastically as the Homeowners. In its first full year, 1951, $777,000 in premiums were written, all by INA. By 1954, with a number of other companies also writing the coverage, the industry received the astounding total of $15,587,-000 in premiums. Two years later the figure reached $178,912,-000. By 1960 it was more than $750,000,000.

In 1950 INA joined with fourteen other companies to form the Multiple Peril Insurance Rating Organization, but three years later the company withdrew because of the reluctance of other members to proceed with Homeowners filings.

Meanwhile, the bureau companies that had not yet written Homeowners policies and did not belong to MPIRO were trying their best to persuade state commissioners that the underlying concept of the policy should be outlawed. The Homeowners policy was a multiple-line coverage written for an indivisible premium. The opposition felt strongly that the policy should be viewed as a fire policy linked with a liability policy, a theft policy, and other coverages. The premium and loss on each component should be figured separately, they insisted.

But the popularity of the Homeowners policy forced them to come up with a competitive product. Through an industry organization, the Interbureau Insurance Advisory Group, they developed a householders' coverage in 1954. The Comprehensive Dwelling policy, as it was called, was based on divisible premiums.

Nevertheless, the Homeowners policy proved much more popular than the Comprehensive Dwelling policy, and soon Interbureau members were writing Homeowners while some MPIRO members were writing the Interbureau policy. The upshot was that MPIRO and the Interbureau group merged forces in 1957, naming the new organization the Multi-Peril Insurance Conference.

The first contract developed by this group was called

the New Homeowners policy. As rates and forms changed in the next few years, that contract was succeeded by policies called, rather humorlessly, the New New Homeowners and then by the New New New Homeowners.

For John Diemand, there was great satisfaction in pulling out of his files the 1944 statement of the Insurance Executives Association that attacked the multiple-line principle, with its complacent assertion, "Most careful inquiry convinces [us] that as a matter of fact there has not been, nor is there now, real public demand for multiple-line underwriting."

The final triumph of Diemand's long crusade came in 1966, when a history of the National Board of Fire Underwriters was published. By that time the board, which had been a bastion of the most conservative element in the industry, had been absorbed into the American Insurance Association, the successor to the old Insurance Executives Association. The National Board's history said: "The business of insurance is never static. In the past twenty-five years it has gone through dynamic changes under which the concepts of underwriting by segregated peril have been superseded by the concepts of multiple-line underwriting."

18: The Senators Take a Look

 FOR THE first time in the company's 160-year history, INA's board of directors in 1953 was meeting outside Philadelphia, all the way across the continent in San Francisco, and *Newsweek* thought the event merited a lengthy article, in the course of which the magazine said:

"In apparent contradiction of the old company's somewhat awesome air of conservatism is an adventuresomeness popularly associated with youth, and an independence which amounts to nonconformism. [INA] belongs to none of the big insurance associations. It has led a long fight to liberalize state laws so that it could write new kinds of insurance, and its officers like to declare now that they will insure anything."

The article conveyed the impression that the company had finally freed itself from the restrictions and obstacles it had then been fighting for more than a decade, and perhaps there were even some in the company who may have harbored that optimistic opinion. If so, they were sorely mistaken.

In fact, the conflict was entering a new phase, which would threaten the company as none of the previous battles had. Up to now, INA had been on the offensive, and the old guard in the industry had been fighting holding actions; but from this point on the opposition would try to seize and maintain the initiative, and INA would often find itself fighting in a dozen places at once.

Because of the victory for multiple-line underwriting implicit in the approval of the Manufacturers Output and Homeowners policies, the opposition moved first to try to block any further breakdown of the barriers between the fire, marine, and casualty branches that had been erected in 1933 by the Nationwide Definition. In 1953 it was decided by the industry's power structure that the Definition should be updated, strengthened, and reaffirmed. For that purpose a hearing was held in Chicago in March.

The representative of one company testified candidly at the hearing that he looked to the Definition to put an end to multiple-line policies. The principal spokesman for the industry advocated modification of the Definition in such a manner that it would, as he put it, prevent independent companies from "flying solo" in competition. (Defending the Joint Committee that enforced the Definition, he declared that it had kept "its virginity pure" in its relations with the state commissioners.)

A few other companies joined INA in opposing the Definition as a threat to multiple-line contracts, which, they argued, should be treated as a new and separate kind of insurance. As the vice president of a Newark, New Jersey, company said, his company had broad charter powers and didn't believe it should be limited "except by the laws of our home state and the laws of the states in which we do business."

The secretary and counsel of a Philadelphia fire company that belonged to all the industry organizations ("We are a bureau company") complained that the Definition had been "unworkable" even before the advent of multiple-line underwriting. His company, which was already writing multiple-line policies, thought that every effort should be made to "avoid putting the industry in a straitjacket."

Appearing for INA, Bradford Smith, Jr., expressed the fear that re-affirmation of the Definition would have the effect of placing "in the hands of a few employees of insurance companies, the power to hinder, if not control, the lawful exercise of the charter powers of other insurance companies in competition with them."

As a result of the protests, the Definition was amended to provide: "This instrument shall not be construed to restrict or limit in any way the exercise of any insuring powers granted under charters and license whether used separately, in combination, or otherwise."

But the Definition was upheld.

By that time trouble in another form had thrown the business into disorder. In 1955 Smith outlined the spread of hostilities as INA had seen them.

"In the latter part of 1952 and 1953," he said, "one company after another announced increased commission scales in the Eastern Underwriters Association territory and to some extent in the Midwest.

"A full scale commission war was on.

"Now the attack came where it really hurt. We had suffered the loss of considerable business in the Excepted Cities territory in order to eliminate the highly discriminatory commissions and to comply with our interpretation of the rating laws, as well as the applicable federal statutes.

"We felt that the elimination of unjust discrimination amongst our agents justified the loss of some of our business in the Excepted Cities. Agents in the ordinary [*i.e.*, not Excepted] territory had stoutly supported us in this period, and it was their steadfastness that enabled us to go through with this program without placing too severe a strain on our production of business.

"But now our business from our agents in the ordinary territory was being attacked by old-line stock companies offering commissions which they themselves had held to exceed a reasonable maximum. One company executive after another openly admitted that while he did not approve of the advance in commissions, he could not afford to hold fast to the old standard commission of twenty per cent. They said they were forced to increase commissions to twenty-five per cent in order to keep the non-hazardous [preferred risk] business from going off their books at a very rapid rate.

"A commission war was on, but INA did not join in it. Our business was openly attacked. Production was falling off. Some proper method of equalizing competitive forces had to be formed.

"We had decided that increasing commissions would inevitably injure the interests of our agents and the public.

"In the fall of 1953 we came to the conclusion that the deviation method of equalizing competition was of extremely doubtful value because of the requirement for annual re-justification and the ability of competitors to harass the deviating company.

"We decided that we must attain freedom of action by making and filing our own rates on the more sought-after lines of business."

On December 7, 1953, INA notified rating bureaus in about forty states that it was cancelling the bureaus' authority to make and file rates on the company's behalf for the "dwelling" classes (a dwelling being defined for insurance purposes as a building occupied principally for residential purposes by not more than two families). The company remained a subscriber to the bureaus for all other classes of risks.

In short, it was changing its relationship with the bureaus from subscriber to partial subscriber.

In San Francisco, Frank Owen received a telephone call

from Philadelphia. Ludwig Lewis, in his terse way, told Owen to design an entirely new dwelling program, and gave him five days to do it. When the program was presented over the telephone to Lewis and to H. Richard Heilman, both approved it, and Owen proceeded to have it printed in the West.

"It was separate and distinct from anything written by the bureau," Owen said. "We did rely on the city classification system or protection classification system of the National Board of Fire Underwriters, but that was all. We made our own rates on the basis of the experience available from our own statistics recorded up to that time. And we made a completely independent program in California.

"This met with tremendous agency resistance, and many agents joined almost every other company in fighting us tooth and nail."

Boycotted by some agents' associations, INA lost well over $1,000,000 worth of business in one year in the fire line alone in just one state, California.

Elsewhere the fighting was equally fierce. The company had made independent filings, identical to those of the bureaus, to become effective March 1, 1954. The filings were accepted in twenty-eight states, rejected in five, and held up in seven states.

The critical contest, in New York, found INA pitted against the New York Fire Insurance Organization (usually referred to by its initials: NYFIRO). Among the arguments advanced by the latter group was the contention that rates should not be based upon the expenses of a single company, but on those of all companies doing business in the state. Any other course, it was pointed out, would prevent rate uniformity.

The state insurance superintendent agreed with INA that the whole intent of the law was to foster competition, which clearly conflicted with the concept of rate uniformity.

After the superintendent approved INA's filing,

NYFIRO appealed the case to the Appellate Division of Supreme Court, where the opposition was supported in an *amicus curiae* brief by the New York State Agents Association. Nevertheless, the court upheld the superintendent. Still unwilling to concede defeat, NYFIRO turned to the Court of Appeals, the state's highest court, but twice that court refused to hear the appeal. When INA's opponents tried to carry the issue to the United States Supreme Court, that body dismissed the appeal.

The battle had been long, time-consuming, and very costly to INA.

There were other clashes, all part of an industry program whose existence INA suspected but could not prove until the Senate Subcommittee on Antitrust and Monopoly called a series of hearings in 1959 and 1960. The subcommittee counsel, Donald P. McHugh, had conducted a thorough investigation before the hearings. And it must be said, to the credit of the men in the leadership of the industry organizations, that every witness invited to testify did so without subpoena, and all the insurance associations opened their files voluntarily to the investigators.

The subcommittee's report at the conclusion of the hearings said that it had compiled an "impressive" record of "the many efforts during the years" after 1945 "to curb competition, with much of it accomplished through utilization of state regulatory channels." Documents found in the files of industry organizations presented "a bleak picture of concerted efforts on a nationwide basis to restrain competition," efforts "which not only went unchallenged by the states, but virtually unnoticed."

According to the subcommittee's findings, which, for the sake of clarity and convenience, we will call the Senate Report, the whole thing started in February 1954, the month in which the New York state insurance superintendent called the first hearing in the challenge by NYFIRO to INA's independent filing.

In that month the National Board of Fire Underwriters appointed a Special Committee of Chief Executives, usually called the North Committee, its chairman being John A. North, president of a major insurance company whose home office was in Hartford.

The National Board was not alone in its campaign to stifle competition. The Senate Report listed as organizations "principally involved in the movement" the NYFIRO, the New York state rating bureau, the Pacific Fire Rating Bureau (PFRB), the Eastern Underwriters Association (EUA), and a multitude of local organizations.

Three fronts were opened in the drive against INA: First, the bureau group tried to prevent the company from exercising its right, under the rating laws of most states, to be merely a partial subscriber to bureau services. Second, an attempt was made to persuade state legislatures to enact measures that would restrict or eliminate the right to compete. Third, the bureaus tried to make independence prohibitively expensive by greatly increasing assessments to partial subscribers— that is, the price charged them for those bureau services that they did use.

Persons outside the insurance industry may wonder why, if INA and a few other companies wanted to be independent, they continued as partial subscribers to the bureaus. The answer has been given by Bertram C. Dedman, who was associate counsel at the time and later became INA's general counsel.

"The argument advanced [by the bureaus]," he said, "was that an insurer must subscribe for *all* bureau classes, or *none*. The bureaus well knew that it was not economically feasible for a single company to make rates for those classes of fire insurance where the technique of individual inspection and rating is employed. [Dwelling class risks are not individually inspected and rated.]

"They reasoned that we would lose our desire to make independent filings for dwellings if by so doing we would be deprived of bureau services for those expensive-to-rate classes."

Although an increasing number of companies were taking independent action similar to INA's, the Philadelphia company was singled out as the primary target for a number of reasons. It was the first to take active steps to assert its independence and thus exposed itself to attack. Then too, as someone pointed out at a meeting of the National Board's subcommittee of lawyers, "other companies . . . would probably follow North America's example."

Even an emotional factor may have figured in the industry's attitude, for the hierarchy felt strongly that, in the light of INA's long-held position as a pillar of the power structure, the company now was guilty of treason to the ruling clique.

No sooner had the NYFIRO challenged INA's independent filing and partial subscribership in New York than the Pacific Fire Rating Bureau attacked the company in the West. This coordination between NYFIRO and PFRB was not difficult to arrange; besides their common links with the National Board and other industry groups, they had interlocking directorates, seven of the sixteen members of NYFIRO's governing committee also serving in the same capacity for PFRB.

"The result," in the words of the Senate Report, "is that the bureaus *are* the companies in another form." [Emphasis added.]

PFRB's initial move was to threaten INA with expulsion, a meeting for that purpose being called for May 1954. The company's general counsel, Perry Epes, flew out to California to join resident vice president Frank Owen and INA's local attorneys at the meeting.

"A great man, Perry Epes," Owen recalled. "He told the bureau that if they wanted to start a fight by throwing us out, we would take every single one of them, individually, to court. And that was the end of that. They never contested it again, never even suggested again that they might throw us out."

At the time, the bureau's constitution and bylaws would not have withstood a court test of INA's expulsion. So the following year PFRB adopted a bylaw which, if approved by the states, would have effectively prevented partial subscribership, although its own legal counsel, the Senate Report later disclosed, "stated he had grave doubt on the position taken by the Pacific Bureau."

Moreover, several of the lawyers on the National Board's own legal subcommittee warned, as the subcommittee's minutes showed, that the proposed "rules are contrary to law" and that the organization was laying itself open to federal prosecution under the antitrust laws, for "when you eliminate the ability of North America to compete, you are involved in economic coercion."

The Senate Report summed up the various industry discussions about PFRB's bylaws change bluntly:

"It would appear that the interested parties were well aware that their activities constituted a conspiracy and a possible restraint [of trade] in violation of the antitrust laws. In the light of the numerous legal opinions by their own attorneys, it is difficult to reconcile the testimony of organization witnesses before this [Senate] subcommittee that they were merely seeking enlightenment as to the meaning of the rating laws. . . .

"It is interesting to note that the industry was not hesitating to enter a conspiracy in restraint of trade and to pervert the state regulatory process, but were boldly relying on the difficulty of proof and the lack of provable damages."

(The Senators may have been unduly harsh on INA's opponents in this statement, for as late as 1967 a major spokesman for the industry's cause, a man respected by INA executives as well as others for his integrity and character, protested to this writer, "Our philosophy was to put the burden of change on the courts. We were certain that somebody was going to get hurt if INA were permitted to follow the course it had charted. Was it to be a fight among the giants, with victory going to the guy with the biggest pockets?"

(INA partisans did not accept that argument at the time, but it is possible that their opponents did rationalize their obstructive tactics that way, if only to justify their actions to themselves.)

Believing, as the PFRB's lawyers said, that it had "the best chance of obtaining approval of the proposed rule in Arizona," a belief based on "a conference with the commissioner of that state during the Los Angeles convention," the organization selected Arizona for its test case.

Opposed by INA and another company at a hearing called by the Arizona insurance commissioner, the PFRB by-law nevertheless was approved as reasonable by the commissioner in November 1955. When INA took the dispute to the courts, the commissioner's ruling was reversed by the Superior Court of Maricopa County. PFRB and the commissioner appealed, with the support of the state agents' association, while INA's position was supported by the National Association of Independent Insurers. On February 18, 1958, the Arizona Supreme Court unanimously upheld the Superior Court's decision sustaining INA's position.

"Thus, the battle for partial subscribership was won," the Senate Report said, "but only after long and expensive legal proceedings against the forces of the major insurers who had joined in a concerted nationwide effort."

There had been other administrative hearings and lawsuits in other states. The brief filed by PFRB in Nevada was a remarkably revealing document. In it the bureau maintained that "everyone . . . is well aware that Public Law 15 was not enacted by Congress, and the all-industry bill was not enacted by the states, in order to 'foster competition in the insurance industry' "—although the sponsors of both those measures specifically declared that to be one of their primary motives.

The PFRB also asserted that it was a quasi-official agency with the authority and duty to "advise the [state] comsioner if it considers such proposals [rate filings] to be improper." Moreover, the PFRB went so far as to claim that the insurance commissioner had no legal right to overrule the bureau on its decisions ("administrative authority does not permit the agency [*i.e.*, commissioner] to substitute its own opinions for those of the management of the utility [the bureau]").

The old, autocratic outlook had not disappeared in the decade or more since the Supreme Court brought insurance under the jurisdiction of the antitrust laws.

While the NYFIRO and PFRB cases were still being argued, the North Committee decided that "legislation [should] be sought to amend, when necessary, the rate law in the fire and allied lines" in all the states. If the amendments it favored were enacted, the law would "be based on the principle of a single rating organization for a state; jurisdiction of this bureau would be limited to fire and allied lines; [and] membership would be mandatory on all insurers writing the coverage rated by that rating organization." So the North Committee said.

North himself regarded this as the best way "to get rid of partial subscriberships," thus eliminating or severely handicapping any attempt at rate competition.

However, four of the six attorneys on the National Board's subcommittee of lawyers expressed the opinion that, in their words, "such legislation is undesirable and impractical" because "the proposal runs counter to the basic philosophy of the all-industry bills" which had become law in most of the states. The National Board's lawyers also feared prosecution under the federal antitrust laws, saying "the plan would coerce all insurers into a single mold of rating."

Despite the attorneys' warnings, attempts to get such measures through the legislatures were made in more than half a dozen states from 1957 to 1959. Thanks to the opposition by INA, the National Association of Independent Insurers, and occasionally some others, all those efforts were defeated.

The third tactic was to raise assessments to partial subscribers to a level which would make independent filings well nigh impossible from an economic point of view.

Not that the independents, including INA, were unwilling to pay a reasonable price. Even the industry, in a document quoted in the Senate Report, said, "Cost is not a basic part of the problem" of stemming the "apparent march toward independence of action." The memorandum conceded "the willingness of some independents to pay a fair share of the cost of developing this material."

"It is probable that rating bureaus could work out mutually satisfactory arrangements for the use of their material [by the independents]," it continued. "But while this would relieve the bureau companies of any unfair cost burden, it would not slow down the movement toward independent action; on the contrary, it might well accelerate such movement."

This device was used to damage the independents. For example, in November 1960—*even after the Senate subcommittee hearings had exposed the coercive drive against the independents*—the National Bureau of Casualty Underwriters announced a boost in the prices for manuals. The Senate Report said:

"One of the large companies estimated that manuals which formerly cost about $5,000 per year would now cost close to $300,000 [an increase of *six thousand per cent!*]. Many smaller companies complained that the increased financial burden resulting from these rules might force them to resign from independent associations."

INA filed objections with the state regulatory authorities in each of the states, about sixteen, in which the new rules for assessments had been adopted. The key test came in Ohio on the company's challenge of the Ohio Inspection Bureau's rules.

"When it became apparent that the [state insurance] superintendent was prepared to set the rules aside," the company's associate counsel, Dedman, said in a review of the dispute, "OIB requested a recess and asked for an arbitration of our differences, [after which] agreement was reached whereby OIB would cost-account and establish separate rates of assessment for each class, and that subscribers would be required to pay only for classes for which they subscribed."

That agreement set the pattern for other bureaus throughout the country, except in the West, where the PFRB proved as intransigent as ever. Negotiations having been fruitless, INA requested a formal hearing before the Arizona insurance director, but the day before the hearing was to begin, PFRB's attorneys agreed to make the assessment changes demanded by the company.

All in all, the Senate investigations gave ample foundation for the Report's belief "that the power to protect the public interest should not be reposed in a private elite."

During the period between 1951 and 1954, the United States Department of Justice stepped into the insurance controversy by initiating antitrust prosecutions in Cleveland and New Orleans against agents' associations, accusing them of illegal boycotts against independent, deviating, and mutual companies.

After five years, the government won a decision on a secondary issue in the Cleveland case, and the agents' groups in those and several other cities agreed to abandon the course of action that underlay the complaints.

About the same time that the Senate hearings were held, one of the biggest bureau companies withdrew from an industry organization.

"The bureau companies woke up to the fact that their chief accomplishment had been to encase themselves in a regulatory straitjacket while the independents walked off with the business," INA's assistant counsel, William B. Pugh, Jr., pointed out. "The breakdown of the industry system of control turned into an accelerated disintegration. Serious arguments erupted among major companies in the dominant trade associations, and major resignations followed.

"It was clear that unless the industry system was relaxed so that bureau members could obtain sufficient flexibility to compete with independents, who had, in effect, won the basic battle to protect their rights, fragmentation of the bureaus could be expected."

By 1962 the industry, of necessity, had changed its own course of action 180 degrees. In a joint statement, the Association of Casualty and Surety Companies, the Inland Marine Underwriters Association, and the National Board of Fire Underwriters told a New York State Joint Legislative Committee on Insurance Rates and Regulations:

"Competition is the best and most efficient regulator of rates. It has proved and will prove a much more effective means of preventing excessiveness than any rate approval mechanism. . . . We do not think that we are wrong in our conviction that competition is the best known way of keeping prices reasonable. . . ."

There was a final irony. In 1967 a company that had been one of the most determined foes of INA's independent drive—the man who was now chairman of the company had been the principal spokesman for the bureau point of view in the most important hearings—withdrew from membership in the bureaus to partial subscribership.

Besides insuring construction of third tube of Lincoln
Tunnel under Hudson River between New York and New
Jersey, INA helped devise safety measures that made it
the first tunnel built without a single fatality.

Disneyland, the safest of all
amusement parks, is insured by INA,
which also maintains a "Carefree
Corner" for visitors there.

INA *Archives*

San Diego Zoo

Even zoo animals are protected by
INA, including the denizens of the
San Diego Zoo (BELOW) and the
Bronx Zoo.

In 1905—about the time this car, now
in the Henry Ford Museum (insured
by INA) at Dearborn, Michigan, was
manufactured—INA wrote its first policy
covering an automobile. By the early
1930s, auto liability and property damage
was the biggest line in its casualty
insurance business. Before the century
reached midpoint, auto insurance also
was the most troublesome problem
confronting the company.

19: A Different Kind of Hospital Blanket

 BY 1961 the company's fight for independence had been largely won, although sporadic clashes occurred for years afterward. The war had been expensive for INA, the industry, and the nation.

"While independent companies have ultimately prevailed in court," the Senate Subcommittee on Antitrust and Monopoly commented that year, "victory has been achieved at great cost, after prolonged delay, and at an expense to the insurance buyer which can never be calculated."

Nevertheless, if the long conflict had not taken place, the cost would have been even greater, for the American economy could not have enjoyed its spectacular expansion without adequate insurance protection, and the insurance industry would have failed its opportunity and its obligation.

Despite the cost of the protracted campaign, INA benefited from it in many ways. As Bradford Smith, Jr., said, "The fights taught us a lot about the business that we otherwise wouldn't have learned."

Morale was lifted, as it is among men in combat. There

[281]

was the heightened *esprit de corps* of men who stand shoulder to shoulder, feeling themselves besieged but certain that what they are fighting for is right. In later years, the memory of having fought together provided a common bond among many INA men, who were proud of having stood firm against odds that often seemed well nigh overwhelming.

Then, too, the attacks of its opponents forced the company to strengthen its own resources and facilities. For example, "this company took the lead in bringing actuarial techniques to property insurance," as L. H. Longley-Cook, who became INA's chief actuary in 1949, recalled.

Of course, the development of the company's actuarial work was a necessity because INA had to be prepared to defend its statistics, projections, and the rates based upon them when it was struggling to win permission to write insurance at rates below those of the bureaus.

Longley-Cook was the ideal person to head the project. A tall, witty Englishman, he has been well described by his successor at INA, Edward J. Hobbs:

"He almost intuitively knows his conclusion. When you first start working with him, this is most disconcerting, because while you are still in the process of reasoning to the conclusion, he puts down the conclusion. You ask him how he arrived at it and he becomes somewhat impatient. A really rare, brilliant individual."

Like many mathematicians (one thinks of Charles Dodgson, who wrote under the name "Lewis Carroll," and of Stephen Leacock), Longley-Cook had a lively and sometimes naughty sense of humor, which he was quite ready to display during the endless administrative hearings and court trials.

Once a college professor testified that he had found statistical correlations "proving," in his opinion, that an insurance company's expense ratio increased with the size of the company. With just a touch of malice, Longley-Cook, spotting a fallacy in the professor's reasoning, had his actuarial assistants at INA run a series of correlations, all of them absurd, which he submitted with a straight face. The calculations appeared to indicate correlations between an insurance company's expense ratios and the total of digits in its telephone number, the number of letters in its president's name, and so on.

He made his point: the mere existence of a correlation does not prove a causal relationship.

"Longley-Cook was INA's secret weapon," an insurance company head who was one of the chief battlers for the bureaus' position at the time complained later. "His English accent impressed the state commissioners, and his logic confounded them."

One of the hearings in which he took part was the Cook County rate deviation case in Illinois. The hearing was presided over by J. Edward Day, who later became Postmaster General of the United States. The decision was in INA's favor, but years later, while Longley-Cook was lunching, Day saw him in the restaurant and crossed the room to greet him.

"Do you know," Day said to him, "during your whole presentation in that case I didn't really manage to understand one word!"

During another hearing an attorney for the bureau was badgering Longley-Cook unmercifully. Demanding "Yes" or "No" answers to questions that were too complex for such replies, the lawyer bellowed that INA's actuary was being too verbose when he attempted to give fully responsive answers. Then the lawyer propounded another long, involved question, winding it up with:

"Can you tell me or not?"

"Yes," replied Longley-Cook with a happy smile.

It didn't answer the question, but it was a one-word response.

The actuarial department that grew in the course of

those battles became a strong arm to top management as it maneuvered the company through the stormy waters of that turbulent period. It also helped to give life to the new concepts being developed within INA.

As the clash of opposing ideas often does, the long struggle between INA and the bureau companies stimulated creative processes. INA, as Simon Whitney pointed out in his antitrust study, "pioneered new forms of fire insurance policy," and not just fire insurance, for in many lines the imagination of the company's men, now unchained from the bonds of industry restrictions, conceived new and needed coverages for the public.

The first of these novel coverages were blanket policies, that is, policies that covered several different properties or risks under one form, instead of separately. INA had introduced the idea of the blanket policy in the late 1930's, and beginning in 1940 the company provided general liability insurance in an individually drawn, manuscript policy with a single premium basis and a single rate.

About the end of World War II, coverages of this type were specially tailored to the requirements of two groups. One was the Morticians Blanket; the other, the Hospital Blanket, a name that must have made for a certain amount of confusion in non-insurance circles.

As it happened, another novelty was being developed in the New York office at that time, a policy covering the mailing of some securities to be sent to stockholders of a utility company which was splitting its stock. Within half a dozen years, drawing on that experience, INA developed a bond coverage indemnifying a transfer agent if non-negotiable securities sent by first class mail or air mail were lost or stolen.

Some of the other innovations that came flooding from INA in those hectic but exciting years included:

In 1947, the first general liability "wrap-up" covering

the owner and all contractors at a taconite (iron-ore) development area in the Mesabi Range of Michigan's upper peninsula. Altogether, 245 contractors took part in the work of building this $300,000,000 project spread over 160 acres, including seventy-four miles of railroad, two large docks, a dam impounding 10,000,000 gallons of water, and a town of 1,200 houses.

At the request of a national brokerage house, INA put together an insurance program providing general liability and workmen's compensation coverage for the owner of the project, the Erie Mining Company, and all of the contractors and their employees, all in one package. With men stationed at the site, INA provided safety engineering to cut losses and handled claims promptly. Technically described as a retrospective rating plan, the program provided that INA would charge the insured his own losses, the cost of administering the insurance protection, the expenses of claims handling and safety work, taxes, and a modest profit for the underwriter. Erie Mining saved $500,000 by this "wrap-up."

In 1950, the Homeowners policy, which by 1966 had soared to $1,500,000,000 in premiums for the entire industry—this for the coverage for which the Insurance Executives Association had seen "no public demand" in 1944!

In 1950, Excess-of-Loss (catastrophe) coverage, which was broadened in 1961 to a combined world-wide policy. This was the large-scale "deductibles" coverage, under which a major corporation may wish to absorb, say, the first $1,000,000 of loss, buying insurance protection for losses above that figure.

In 1955, the first policy covering the operation of a utilitarian nuclear reactor. This policy was written by INA when no other American company was willing to undertake such a risk.

In 1956, establishment of the first Commercial Multiple-Line Department.

In 1957, blanket catastrophe policies, often described in

the industry as "umbrellas"; INA's version was called the Big Top Policy. This provided large buyers of insurance with protection for any exposed gaps in their primary coverage (or their self-insurance); essentially, a variation on the Excess-of-Loss protection. Like a number of the other developments in this list, this sort of policy was not originated by INA, but by the London underwriters; however, INA was the first American company to offer this protection.

In 1957, commercial package policies, beginning with a program designed for funeral directors; in a short time similar policies were written for motels and apartments, schools and churches, and retailers and wholesalers. A package policy combines several coverages in one contract, as the Homeowners does.

In 1960, Simplematic Re, a unique, simplified method for reinsuring other life insurance companies.

In 1961, development of several original forms of protection for employees of business concerns, including Salary Continuance and Voluntary Accidental Death and Dismemberment for groups.

In 1961, packaged catastrophe personal liability insurance for executives, community and business leaders, professional men and women, and their families.

In 1961, direct "named perils" coverage (excluding nuclear perils) on nuclear risks. That year two policies were written to cover electric power plants using nuclear reactors.

In 1962, a Mortgage Impairment Insurance form. First developed for the country's largest life insurance company to cover buildings on which it held a mortgage, this type of insurance quickly became very popular. INA remained the leading underwriter in this coverage, which protects the lender against loss by reason of the failure of the mortgagor to maintain insurance on the property.

These innovations and the spirit of exhilaration and

enthusiasm they connoted helped INA to prosper during those years despite boycotts, loss of some agents, crippling litigation, and whispering campaigns.

And prosper it did. Beginning in 1945, the company enjoyed an underwriting profit in all but six years through 1961. In some of those six years the statutory underwriting loss was painfully big; in 1946 it was more than $5,000,000, in 1947 almost $9,000,000 and in 1957 a walloping $11,000,000 ("the worst year since the Depression days of the 1930's," said the company).

The eleven profitable years, however, more than made up for the lean years; in seven of those years the statutory underwriting profit was upwards of $6,000,000. Oddly enough, the second most profitable year was 1953, the year when the campaign against the company reached a peak of intensity, and even the next two years were fruitful.

It was a period marked by many changes within the company, as well as by its changed relationship to the rest of the industry. In 1947 John O. Platt died, and his death was followed a year later by that of Benjamin Rush.

The national economy was thriving, and so was the company. But prosperity went hand in hand with inflation, which worked a hardship on many people. To compensate for the diminished purchasing value of the dollar, the company provided supplementary cost-of-living payments year after year until finally, acknowledging that monetary conditions were unlikely to change in the foreseeable future, the supplementary pay was incorporated into the regular salary scale.

The impact of inflation was discernible in other ways. As the 1956 annual report observed: "Inflation is still having its effect on fidelity losses, as the embezzler steals larger amounts in an effort to keep pace with his questionable fashion of living."

That was the year a number of the directors and senior

[287]

officers went to Europe to dedicate INA's Continental head-quarters at the Hague. A year earlier the board had held its first meeting outside the United States in Toronto, during a business tour of our neighboring country that took the directors from Montreal to Vancouver, covering 7,000 miles in less than two weeks' time.

Hailing the visit of the "directors and top executives of the Insurance Company of North America, the largest, from the point of view of assets, fire and casualty insurance company in the United States," the *Financial Times* of Canada said: "To say that Canada and Canadians welcome such visits as this is to use an understatement. They demonstrate that business leaders across the line are not only fully aware of Canada's growing importance in the scheme of things, but are anxious to learn more about us at first hand."

Arrangements for the Canadian trip had been made by Frank G. Harrington, who was then public relations director for the company, a dynamic and remarkably creative man who would ultimately rise to senior vice president. Harrington had no sooner returned to Philadelphia than he found that INA was to be host six weeks later to more than 3,500 members of the American Bar Association and their guests, including President Dwight D. Eisenhower and Chief Justice Earl Warren.

And Harrington had to make all the arrangements.

That evening, when he arrived home, he joined his pretty wife, Jeanne, on their terrace. After inquiring about his day, she said, "The girls are coming tomorrow for lunch and bridge. What do you think I should give them for lunch?"

It had been a stock question for years, and Harrington replied with the stock answer that had become a family joke:

"Tuna fish salad, hot rolls, coffee, and ice cream."

"You don't have any imagination," Jeanne commented, as she had for years when he made that suggestion.

Her husband said:

"Well, I want you to listen to me for a minute. You've got three girls coming for lunch tomorrow. On August 14 I have 3,500 people coming for lunch. They include the President of the United States, the Chief Justice of the United States, the Chief Justice of England. And we are going to have it on the Mall across from Independence Hall, where they don't even have a hot plate. And you're asking what to serve three girls!"

"Are you serious?" she asked.

"I couldn't be more serious."

"Well, I have one word of advice for you," she said.

"What's that?"

"Quit."

Harrington didn't quit. He arranged matters so well that there wasn't a hitch in the proceedings. Indeed, the Secret Service judged it the best-planned event at which they had ever guarded the Chief Executive.

The President's bodyguards were not alone in that feeling. The *Philadelphia Inquirer* called it "an event unique in the city's history," and *Printer's Ink*, the advertising trade journal, called it "top drawer public relations." All the guests echoed Lord Justice Denning of England when he said, "Never have I witnessed such a perfectly executed affair."

The menu?

—Chicken salad, rolls, coffee, and ice cream, not very different from the lunch served to Jeanne Harrington's bridge players.

20: 'Noisy, Stinking Things'

 THERE WERE PROBABLY not more than a dozen automobiles in New York City in 1890, all of them
apparently steam driven. But in September of that
year a man by the name of H. H. Bliss was assisting
a woman alighting from a trolley car when he was struck by
one of the new "horseless carriages." Bliss died the following
day, the first recorded victim of what was to become America's
most lethal weapon.

By 1904 the nation's supply of automobiles was still
scattered thinly across the country. In Kansas City, Missouri,
there were only two, but that turned out to be one too many—
they collided at an intersection.

Even without pedestrians or other motorists as targets,
the early drivers set a ruinous example to the millions who
followed them. They quickly discovered the most efficient
means for destroying their vehicles and maiming or slaying
themselves.

Like speed. One pioneer in a Stanley Steamer, dubbed
"the Flying Teapot" by the press, rolled onto the sand at
Ormond Beach, Florida, in 1907 and, before a large and ex-
pectant crowd, provided the thrill of the day by keeping the

throttle open until his "horseless carriage," having reached a speed of 197 miles per hour, bounced off a mound of sand, soared through the air ten feet above the beach for 100 feet, and then exploded against the ground in steam and flames. The driver, flung clear, was seriously injured but not killed.

Thus began the carnage.

By 1966, motor vehicle accidents ranked sixth among the causes of death in the United States. Car crashes were causing an injury to someone in the country every eighteen seconds and a death every eleven minutes. Unless the trend were reversed, half the people alive in the nation that year would be injured in an auto accident sooner or later, and nearly 2,800,000 of them would lose their lives on the roads.

Although most Americans were still afraid of flying, statistics showed the death rate for travelers in cars substantially higher than in airplanes (2.4 fatalities per 100,000,000 passenger-miles against 0.38). About 49,000 Americans each year were dying in highway tragedies, and about 4,000,000 were being injured, with nearly 250,000 of them suffering permanent disabilities.

Since the death of Bliss ushered in the Age of the Automobile, more than 1,500,000 Americans had been killed in crashes, more than the toll in all our wars.

So astronomical were the statistics that for most people the enormity of the catastrophe, for that was what it had become, was beyond true comprehension. To borrow a thought from Hannah Arendt, the vast dimensions of the slaughter on the highways had perhaps harmed us most by making sudden, violent death banal.

One of the earliest organizations to attempt to deal with the problem was INA, although it could not claim to have pioneered in auto insurance. The first automobile liability policy had been written by another company in 1898 at the request of a Buffalo, New York, physician. Four years later a second company issued the first policy protecting an auto against damage, and within months motorists could buy fire and theft insurance for their cars.

An insurance trade journal, *Spectator*, appealed for a boycott of the newfangled contraptions: "The motormen— chauffeurs is the general term—driving automobiles are usually reckless, rushing madly past frightened teams [of horses] without attempting to slow down, or frequently coming up from behind and passing without giving any warning whatever. Nervous horses are sure to be alarmed at such apparitions. . . . While they cannot prevent their policyholders from being run over by reckless chauffeurs . . . [underwriters] might serve the cause of public safety by refusing to insure anyone who has acquired the automobile habit."

INA's president, Charles Platt, was of the same frame of mind. When it was suggested that the company should begin insuring "horseless carriages," Platt snorted: "I'll never insure a gasoline can on wheels—the noisy, stinking things!"

However, the brightest of the young men about him, Benjamin Rush, saw the opportunities in auto coverages (although he might have felt differently a half century later). Discreetly urging agents to try placing their automobile business with the company, Rush kept advancing, as tactfully as possible, his arguments for getting into this new field.

The attack on two fronts succeeded, and in 1905 INA began writing fire and theft coverage for cars. Two years later collision insurance was added, but it was not until 1920, when INA's casualty affiliate, the Indemnity Insurance Company of North America, was established, that it could also offer third-party liability protection.

By the early 1930's the biggest item in INA's casualty business was automobile liability and property damage insurance, protecting motorists against losses for damaging other people or property with a car. In those days it was true, as

Fortune reported, "that most companies will cover only a stipulated car driven by the insured and by others with his permission, but [INA], if satisfied with the 'moral hazard,' will cover you for any car, whether you own, borrow, or hire it, and also will cover you while someone else is driving your car." This innovation by the company was widely copied in later years.

It was the automobile business that caused the Indemnity to withdraw from the National Bureau of Casualty and Surety Underwriters in 1929. The rupture occurred over another new INA idea, "merit rating," which allowed a credit in the form of rate reduction to drivers with good safety records.

As a matter of fact, the bureau itself did come out with such a policy, but dropped it in 1932 because of protests that many member companies were using the discount system as a disguised means of giving rebates by awarding premium cuts to drivers whose records did not support such treatment. The bureau companies never quite made up their minds about merit rating; they revived the idea, dropped it, brought it up again. About 1960 the bureau companies with a great fanfare of publicity "introduced" the program as the "Safe Driver Plan."

Over the years every state enacted laws of one kind or another designed to force motorists to obtain liability insurance. The rationale underlying those laws was commendable: to protect innocent traffic victims whose persons or property had been damaged by motorists who did not have the financial resources to pay the resulting judgments.

According to Dr. C. A. Kulp, dean and professor of insurance at the Wharton School of Finance and Commerce of the University of Pennsylvania, "The chances of collecting any damages at all when the other party is insured are roughly nine out of ten; when he is not, only one out of five. . . . Of tremendous social import is the cold fact that when there is no liability insurance legal rights and remedies are largely meaningless."

Some of those laws were good; a few were ill-conceived. But good or bad, they were one of the factors that made auto insurance the largest single classification of the non-life insurance business in the seventh decade of the century. For the industry as a whole forty-one per cent of all property-liability premiums covered motor vehicles. More important to the policyholders was the fact that motorists were paying auto insurance premiums at the rate of $8,300,000,000 in 1965.

Everything should have been sunny for the underwriters, but it wasn't. John T. Gurash, president of the Pacific Employers Insurance Company, an INA subsidiary, expressed alarm at "the continuing deterioration of the public image of auto insurance" and added with candor, "Many people, including many within our own business, are convinced that our present system of providing automobile insurance coverage is not working as it should."

More people held auto insurance than any other kind of insurance protection, and they were finding it increasingly expensive. From 1957 to 1967 their premiums had shot up between thirty-five and fifty per cent. Drivers in thirty-two states had seen their rates rise in just one year, 1966, and in the first quarter of 1967 auto insurance prices moved upward again in seven states.

"A crisis appears to be developing in the field of automobile insurance," *U. S. News & World Report* said in April 1967. "Screams from drivers reach Congress as insurance premiums rise. Drivers seem to feel premiums already are in the stratosphere."

Understandably, the motorists, hard hit by a series of rate increases, found it hard to believe in 1967 that insurance companies had lost nearly $1,400,000,000 on their auto business in the previous ten years. But an examination of INA's records beginning in 1944 and ending in 1966 showed that the company suffered a statutory underwriting loss on its automobile policies in thirteen of those years, only eight years producing a profit.

The widespread public skepticism reflected a general lack of understanding of the peculiar nature of the insurance business and the specific pressures to which it was subject during the postwar period. It was the sensitivity of insurance to social, political, and economic changes that plunged the business into its automobile underwriting predicament.

After World War II the United States enjoyed a long period of prosperity that blessed us with a standard of living higher than anyone had ever dreamed possible. Analyzing the shifting patterns of income tax returns between 1939 and 1960, John Brooks wrote in *The Great Leap*:

"These figures, I am convinced, attest to one of the most dramatic redistributions of income that any nation ever went through in so short a time. The very rich we still have with us, but they are increasingly insignificant as to relative numbers and relative economic importance . . . ; the moderately rich have increased in number moderately; the distinctly well-to-do have become commonplace; and the comfortably-off have become our great central mass."

In two decades, from 1940 to 1960, the population rose by more than one-third, to 179,323,175, which meant that there were more drivers. And more cars, for registrations had increased even more rapidly, from 27,465,826 in 1940 to 74,904,000 in 1965, or about two and one-half times as many.

Like the distribution of income, the spread of cars changed, too, in those years. Four out of five American households owned at least one car in 1960, and one out of five were two-car families.

The spread of population to the suburbs made the auto a real necessity for millions of people, for mass transportation in those areas was generally inadequate, and little was done to improve it in most places.

Moreover, people had discovered the automobile offered, as Ben J. Wattenberg observed, "a degree of personal freedom not experienced by any other people in any other place. The private car means privacy and freedom. Freedom to be alone, to travel, to move, to explore. . . . The automobile is the true non-scheduled common carrier to almost everywhere."

In fact, ninety per cent of all travel between cities in 1967 was done by car.

Nobody had been prepared for this fantastic growth in automobile use, so there was a long and lethal lag in time before all the elements in our society which were concerned in the problem began to take action. And even then many of the initial efforts were directed at symptoms rather than causes. In 1967 far less money and energy were being put into research on traffic safety than into many less tragic and costly problems.

It was estimated that uniform road signs throughout the nation would save 2,000 lives a year, for one traffic fatality in eight involves an out-of-state driver.

Licensing, control, and disciplining of motorists was nothing less than a national scandal in 1967. Scarcely any state tested drivers more than the one time they applied for a license, and that test was almost always given at slow speeds under close to ideal conditions. Furthermore, "some states and localities are inexcusably lax in granting drivers' licenses to obvious incompetents," as *Time* pointed out.

"In New York, Massachusetts, Maine, and Wyoming, drug addicts and mental defectives can get licenses," the magazine said. "In Kansas, one state official discovered not long ago that ten per cent of the people receiving Aid-to-the-Blind payments were licensed to take the wheel. Children of fourteen can be licensed in many states; in Montana, some thirteen-year-olds are permitted to drive—although one study by New York State showed that drivers under eighteen have an accident rate seventy per cent higher than older ones."

Law enforcement in most states was deplorably lax at all levels—motor vehicle departments, the judiciary, and the police. Half of all fatally injured drivers were found to have been drinking, but drunk drivers rarely suffered heavy penalties. Thirty states did not inspect cars at regular intervals.

Automobile design, too, was a factor. Although relatively few accidents were caused by faulty construction of the cars involved, serious injuries and deaths could be reduced by making the vehicles more "crashworthy." Some experts estimated that casualties could be lessened fifty per cent by better safety engineering in design of the car.

Obviously, many factors contributed to the mass slaughter on the highways. And it was that terrible toll that pushed insurance premiums so high.

The costs of medical care, including physicians' fees and hospital rates, went up nearly twenty-five per cent in the decade beginning in 1957. During the same period, the cost of auto repairs rose more than thirteen per cent. And auto thefts nearly doubled. As the concept of negligence in liability law diminished, jury verdicts increased at the rate of nearly fourteen per cent a year, outstripping the cost of living and the economic growth of the country.

All of these elements pushed up the size of automobile claims. At the end of World War II, the average bodily injury incurred claim cost was $621; in 1963, $1,143. At the same time, property damage claims costs rose, on an average, from $87 to $183. By 1966, claims settlements by all insurance companies were approaching $4,000,000,000 a year.

[297]

Almost everyone agreed that Americans had become highly "claims-conscious." But not all of them.

One INA claims man investigated the death of a youth in the Amish country of Pennsylvania. The boy had been pushing a motorcycle along the shoulder of a road when a motorist insured by the company struck and killed him.

Visiting the family, the claims man asked the father, as delicately as possible, if he could suggest a figure for settlement of the liability for the death of his son.

"I don't want to make a profit on my son's death," the man said. "But would you pay the funeral expense?"

"Of course," said the claims man.

"Is there any damage to the car that hit my boy?" the father asked.

Puzzled, the claims man said, "Yes, there is damage to the bumper, a fender, and the hood."

"Well," said the man, "could you arrange under my claim to pay for his car?"

Afterward the claims man told his associates that "in this day and age, I think it's a pretty touching story."

Because insurance rates are based on experience (the claims and losses of the past) and not on forecasts (the losses of the future), premium levels tend to lag behind losses. But the spread between the rates required to meet the losses and the rates actually charged to policyholders widened more than usual during the 1950's and 1960's. The reason was political: state officials were more and more reluctant to permit rate increases because of the growing public resentment against frequent premium boosts.

On their part the insurance companies, unable to obtain timely rate increases and anxious to eliminate the red ink from their ledgers, became highly selective in their underwriting.

In some areas, where they were losing too much money, many underwriters stopped doing business altogether. One hundred companies were reported to have stopped writing liability insurance in Miami by the first quarter of 1967.

In Louisiana, the Public Affairs Research Council, a private group of legislators, educators, businessmen, labor leaders, and other prominent citizens, reported that many residents of the state were unable to buy protection for their cars because of "a reluctance on the part of companies to sell insurance under present rate structure," a state of affairs that "culminated in a near crisis in the years 1965 and 1966."

For companies like INA that were part of the American Agency System, the problem was complicated still further by the competition of the "direct writers"—companies that sold directly to the public, not through independent agents.

In an effort to cut administrative expenses in order to compete on price with the direct writers, INA in 1959 introduced a plan called the Champion Automobile Policy.

Designed for the more desirable risks (drivers least likely to be involved in costly accidents) the Champion was a package policy providing complete coverage at a premium usually twenty per cent below bureau rates, payable semi-annually.

The major administrative economy was in the billing and collection, which were handled by mail by the company rather than the agent, although the latter retained control of the account. Direct billing enabled the company to employ electronic data processing equipment, thus reducing clerical costs.

Shortly after the Champion policy was offered to the public, the bureau companies and several independents announced somewhat similar programs.

The popularity of the Champion policy led INA later to develop a similar plan, called the Challenger Automobile

Policy, for good risks who could not, for one reason or another, qualify for the Champion. The Challenger, too, featured direct billing of the customer by the company.

Nevertheless, the broader problem of auto insurance was too big to be solved by new policies, no matter how attractive.

Insurance companies continued to lose money on their automobile business and rates continued to rise. Furthermore, the money being lost on auto insurance compelled underwriters to become even more selective in accepting risks.

Some companies shortsightedly exposed the industry to public criticism by lengthening their lists of "undesirable" risks to include far too many groups. The elderly, for example, found many companies refusing to renew their policies even if they had excellent safety records. This discrimination against older men and women was condemned as "grossly unfair" by a Florida state committee of businessmen.

In keeping with its tradition of concern for the public interest, INA continued to insure many people in categories shunned by its competitors, although it examined such risks very carefully. Policyholders who were past retirement age had their insurance renewed, most of them being asked to submit a physician's statement attesting to their fitness to drive.

"The public clamor for something to be done about automobile insurance rates which are alleged to be exorbitant, delay in settlements, cancellations and refusals to renew, insolvencies, public hearings on rates, and inability to obtain insurance in some quarters" was discussed by Bradford Smith, Jr., of INA in a speech which attracted national attention.

As he had for more than twenty years, Smith tried to make his colleagues in the industry face the harsh realities.

"I would like to be able to feel that none of these complaints is justified," he said, "and make a convincing case that they are capricious and without merit. Regretfully, I cannot do so in every case, although some are clearly the result of our failure to communicate adequately with the public."

Nevertheless, Smith was not disposed to suffer in silence the pious proclamations of some public officials and legislators "who are so quick to criticize insurance companies for their unwillingness to insure a very small percentage of licensed drivers." He suggested:

"They should ask themselves whether or not they are serving the public interest by permitting the issuance of driver's licenses to individuals who are judged to be such high-risk drivers that no company feels it can insure them. They should ask themselves why they are not promoting legislation, even if unpopular, which will, in fact, eliminate the unsafe driver and reduce the holocaust on the highways. They should ask themselves if shortcomings in these matters, including the regulation of insurance, are not inviting the federal government to invade these areas heretofore under the purview of the states."

Then, turning to the attitude of the insurance industry, he said:

"Insurance companies have in the past opposed 'compulsory insurance' for valid reasons which appeared to outweigh the public good that would result. Many still do. But times have changed; and I feel that we must re-evaluate the known problems of requiring all licensed drivers to be financially responsible for the damage they may do to others. Insurance is the appropriate medium for attaining this sound objective, and, if it is to remain in the realm of private enterprise, it is up to us to find a way to satisfy the public interest even if it means compulsory insurance."

Next Smith considered the problem of "compensating the traffic victim speedily, equitably, and economically." Noting the gradual drift away from the concept of negligence liability, he pointed out that "the trend of thinking in our modern society is security for all, which calls for compensating the injured regardless of fault."

This, in turn, raised "the possibility of abandoning our present tort system" involving negligence lawsuits "for a new system of compensating the victims of automobile accidents."

This was a reference to several proposals which had been advanced for dealing with traffic victims through a system similar to workmen's compensation with a schedule of payments for injuries. The suggestion had been made that the compensation and tort systems might be combined, with compensation awards covering claims up to a certain level, say $10,000, and lawsuits permitted to recover damages over that amount.

In his speech Smith did not go into any details of the proposals to move away from the tort system. Instead, he said:

"Preliminary studies of [these] proposals . . . reveal some sweeping and startling changes which must be given the most objective consideration. It is for this reason that I am in favor of a study in depth by an appropriate research organization with the capability of sorting the practical from the impractical [and] of making a determination on a purely objective basis. . . ."

About the time that Smith delivered that speech, federal safety standards for automobiles were established for the first time.

A few months later the new United States Department of Transportation made public the first safety standards to be met by states which desired their share of federal highway grants. Among other things the federal code called for annual inspection of motor vehicles, driver-training programs for youths, re-examination of licensed drivers at least every four years, uniform traffic rules, centralized state recording of moving-vehicle violations, blood tests of all persons arrested for drunken driving, programs for providing medical care to traffic victims quickly, and improvement of roads and signs.

For the first time since the ironically named Bliss became the first of millions of traffic victims, there was reason to hope for a decline in the slaughter on the highways.

21: Ninety-Cent Claim for a Piece of Pie

 AT THE BEGINNING of World War II, INA's vice president in charge of claims had to be briefed on any case which was reserved at $4,000 or more.

"Now I get briefed at the $100,000 level," C. Sumner Katz, assistant vice president, said in 1967, "and it's pretty difficult to keep on top of that."

During the seventh quarter-century of the company's history, no area of its activities reflected the changes taking place in the country more than its claim and loss service.

The atom was being put to peaceful uses. In the booming construction business, contractors found that radioactive cobalt could be used to examine welding. At one building site a workman had a piece of cobalt suspended on a long string. When the quitting-time whistle blew, the workman simply went home.

A carpenter happened to notice the string. A compulsive string saver, he wound it up, not realizing that the cube at the end of it was radioactive, and put it in his hip pocket.

When he reached his car, he put the string and the

cube of cobalt into the glove compartment, just as the other men he drove as part of a car pool arrived. Unaware of the hazard, they all drove home that evening and back to work the next day in the car with the cobalt.

In the meantime, an alarm had been sounded about the missing cobalt. When the carpenter drove up to the construction site, an emergency crew was moving slowly over the ground with Geiger counters, which quickly focused attention on the now "hot" car. Sheepishly, the carpenter turned over his rolled-up string to the searchers. None of his passengers suffered any harm, but by the time he arrived at a hospital for a medical examination, the carpenter had severe burns in a part of his anatomy that made sitting an ordeal for weeks afterward.

Fortunately, INA's increasing participation in the insuring of nuclear risks produced few claims. Early in 1954 the company's underwriters, legal counsel, and engineers began working with the shipyard that was building the first nuclear submarine, the *Nautilus*. Late that year the company submitted a proposal for insurance covering public liability, workmen's compensation, and employer's liability exposures arising out of operation of the nuclear reactor then being installed in the sub.

Until then, another company had insured the shipbuilder. The other insurer, "a very fine company, and usually quite venturesome," as INA vice president Robert S. Gillespie observed, couldn't make up its collective mind whether to underwrite this particular risk, "primarily because they didn't know anything about it and weren't permitted to know anything about it."

Finally, just before midnight on New Year's Eve, the other insurer decided not to insure the *Nautilus*, although it meant losing the other insurance business of the great corporation which was building the undersea vessel.

In Philadelphia, there had been a good many troubled meetings about the nuclear submarine. Was it prudent to trust the scientists who had designed the vessel, without knowing the details of their work and their projections?

"We decided that the best brains in America were working over this thing and that we should have a go at it," Gillespie said. "We did, and it worked out very well. We insured a succession of nuclear vessels after that."

INA's coverage of the *Nautilus* took effect at 12:01 A.M. on January 1, 1955, and two hours later the reactor became "critical." There were never any nuclear claims arising out of the coverage, which enabled INA to boast that it was "always among the first to brave the hazards of new and untried fields."

Subsequently the company joined with other underwriters to form an organization to pool nuclear energy risks.

The newest industrial frontier proved remarkably safe, but the same could not be said for some other activities of the postwar world. To go from the cosmic to the microcosmic, from reactors to recreation, consider the pastime that grew to enormous popularity in those years, golf.

The war was not yet over when the company was confronted by the first claims growing out of the pursuit of the little white ball. In one case, a duffer addressed the ball, swung, and silently watched the ball hit a caddy. It turned out to be a hole in one wallet, for the caddy was awarded damages of $2,000 because the golfer had neglected to yell "Fore!"

Another claim involved three criticisms of a golfer's game. He was one of seven men playing together. At the fourteenth hole, the last man to tee off dubbed his shot into the rough about six feet to the left of the tee. Taking a second stroke with his driver, the golfer drove his ball into the clear, but it struck the head of one of the caddies, who was about thirty-five yards along on the fairway. The caddie sued, asserting that the golfer had been negligent in three ways: he should not have been playing in a group of seven; he should not have used a driver in the rough; and he failed to shout "Fore!" The judge tossed out the first two charges, possibly being a duffer himself, but awarded damages of $10,000 because the player did not give adequate warning to the caddy and others on the course.

Some golfers are able to get in trouble when they're just practicing. In Maplecrest, Ohio, a man was trying to improve his wood shots one day in 1961 when he sliced a shot wildly. The ball whistled through the air and smashed through both the storm and the regular windows of a house. They happened to be kitchen windows, and the ball came to rest in the middle of a freshly baked apple pie which the lady of the house had set out to cool. After paying $5.60 for the windows and ninety cents for the pie, INA issued a warning to golfers to "watch those half baked shots."

That total claim, for $6.50, reflected one of the developments of the period, the tendency to file claims for the most trivial losses. One of the basic purposes of insurance is to protect the policyholder against a loss which would be inordinately uncomfortable, expensive, or inconvenient for him to bear unassisted, as well as against catastrophic damage. It has never been assumed that insurance could or should provide coverage against all unexpected costs, no matter how minor.

However, millions of men and women who had never purchased insurance before and who had not grown up in an "insurance-conscious" environment—their parents usually only buying life insurance (only a minority of the automobiles and houses were insured before the war)—now were seeking protection, and nobody tried to educate this huge group to the role that insurance should play in their lives as a cushion against the hard blow, rather than a cocoon against every adverse breeze.

Thus, thousands of claims were submitted which were so petty that the costs of processing them were a good deal more than the initial loss. Both the administrative expense and the sum paid to the policyholder went into the making of rates, and the flood of picayune claims pushed premiums higher and higher.

Unfortunately, not enough policyholders availed themselves of the deductible clauses available to them, which, by eliminating the small claim, enabled the company to reduce their premiums by a sizable percentage.

During its long history, the company had always taken pride in prompt claims settlement without hairsplitting, but in these years there was greatly increased emphasis on this.

In Waskom, Texas, INA technical experts, called in by the company's agency at Marshall, Texas, appraised the Waskom Independent School District and found its properties to be dangerously under-insured, a not uncommon problem. For the brick high school, the survey recommended that fire and extended coverage be lifted from the $45,000 then in force to at least $92,000, representing eighty per cent of the value of the building and its contents.

On the night of January 7, 1958, the school board discussed the survey and voted to insure the high school at seventy-five per cent of the recommended $92,000—in other words, for $69,000.

Not long after midnight, a few hours after the school board meeting, fire raged through the building, leaving it an empty, rubble-strewn shell in the cold light of dawn.

Although INA's only commitment was an oral agreement between the independent agent and the school board, the company paid its share of the loss within a few days. A local newspaper considered it headline news: "Insurance Company Upholds Binder Approved by School Board Without Notification."

The size of the account was not a factor in this claims

policy; for the small, individual policyholder the company's claims philosophy was as effective as for the large, corporate customer. Resident manager Joseph J. Graham of the San Francisco Service Office recalled an incident that occurred in the late 194c's when he was working as Edwin H. Marshall's assistant in New York City. At the time, Marshall was field underwriter in the new Group Department, which also wrote some individual policies, like travel insurance.

"One day an applicant for a $10,000 individual travel accident policy came into our office," Graham said, "and ordered a policy directly from the young lady in our department. She took down the information needed for policy issuance but did not ask for a formal application, nor did she get in touch with the insured man's broker to arrange for premium payment.

"The man was killed in an airplane accident the following day, well before the policy had even reached the typing department. The young lady who took the order saw the insured man's name in the casualty list published in the newspaper. The frightened young lady realized she had made a couple of mistakes (the application and the payment), but she came to me to tell me that she felt the man in the casualty list was the same one who had ordered the insurance. She wanted to know what to do.

"Within minutes we verified, by contacting the broker, that our young lady was correct. Surprisingly, the broker did not know that the man had ordered the policy.

"Under Mr. Marshall's direction, the policy was issued within the hour and delivered to the broker along with a letter of sympathy addressed to the widow. Instructions were also given as to how to proceed with the claim.

"As it had been with the broker, the widow did not know of the policy either, and she sent her lawyer to investigate what we were talking about.

"Needless to say, all concerned were flabbergasted at a

company that did not 'lie in the weeds' waiting for a claim to be presented but, rather, recognized its obligation and sought to pay it promptly."

In insurance, as in law, justice delayed is justice denied, and INA stressed speed in settling claims. For a time it seemed as though the company's claims men across the country were in a race to see who could pay claims fastest.

One summer day in 1961 a man drove up in front of the First National Bank in Saxton, Pennsylvania. Leaving his wife and two children in the car, he ambled into the bank, rifle in hand, announced that it was a holdup, grabbed $19,262, ran out to his car, and drove off.

Precisely two hours later William T. Phillipy, claims representative from INA's Harrisburg office, presented a draft for the full amount that had been stolen to the manager of the bank, which was protected under a Bankers Blanket Policy.

On the surface, this might appear to be an irrational eagerness on the part of the company to hand out money as quickly as possible. In fact, however, the company was protecting its own best interests. For one thing, it had found that claimants were more cooperative in settling claims when fair offers were made promptly. For another, it was aware, as Frank G. Harrington, then newly promoted to vice president in charge of the Business Development Department, pointed out, that a deserved reputation for fair and fast claims settlement attracted more business to the company.

For a time it looked as though Phillipy's time would stand as the speed record, but in May 1962, it fell. At ten o'clock one morning fire broke out in a flat in the sixty-four-unit apartment house at 3201 St. Charles Street in New Orleans. Although the blaze was quickly extinguished, the flames did cause a certain amount of damage.

At 11:30 A.M., just ninety minutes after the fire was discovered, Dean Garrison, claim and loss adjustor for the company's New Orleans Service Office, presented a draft covering all damages to the building's owner. The structure was insured under the Apartment Owners Policy, a package policy.

But INA recognized that "promptness alone is not enough," as John C. Phillips, later senior vice president in charge of the Policyholders Service Division, said when he was claims secretary. Phillips explained: "Our field men know the coverage and the values of property, so there are few disputes or delays because of disagreements. For decades it has been INA's policy to resolve all reasonable doubts in favor of the policyholder and to be liberal in arriving at the value of the damaged or lost property.

"And while we seek to act promptly and to be fair in the process, we do not push the policyholder to settle before he knows the full measure of his loss. Some direct-writing companies have made considerable propaganda out of the speed with which they paid disaster claims. This is reminiscent of the late and unlamented days when personal injury claims were settled at the scene of the accident.

"We prefer to give the policyholder time to gather all the data required to establish his loss and, if he needs money meanwhile, to make an advance against the final payment."

Thus, 169 policyholders received money from INA, many of them under the additional living expense portion of their Homeowners policies, immediately after the four-day fire that raged through the expensive Bel Air-Brentwood area in the hills north of Los Angeles in November 1961, the most costly conflagration in the history of Los Angeles.

Strictly speaking, these were covered, not by "fire" insurance, but by "property" insurance. Even in the 1920's and 1930's, senior vice president Russell H. Petefish once pointed out, fire insurance policies offered extended protection against many other perils, among them windstorm, cyclones, hurricanes, explosions, and earthquakes. The introduction of mul-

tiple-line underwriting on a broad scale with INA's first Homeowners policy completed the process of establishing "property"
insurance. During the 1950's and 1960's, many of the company's largest losses occurred under these broader coverages,
as a result of violent storms.

The Northeastern part of the country, which had always
viewed hurricanes as a phenomenon peculiar to Florida, was
swept by the gigantic cyclonic air masses year after year, with
mounting losses. When three hurricanes roared up the Atlantic
Coast in one year—Carol, Edna, and Hazel, in 1954—INA paid
out $15,879,048 in direct insurance and through reinsurance.

Oddly enough, until 1966 the largest loss sustained by
the company or the industry was not inflicted by a hurricane,
but by an extremely severe windstorm in late November, 1950.
Although this weather oddity is not to be found in most
almanacs and other lists of disasters, that storm has gone down
in history as Catastrophe No. 15 in the records of the National
Insurance Actuarial and Statistical Association. The industry
as a whole paid losses amounting to some $173,900,000, of
which INA's net share amounted to about $9,009,576.

From 1954 to 1962 the company's claims men "fielded
ninety-one catastrophes," according to John Phillips, who
added, "This enormous depth in experience is not shared by
any other insurer."

Catastrophes were handled "by the book"—the book,
in this case, being a manual detailing every step to be taken
by the company's claims men, covering advertising, work with
agents and brokers, claims procedures and advance payments,
personnel, the setting up of a temporary office if needed,
records, price lists, even samples of letters to be sent and
notices to be inserted in newspapers.

"Because we know what must be done to aid our policyholders," Phillips said, "we customarily pay storm and other
losses much ahead of our competitors. While Hurricane Donna

was still blowing up the New Jersey coast in September 1960, INA was settling claims Donna had produced earlier in Florida and other parts of the South."

On the Gulf Coast, the first of INA's "storm troopers," as claims men assigned to catastrophe duty were called, started processing claims from Hurricane Carla in September 1961, while the storm was still wreaking havoc. Twenty-seven men from as far away as Portland, Oregon, moved into the stricken area to handle claims against the company, working sixteen hours a day and more, in rain, ankle-deep mud, and clouds of mosquitoes and bees, trying to avoid the ubiquitous rattle-snakes that had been forced up out of the bayous by the high waters.

"Bless you," said a weary homeowner in Galveston to INA claim and loss man Bob Smith, of Rochester, New York. "I don't know where half this town would be today without you people."

At the home office, or world headquarters, as it was now called, in Philadelphia, the course of every hurricane was plotted hourly from its first report as a tropical disturbance to its dissipation as a dying storm, often far inland over the continental United States or at sea in the Atlantic in the upper latitudes, and the company usually had a few hours' or even a couple of days' warning, so that it could prepare to dispatch its "storm troopers."

Tornadoes were another matter. Despite improved forecasting by the United States Weather Bureau, the dread twisters often struck without notice, blasting buildings apart with their explosive drop in atmospheric pressure and turning the most commonplace objects into lethal weapons with their wind velocity, estimated to accelerate close to the speed of sound itself.

In June 1966, Frank G. Harrington flew into Topeka, Kansas, three days after the city was devastated by a tornado labelled "Catastrophe Number 12." He later described what the tornado had done.

"With the thundering, grinding noise of a hundred freight trains it bulldozed a swath two to four blocks wide for twelve miles, plowing diagonally through the heart of the city from the Southwest to the northeastern suburbs.

"It demolished homes, apartment houses, shopping centers, and commercial buildings. Automobiles, buses, airplanes, and freight cars were tossed and tumbled into total wreckage. . . . Trees and poles were uprooted and shredded. Topeka looked like a bombed-out European city in World War II."

Thanks to the government's tornado-tracking radar system, which alerted the city fifteen minutes before the funnel screamed through it, only seventeen persons, including one child, were killed. But the property damage was incredible. Harrington noticed that on a ten-story life insurance building which had been left a broken, contorted shell there still was legible an ironic sign: "A Refuge in Time of Storm."

While the National Guard was still being mobilized for rescue and guard work, INA's "storm troopers" were swinging into action under the leadership of Edgar R. Phinney and Eugene Thaney, with direct supervision of the catastrophe crew assigned to Wally Redmond. Men flew to the scene from cities as far away as Buffalo and San Diego.

Almost immediately claims began to be paid. The first fifty-eight claims averaged more than $10,000 each. Within six weeks ninety per cent of the company's claims, about 300 in all, had been settled, with more than $1,500,000 paid out.

"A disaster of this kind," Harrington wrote, "brought about by the worst in nature, seems to bring out the best in men and women. Insurance men can be proud of the part they and their fellow workers played in alleviating the suffering of the hurt and homeless. . . .

[314]

Ninety-Cent Claim for a Piece of Pie

"We are truly engaged in meaningful work. When you see a family of fine pioneer stock keeping a stiff upper lip through this personal tragedy, and then you see a man and wife break down and weep when the INA claims man presents the loss draft, you know how deeply insurance touches the lives of America's families . . . and you can feel special pride in the way INA responds."

22: *Traffic Jams Afloat*

 JANUARY 8, 1952. For ten days the attention of the whole world has been focused on an area in the North Atlantic, southwest of Ireland, where a crippled ship is wallowing helplessly in mountainous seas. Stricken during an unseasonal hurricane, the *Flying Enterprise* sent out an SOS December 28, and a few hours later the passengers and crew were taken off by rescue vessels—all the crew, that is, except the taciturn skipper, Captain Henrik Kurt Carlsen, who insists on remaining aboard his dangerously listing freighter, whose main deck is awash.

A tug gets a line aboard the ship 250 miles from Ireland. Gradually it draws the helpless vessel toward England. After eight days alone on the lurching ship, Carlsen gets company; headlines cry: "Tug's Mate Joins Carlsen on Enterprise." The *Flying Enterprise* is 190 miles off Falmouth, England.

Two days later France announces Carlsen will be honored with a medal for valor. The land of his ancestors, Denmark, says it will offer similar tribute. Then bad news: the towline parts in heavy seas. Falmouth is only fifty heart-breaking miles away.

For another forty-eight hours Carlsen and the mate

from the tug, Kenneth R. Dancy, cling to the battered hulk as green-black waves tower above it before crashing down in foaming savagery. The degree of list rises—sixty-five degrees, seventy, seventy-five. . . .

Every newspaper reader, even the driest landlubber, knows the inevitable is near. A dispatch from London reports Lloyd's clerks are waiting for the news that will tell them to enter the *Flying Enterprise* in the "Lost Book" as the Lutine Bell is rung once.

*   *   *

In Philadelphia, Frank G. Harrington, INA's new advertising manager and director of public relations, deeply moved by the continuing story of the heroic captain's lonely battle against the sea, wandered into the office of G. Brinton Lucas, who had become marine vice president on the retirement of T. Leaming Smith.

"I guess those fellows at Lloyd's must be pretty upset about this Flying Enterprise thing," Harrington said.

"Why should they be upset?" Lucas said. "We have the largest share of the syndicate's policy on the hull, and we independently insured a substantial part of the cargo, which includes rare art objects."

*   *   *

January 11. The *Flying Enterprise* slips further over on to its side, listing eighty-five degrees. All hope is gone. Carlsen and Dancy leap from the funnel into the icy waters below, are picked up quickly by the rescue tug. Forty minutes later the derelict vessel up-ends, slides with a roar down to the bottom. The tug heads for Britain and the first of many hero's welcomes for Carlsen.

*   *   *

Newspapers throughout the country reported the first claims payment on the cargo of the Flying Enterprise as INA's A. Henry Smith presented a check for $121,000 to insurance broker Manfred H. Mayer. *The broker, who preferred not to make public the name of his client, said "they had expected to wait much longer for the claim to be made good," according to* The New York Times.

* * *

Obviously, all of the drama inherent in marine insurance did not center on the *quondam* coffee houses of London. Most of the losses were not as spine-tingling as the death of the *Flying Enterprise*, but year in and year out ships sank for one reason or another. The number of vessels lost at sea in peacetime is one of those astonishing facts known only to the handful of men directly concerned with such matters. For example, in 1953 a total of 181 ships, twenty-eight of them of American registry, went to the bottom—and that aggregate represented the lowest tonnage (219,429) since 1928, and the second lowest number of ships for any one year in that period!

However, the most serious problems confronting the marine branch in the two decades after the end of the war had little to do with the number of ships sinking.

As always, the first stumbling block was rates. In marine insurance, there are no regulatory agencies, for the underwriters of every country must compete on a worldwide scale. For several years marine insurance was very profitable. Its very success brought on its later troubles, for many companies which had not hitherto written hull or cargo covers now plunged into the field, where some of the most sophisticated brokers in the world are to be found. The brokers were quick to seize on the inexperience of the newcomers to drive rates down to an unprofitable level. Not until the mid-1960's did the marine line show signs of improvement, as most of the newcomers withdrew from the field, sadder but wiser, and rates stiffened.

In the meantime our merchant marine, floundering for lack of a coherent and consistent national policy, was allowed to deteriorate. At the end of World War II, the United States had the greatest merchant marine in the world; twenty-two years later, only 944 ships flying the American flag were in the active merchant fleet, with another 474 vessels under the "effective control" of the United States flying "flags of necessity" —mostly Liberia, Panama, and Honduras—to cut costs by evading American union requirements and some governmental controls.

Moreover, the ships of the American merchant marine were the oldest, on an average, of any nation's in the world except for Argentina and Spain. For example, almost sixty-five per cent of the tankers were more than ten years old, although the United States accounts for more than thirty-five per cent of the world's oil consumption. A seventeen-year-old vessel is regarded as over-aged, but by 1972, it was said, 560 of the nation's ships would have had at least fifty-five years of service.

Despite pleas from many quarters, there seemed little likelihood of a change in government policy to encourage renewal, expansion, and development of the merchant fleet. The root of the difficulty, of course, lay in the inability of the American people to understand that their country is a maritime power.

This was reflected in marine insurance. In former times, eighty per cent of American exports were insured by companies here. By 1967 the ratio had dropped to one-third.

With gold flowing out of the United States, the pressure on the dollar was heightened by the payment of marine insurance premiums abroad. Estimates of the money that could be retained in the United States if most marine insurance covering our own foreign trade were written by American companies ran as high as $500,000,000.

This would be to the advantage of American commerce and industry for another reason, it was pointed out by Francis A. Lewis, vice president in charge of INA's Transportation Department, established in 1966 to bring together under one grouping the marine, inland marine, and aviation lines. Lewis said that many American exporters permitted their foreign customers to arrange the insurance for shipments, placing the business with insurance companies in other countries. Often this meant that the shipments were utterly without insurance protection during at least part of their journey abroad. And many sellers here did not realize that foreign insurance contracts frequently did not include all the coverages customary in an American policy.

There were other changes in the marine line. Where almost three-fourths of all INA marine business had formerly been written in New York, the percentage dropped to little more than half by 1967, the rest being handled through the company's service offices throughout the country.

During that period INA also helped to organize a cargo reinsurance pool and waged a successful campaign to win back from the London insurers most of the American export cotton business which had been written there. Most important of all, the company, treading where most other American underwriters feared to venture, began insuring off-shore oil-drilling operations. By the mid-1960's, the company had "become the absolutely recognized American authority in this area of enterprise," Lewis observed with pride.

When Lewis became chief of all transportation insurance, he was succeeded as head of the marine branch by John Armstrong, Jr., an exuberant former sea captain, who was confronted with a difficult development, the rise in popularity of boating.

By 1965 more than 50,000,000 Americans were participating in some form of boating, an increase of nearly 10,000,000 in just five years. Three billion dollars a year was being spent on some 8,000,000 boats, and the traffic jams in lakes and harbors across the country began to resemble rush-hour bottlenecks on a city highway.

Traffic Jams Afloat

There was little policing of the waterways and a great need for strict enforcement of the maritime rules of the road. Most of the new boating enthusiasts not only did not know the rules, but also lacked training in the handling of boats. Many appeared to believe that a vessel was like a car, to be parked at the curb, started up without preparation, and driven off.

"A lot of the people who go down to the sea in ships are nuts," grumbled *The Wall Street Journal.*

The results, predictably, were often tragic. In 1966 there were 1,318 boating fatalities. Accidents on the waterways came to 4,350, a sixteen per cent increase over the previous year; incapacitating personal injuries, 1,555, up sixty-seven per cent; and property damage, $7,000,000, up fifty-five per cent.

The growth of boating had already exceeded official government forecasts, which predicted a two hundred and fifteen per cent increase by the end of the century. Water-skiing was increasing in popularity at an even faster pace, and many of the worst accidents involved water-skiers.

One of the most touching of the hundreds of boating claims handled by INA involved several boys who ventured out in an inboard motorboat. The son of a man insured by the company was at the wheel of the speedboat, although it belonged to the father of another boy. Somehow, the boat flipped over at high speed. One boy suffered a broken neck and died instantly. Ultimately, the insurer of the boat and INA put up the money for a joint settlement of $15,000 to the dead boy's family.

"Then the father of the dead boy decided he wanted to devote more time to helping other boys," one of INA's claims managers said. "He began to work with boys of approximately the same age as his son, and he's been engaged in those efforts several years now. Recently he was instrumental in getting an appointment to Annapolis for the son of our resident manager."

For its part, INA did everything it could to encourage safe boating, including stimulating attendance at boat-handling classes sponsored by the Power Squadrons and other groups.

To cut down on property damage in storms, the company inaugurated what the *United States Review* called an "extraordinary service."

This was the "Security Watch," a program under which INA made agreements with the operators of hundreds of boat-yards and marinas. They promised to take whatever steps might be necessary at the first sign or warning of a storm to provide special protection to boats insured by INA, as indicated by the company's decal on a cabin window. This extra help might range from securing additional lines to the boat to actually taking it out of the water. INA agreed to pay the cost of this service whenever it was needed. The "Security Watch" was welcomed enthusiastically by East Coast boat owners.

Storms cause damage to more than boatmen, of course. Hurricanes and other severe storms often wreak havoc on thousands of buildings in their path. When the destruction was caused by high wind, it was covered in most insurance policies. But none of the customary insurance policies protected property owners against financial loss resulting from floods in river valleys or "wave wash" along the coasts. ("Wave wash" encompasses all destructive flowing water—high waves, tidal waves, high tides, and tidal surge.)

A great many policyholders were not aware that this protection was not included in their regular coverage. Thousands of people made this discovery belatedly in the middle of September 1944, after a hurricane swept the Atlantic seaboard from Cape Hatteras to the eastern tip of Long Island.

The worst damage was inflicted on New Jersey, whose shore communities were cut off from the rest of the world. The fishing pier at Asbury Park was washed away, the Steel Pier at Atlantic City damaged, and the boardwalks in both those cities were battered. Ocean City was under several feet of water, and the damage there was estimated at $1,500,000. The hurricane left twenty-seven dead in five states and caused property damage estimated at $50,000,000.

One of those beach-front home owners who found that his insurance would not make good his loss was Governor Walter E. Edge of New Jersey. In an angry mood, he hinted that he would compel insurance companies doing business in his state to write Wave Wash and Flood insurance unless the industry provided this coverage voluntarily. When the rest of the industry dragged its heels and finally decided to do nothing, despite the obvious public relations danger inherent in the failure to meet this public need, INA (as we have seen in Chapter 11) went ahead on its own and offered this coverage.

Unfortunately, INA's effort ended in failure. The large numbers and spread of risk needed in any insurance program were not there. INA could not get the broad distribution required to make the plan succeed. INA proved that the only people who tended to buy this protection were persons whose homes were so close to the water that damage to their property was virtually inevitable. And nobody, including INA, could expect to sell the policy if the frequent storms produced so many big losses that the premium, adjusted to the true loss experience, soared to an unrealistically high level.

From time to time, as successive storms created new disaster areas, various proposals for making Wave Wash and Flood protection available to the public were outlined in Congress.

It was not until 1967, however, that everyone concerned with this matter—bureau stock companies, mutuals, independent stock companies, agents, home-builders, and many others —agreed on a legislative measure, which had been one result of a study conducted for the United States Department of Housing and Urban Development. To underline the need, just about the time the printed study was distributed to members of Congress in 1965, Hurricane Betsy, the most costly disaster in the nation's recorded history, ripped into the Gulf Coast.

After Senate hearings, at which INA was recorded, along with the rest of the industry, in support of the Wave Wash and Flood insurance bill, chances were favorable that the measure might be enacted into law, if not in 1967, then within a few years. The bill envisioned federal subsidies to keep premiums within reason and the establishment of a federal reinsurance fund to cope with catastrophic storms.

In Philadelphia, an INA man said: "We failed twenty-three years ago, but at least we *tried* to give the public what it wanted and needed. And our willingness to experiment with this type of coverage gave us the experience to be able to judge the provisions of the Senate bill."

23: The Birds, the Bees—and the Onions

 BY THE 1960's it could truly be said that INA was offering insurance protection from the womb to the tomb: among manufacturers covered against product liability claims were corporations engaged in making contraceptives in response to the worldwide reaction against the population explosion, while the rising tide of malpractice cases—once limited to doctors but now extended to many other fields of endeavor—produced claims against some funeral directors.

Architects, engineers, accountants, even insurance agents, found themselves in need of malpractice protection as a result of broadened judicial interpretations of responsibility.

"So, ironically, [did] lawyers, who probably have done more than any group to make Americans claim-conscious," commented *The Wall Street Journal.*

One enterprising salvor insured by INA figured out a way to make a profit out of two freight carloads of loose sugar which had been spilled in a railroad derailment. Scooping up the sugar, his firm proceeded to bag it and sell it through the

Midwest and parts of the South as a feed for bees, which must be fed in winter lest they die.

"Unfortunately," said James Wantland, INA's claims manager in Chicago, "there were some cars in the train that had chemicals in them, and just enough chemical had been scooped up with the sugar to contaminate it. As a result, I think the stuff killed every bee in Nebraska, Kansas, Oklahoma, and all the way down into Florida, and it cost INA between $100,000 and $150,000."

In the course of his work, the claims adjuster assigned to the case donned a bee-keeper's hood and gown and became quite proficient at handling the insects. Bees became so intriguing to him that he acquired a couple of hives of his own.

Bees figured in another case when they refused to carry out their part in the floral system of reproduction. Onion seeds were sprayed with pesticide before planting. Later, as the onion plants grew, bees were released near them for pollination, but to no avail. Because of the pesticide residue in the plants, the bees refused to go near them.

The legal doctrine that a manufacturer is *absolutely* liable for untoward effects of his products, and not merely when he has been negligent in making them, became widespread after World War II and caused many corporations to re-examine their insurance policies. This development, like the sudden expansion of malpractice litigation, was to a considerable degree the result of the work of attorneys banded together in an organization called the American Trial Lawyers Association.

These lawyers customarily entered into a contingent fee arrangement with the claimant, under which the legal fees and the expenses would be paid out of the damages award if he won.

"This is a universal practice," John C. Phillips of INA,

an attorney himself, said, "and [it] has the virtue of making the courts and good counsel available to claimants who could not otherwise afford them.

"But in abuse, the contingent fee is vicious. Rarely is the contingency fee less than one-third after expenses, and in some instances it runs beyond fifty per cent. INA has files indicating that the claimant received *less* than his lawyer in cases which were settled out of court. This can happen where the contingent fee is a high percentage, the expenses are substantial, and the settlement agreed upon is low."

Abuse of the contingent fee device caused the New York City courts and the federal Court of Claims to regulate the fees, but elsewhere fees were regulated, as Phillips put it, only by "the appetite of claimants' lawyers."

The very mention of ATLA and the lawyers who specialize in claims was enough to cause apoplexy in most insurance men. It could be argued that these lawyers helped to make manufacturers and professional men more conscious of their responsibility to market safe products and to take the utmost care in fulfilling their obligations to their clients. It was when claimants' lawyers went beyond reasonable claims, when they attempted to obtain unjustifiably large judgments or awards based on outlandish and exaggerated claims, that they deserved censure. Unfortunately, this too often was the case.

Product liability cases could occur in almost any field, INA found. A cosmetics maker got into difficulties with a liquid designed to harden nails; it was withdrawn from the market after a number of women complained that their fingernails fell off. An anti-freeze was found to function in reverse— regardless of the temperature, it caused the automobile motor to freeze after the liquid had circulated a short time. A weed killer marketed by another company did the job that was claimed for it, but it killed the cattle that ate the weeds too.

Perils: Named and Unnamed

Tragically, a salt substitute for elderly people contained a chemical which, it was discovered belatedly, caused aplastic anemia by acting on the marrow in bones.

To prevent such misfortunes whenever possible INA established its own laboratory in the early 1950's. Using an impressive array of instruments, chemicals, and devices, the lab technicians subjected all manner of products to tests to determine whether they could be used safely.

But the testing did not stop at the lab's doors on the eighth floor of the INA world headquarters building. Often the technicians went out to the site of possible hazards. In hospital operating rooms, tests were conducted to determine whether the flooring adequately dissipated static electricity which could cause combustible anesthetics to explode. Sewers and sump wells were checked for possible concentrations of deadly gases. The air in cement factories was examined as a possible cause of silicosis.

There were other industrial liability claims that could not be foreseen. Some of them reflected the increasing concern with pollution of the air and the waters.

When an airliner coming in for a landing at New Orleans missed the runway and cracked up—a total loss, although, fortunately, there were few injuries—the airline sued a nearby factory, asserting that smoke from the plant drifted over the airport, obscuring the runway at the critical moment of landing. When the $1,250,000 suit came to trial, however, the airline lost. The jury held that the cause of the crash was pilot error.

In another city, it was alleged that fumes from a distillery drifted over a bridge and remained in the air there, building up such a concentration that one driver (a teetotaler, no doubt) found his senses affected, as a result of which his car collided with two other vehicles.

Water pollution presented more serious problems.

The Birds, the Bees—and the Onions

Senior vice president James Crawford recalled a costly mishap in Perry Sound, in Ontario:

"An oil company insured by us brought a tanker in there and was discharging crude oil into an installation on the shore. The bottom of the installation gave way and before they knew it they had put 200,000 gallons or more of crude oil into Perry Sound.

"It cost us $1,000,000. We spent our million on what was probably the biggest laundry job that had ever been performed until then. We were restoring beaches, cleaning shoreside installations, washing boats. The damage was so severe that the oil company spent another $2,000,000 or $3,000,000 of its own money after the limit of our obligation was reached."

When the supertanker *Torrey Canyon*, more than three times the length of a football field, broke up on rocks off the Cornish coast of Britain in 1967, spilling more than 90,000 tons of crude oil into the sea, INA men knew just how difficult a task confronted the British authorities as they attempted to remove the oil from their beaches. (The company's loss in the *Torrey Canyon* disaster was approximately $600,000 because of its share in the American Hull Insurance Syndicate, which insured fifty per cent of the hull.)

One day Los Angeles claims manager John Hinds was asked by William Little, of INA's Houston office, how much a cow's moo was worth. Little had been presented with a claim by a farmer who complained that two of his cows had "lost their moo" by drinking water from a stream into which an INA-insured factory had discharged some chemicals.

Settling the claim for $200, Little wrote a release in longhand, and it was signed by the farmer. The release read: "This is in full and final release for two cows (even though they may die) who have lost their moo."

In the New York area, a couple moved into a new house. Smelling gas, the wife called the local utility company to report a possible gas leak. The gas company sent men on three separate occasions, but none of them could detect any gas. After her fourth telephone call, according to New York claims manager Clifford Whiteford, one of the utility's executives offered to stop by on his way home from the office.

After checking throughout the house, the man walked out into the breezeway between the house and the garage, stopped, sniffed again, and said, "Everything's perfectly all right. There's no gas here."

And he pulled a cigar from his pocket and unwrapped it.

"Please don't light that cigar," the woman pleaded. "I smell gas right now."

Smiling indulgently, the man said, "Now, don't you worry," and struck a match.

The resulting explosion caused a total loss of the house, although neither the gas company executive nor the woman was seriously injured.

INA was, as assistant vice president Joseph E. Johnson pointed out, "the leading American market for gas risks." At a meeting of the insurance committee of the American Gas Association, Johnson found that "at least seventy per cent of the membership" was covered for third-party liability by his company.

Malpractice suits were as widespread as product liability cases. In 1965 the law department of the American Medical Association studied the problem and reported that one out of every six physicians in the United States had been forced to defend himself against at least one malpractice complaint during his lifetime. Litigation had reached the point where some doctors were even suing each other. At the same time, judgments reached hitherto unheard-of heights.

"Most policies aren't geared to meet the hazards of outsize awards," an article in *Medical Economics* said in 1962.

"But now [physicians] can get that added protection through personal-catastrophe liability insurance, commonly called an 'umbrella' policy."

The magazine listed INA among five companies offering such coverage.

Although many medical malpractice claims involved allegations of mistakes by doctors—like the surgeon who was found to have sewn shut the duodenal tract during an abdominal operation—a surprising number had to do with errors said to have been committed by other hospital personnel. Hospitals were particularly vulnerable to these complaints because they were responsible for so many employees—nurses, technicians, laboratory assistants, ambulance drivers, orderlies—any of whom might make an unfortunate error.

One Florida hospital insured by INA got into trouble because of two women patients. One was scheduled for surgery on an ingrown toenail; the other, for removal of a lump from a breast. Somehow, the patients were switched on their way to the operating rooms. The woman with the ingrown toenail had a lump excised from a breast (she did have a lump) before it was learned that she was the wrong woman, a discovery made when the other woman's toes were found to be without need of surgery.

In another hospital, during an operation, the anesthetist saw that the patient was failing, so he increased the flow of oxygen. But his efforts caused the patient's death, for, without his knowledge, the anesthesia supply lines had been incorrectly connected by a hospital maintenance man. When the anesthetist thought he was applying more oxygen, he was actually cutting the supply of that vital gas while increasing the flow of nitrous oxide.

The spread of malpractice suits to other professions hit an accountant insured by INA. A supermarket chain argued that in auditing the books of each store, the accountant ought to have detected a dishonest manager who later was found to have been kiting checks.

Probably no group has been more astonished by malpractice suits than the architects. After all, one of the legends, possibly apocryphal, about the great Frank Lloyd Wright had to do with his offhand reply to a client who complained that the roof of his expensive new office leaked during rainstorms.

"Put a bucket under the leak," Wright was said to have suggested.

The new attitude toward professional responsibilities was expressed by a federal judge presiding over a successful lawsuit against an insurance agent on the West Coast.

"This is an age of specialists," said the judge, "and as more occupations divide into various specialties and strive toward 'professional' status, the law requires an ever higher standard of care in the performance of their duties."

24: Departures and Arrivals

 LUDWIG C. LEWIS had always insisted that when he reached the age of sixty-five he would retire. In December 1955 he submitted his request for retirement after forty-six eventful years with the company.

Starting in the marine branch, Lewis had devoted most of his apparently limitless energies to the inland marine business during and after World War I. It was his proud assertion that INA had been the first company writing inland marine business to take advantage of the enormous potential in truck transportation. He had also been the first to write insurance on bridges.

According to a company statement in 1950, Lewis was "responsible for the establishment of the . . . service offices which now give home office service to agents in all parts of the United States and Canada."

When it was decided to decentralize as much of the company's record-keeping as possible by establishing regional processing offices, Lewis played a major part in that development, too, even to site selection. Driving across the country in a station wagon, he personally chose most of the locations.

[333]

An exception was the first processing office, established in 1949 in San Jose, California, on the recommendation of resident vice president Francis F. Owen, to serve the entire Pacific Coast region. The San Jose center was housed in what Lewis described as "a beautiful plant"; designed by Wurster, Bernardi, and Emmons, the strikingly modern building won an Award of Merit from the American Institute of Architects in 1957 and was a financial as well as an aesthetic success—the top floor was rented to another company, the income representing a thirteen per cent return on INA's investment in the property.

The Macon Processing Office was erected on a hill just above the center of the city. After INA acquired the site, a local banker told Lewis that Confederate leaders had stood there as their troops passed in review for the last time at the end of the War Between the States, and that a local group was insisting on raising a monument to the historic event.

"If you put up a Confederate monument," the peppery Lewis shot back, "we'll put up a statue of Lincoln. We're not involved in the Civil War, and we're not going to get involved in it."

Other disagreements revolved about the building. The first architect consulted on the design withdrew in protest because Lewis insisted that the structure had to feature a colonnade of fifteen pillars, one for each of the states in the Union at the time INA was founded. Another architect gave Lewis his pillars on a Colonial building with a clock tower that was a copy of Independence Hall's superstructure in Philadelphia. Some irreverent wags in the company dubbed it "Tara Hall," after Scarlett O'Hara's plantation home in *Gone with the Wind*.

Lewis retired as an officer in March 1956, although he remained a director for another three years. At a party tendered him on his retirement, Lewis predicted that the company, whose premium volume was then $270,000,000 a year, would be doing a business of $400,000,000 before another ten years rolled around. In 1961 Bradford Smith, Jr., by then president, sent Lewis a ceremonial bowl as a tribute to his forecasting, with a note that read, "This month we passed the $400,000,000 [mark]."

Nine months after Lewis' retirement, Smith was elected executive vice president.

It seemed evident that the next president would be either Smith or Herbert P. Stellwagen, who had been closely associated with John A. Diemand since the latter first joined INA. After Diemand's rise to the presidency, Stellwagen had become executive vice president of the Indemnity company, INA's casualty affiliate.

However, Stellwagen, at sixty, was five years older than Smith, and he had not been in the best of health. Although Diemand had earlier looked to his casualty aide to succeed him, the president began to change his mind after Stellwagen underwent several operations.

"I love Herbert Stellwagen," Diemand said later, "but I felt I had a job to do for this company.

"Now, Brad Smith had always impressed me as having his feet on the ground. He had some very definite opinions as to how problems in the fire business should be handled, and wasn't afraid to stand up and advocate them."

It was not easy for Diemand to acknowledge Smith's strong points, for the older man was thoroughly imbued, although he may not have been aware of it, with the typical casualty man's prejudice against his fire colleagues.

But Smith, an early supporter of the multiple-line campaign, had proved himself in the long fight for independence. He had shown himself to be a man who could think for himself, remain open to new ideas, act decisively, and fight like a bull terrier for what he thought was right. For years Smith had been troubled by the divisions among insurance men. Now he had an opportunity to do something about them.

Starting with regular Monday morning breakfast meetings with his property executives, Smith soon extended invitations to the key men in the casualty branch.

"My purpose was to get each group to understand the other's problems," Smith said. "At first the meetings were very difficult. The men were very reluctant to speak out. I had to drag out their ideas by going around the table, asking each man questions. It was somewhat disheartening at first, but I kept at it because I believed strongly that INA couldn't realize its potential for leadership as long as the separation between the various branches existed.

"After a while, the meetings achieved their purpose. We did establish a mutual understanding."

The property men had been writing a little casualty business, including auto insurance, and the Indemnity group wanted to begin writing Homeowners policies, because that type of coverage had been cutting into the casualty area. Smith got together with Stellwagen, and they came to an agreement: the Indemnity men would keep their hands off the Homeowners, and the automobile and other liability insurance written by the property men would be turned over to the casualty group. It was a simple, obvious solution, but matters had rarely been handled on such a cooperative basis before.

Like the rest of the economy, the company had been growing fantastically through the 1950's. At the beginning of 1942, its 150th anniversary, the company's assets totaled less than $151,000,000. By the end of 1959 INA had moved into the exclusive ranks of American corporations with assets of more than $1,000,000,000. Only ninety-six other corporations in this country were bigger.

But INA's corporate structure, still geared for the old, prewar level of business, was not organized to handle the growth that had been thrust upon it. The Education Department was providing a steady supply of first-rate men and women, and the service office network, along with the processing officers, improved the handling of business. But throughout the mushrooming company there were hundreds of examples of duplication, overlapping, cannibalistic competition, intramural rivalries, diffusion of authority, obscuration of responsibility. It wasn't quite administrative chaos, but it certainly wasn't efficient.

In his weekend retreat at Reed Creek on the Eastern Shore of Maryland, Smith studied the most authoritative texts on scientific management theories and methods whenever he could get away from Philadelphia. After sailing on Chesapeake Bay, he would put in at the creek and tie up, then stroll up to the cottage with his wife. While Henrietta prepared one of her unusual, appetizing dishes, Smith would open oysters he had gathered locally. Afterwards, he would pore over thought-provoking books on management.

He had already decided that good management didn't just happen; it had to be planned, designed, constructed. Smith recognized, as every great corporate leader of modern times has come to realize, that management is both an art and a science, a combination of business, academic, and even political disciplines.

Gradually his ideas began to take shape. He could discern the reorganizaton through which INA must pass if it was to realize its full potential. But it would take time.

Before anything else, INA had to be unified structurally. At the end of the war, the "fleet" had consisted of five subsidiaries: the Alliance Insurance Company of Philadelphia, the Central Insurance Company of Baltimore, the National Security Insurance Company, the Philadelphia Fire and Marine Insurance Company, and the Indemnity Insurance Company of North America.

Two of the "pups," the Central and the National Security, had been liquidated at the end of 1945, and the Alliance in 1950. All three companies had become INA properties by purchase years before, and a few of the employees, not indoctrinated in the INA way of doing business, had proved troublesome. Inevitably, INA found it had what Russell H. Petefish called "a clean-up job" to do.

For example, Petefish found in Omaha in 1941 that the local representative of one "pup" had obtained new accounts by paying excessive commissions and rebates.

"These were God-awful situations," Petefish said. "They just weren't decent. They weren't ethical. In fact, they were downright illegal!"

In some areas it was even discovered that unscrupulous representatives of subsidiaries which had not yet been "cleaned up" were even luring customers away from the parent company, INA, by offering improper inducements.

Long before the liquidation of the first three "pups," those problems had been taken care of. And the remaining subsidiaries, Philadelphia Fire and Marine, and the Indemnity, had never caused any difficulties.

The year after Smith was elected executive vice president, the company set to work to develop a new symbol, or "service mark," as it was technically called (as opposed to a "trade mark," which is applied to products rather than companies and their services). Originally, the company had been identified by a six-pointed star, and later, for more than a century and a half, by an eagle. But so many companies displayed eagle symbols that the national bird was useless for business purposes.

Officially the "fleet" was called "the Insurance Company of North America Companies," not the snappiest of names. Unofficially, the parent had always been called "the North America," which could be misunderstood to mean a continent or any number of other things, depending on the context. And if one attempted to string the initials of the "fleet" name together, the result was "ICNAC," which sounded like a character in a science-fiction novel, a collection of small objects on an elderly spinster's shelf, a new data processing machine, or a Navy command post.

Finally, the new symbol emerged from the company's function: "Insurance by North America," a phrase that could be cut down to its initials, INA.

It was a modern symbol, reflecting the still subterranean drive for streamlining the company's operations and outlook.

In 1958, a year after the new symbol made its first appearance, the Philadelphia Fire and Marine was absorbed into the parent company.

But the Indemnity was still a separate entity, a living contradiction of the multiple-line concept which had been at the heart of INA's long struggle against the power structure of the industry.

Before his retirement Lewis had urged the merger of the Indemnity into INA.

"They had to become one," he insisted.

Years later he protested that Diemand "did not appear to be willing to take a positive position" on the issue.

One reason for Diemand's reluctance, while Lewis was still an officer, was probably his unwillingness to create a situation in which Lewis and Stellwagen would have equal and overlapping authority in the same organization, a circumstance likely to lead to friction. But that fear was no longer a factor after Lewis' retirement.

When Smith pressed Diemand to attempt the consolidation in 1960, the older man said it couldn't be done. Knowing that relations between the property and casualty executives had improved greatly as a result of the Monday morning breakfasts, Smith told him that he was certain that Stellwagen would agree to the merger.

He was right. Stellwagen did go along with the proposal, but he felt that another factor made resistance useless. That was the Indemnity's prosperity.

"I often thought it was ironic," Stellwagen recalled, "that one of the factors leading to the merger was our threat to increase the dividends. We had been paying, I think, a $4,500,000 dividend to the parent company and I recommended we go to $6,000,000. Well, that was taxable to the parent company. They looked at that tax and said nothing doing.

"So the Indemnity is one of the few companies that was liquidated because it promised to do better for its stockholders [*i.e.*, INA]. There were other reasons, of course, but that was one powerful reason."

On May 23, 1960, announcing the consolidation, Diemand said: "The joining of the two companies is the culmination of an effort begun several years ago to coordinate the companies' operations in the best interests of INA agents and policyholders."

He pointed out that the uniting of the companies would bring about "substantial savings in taxes and operating costs, providing a most effective medium of satisfying policyholders' and producers' needs, and providing expanded opportunity to all INA employees."

"We have been one in fact," Diemand concluded. "We shall soon be one in name."

When the Indemnity ceased to exist at the end of 1960, Stellwagen became executive vice president of INA. Three years later he retired as an officer, although he remained a director for several years beyond that. At the time of his retirement, after thirty-four years with INA, a company publication said:

"Although his quiet dignity is sometimes mistaken for austerity, he is, in fact, a man whose wisdom, wit, and warmth have won him thousands of friends among agents, brokers, and company personnel across America."

That sort of comment is not unusual when a top executive of any organization retires, and in many cases it smacks more of fiction than of fact. But not in Stellwagen's case. The feeling of most of his associates toward him was one of genuine affection.

This was, in part, because of his down-to-earth attitude.

"Some people think that all wisdom resides at 1600 Arch Street [INA world headquarters]," he once said. "I know better."

Three months after the merger, Diemand was elected chairman of the board of directors and Smith was raised to the presidency. However, Diemand also was designated chief executive officer; Smith, chief administrative officer. In other words, Diemand, now seventy-five years old, was still running the company.

This was an unusual and unwise division of authority. In practice, it was unlikely that anyone would be able to determine what were administrative matters subject to Smith, or at what point Diemand's powers should be invoked. The confusion was heightened by the lack of position descriptions.

Moreover, Diemand, since the middle of the 1950's, had been drawn increasingly into civic activities, which diverted a good deal of his attention from the company. A man of social conscience, involved in many worthy endeavors for the public good, he was in constant demand. Without realizing it, he became detached, to some extent, from the great corporation of which he was head. At least that was the impression of many observers outside the company.

"INA had been plunging ahead like a rogue elephant ever since the war," one industry authority said. "Then it seemed to slow down, as though it wanted to graze for a while and take it easy. And I said to one of my friends, 'John Diemand is a great man and a wonderful human being, but I hope he decides to retire and enjoy the fruits of his labors.'"

Diemand's reluctance to retire was understandable. He

had admired Benjamin Rush deeply—and Benjamin Rush was still chairman when he died (although Rush did not retain day-to-day control of the company while he was chairman the way Diemand did).

A story that Diemand sometimes told indicated a good deal about his emotions in this situation.

"Two days before Benjamin Rush died I went up to see him," he said. "He was in bed, in terrific pain. He said to me, 'The doctors can't find out what's wrong with me. I'll tell you— it isn't *anno Domini*. It's something else.'

"Well, I went there to show him our annual statement, to show him that we had done better than our biggest competitors as to assets and so on. And he said, 'John, I'll die happy.'"

It wasn't age (*anno Domini*) that had ended Rush's life as well as his tenure as chairman. There was a suggestion that age needn't have ended Diemand's administration, either. His great predecessor had died still in office, so. . . .

There was good reason why Diemand could discount his age, for he was far more active, vigorous, and alert, even after his retirement, than many a younger man. When he was eighty-one, an acquaintance telephoned Diemand at his farm in Bucks County, Pennsylvania. "Can you call back at noon?" said the voice on the other end of the line. "He's out on the tractor now, plowing."

Nevertheless, Diemand finally came to the conclusion that he should retire. On October 20, 1964, in a graceful statement to the board at its meeting, Diemand reviewed the status of the company and then said:

"At this time, I should like to move towards retirement which will afford me greater opportunity to devote myself to personal and civic interests. Consequently, I now request the board to allow me to retire as chairman and chief executive officer, effective as of the close of business today."

Acceding to his wishes, the board relieved him of those duties but elected him chairman of its executive committee, a post he held until his retirement from the board in 1967.

In a unanimous resolution, the board hailed Diemand's thirty-one years of service to INA, which had "contributed immeasurably to the growth, progress, and reputation" of the company. It said that he had "earned the respect, esteem, and affection" of everyone at INA "for his integrity, his leadership, his wisdom, and understanding."

"He is a figure of world stature in many fields," the board said, "particularly in the field of insurance, known for his effective and progressive views. . . . [He has] been honored by induction in the Insurance Hall of Fame and [has] been the recipient of many other honors and degrees from insurance organizations and institutions of learning, and [has] earned the admiration and respect of his colleagues in the insurance business."

In his statement to the board, Diemand also had referred to Bradford Smith. "I am sure you all know my high regard, respect, and affection for the president of the company," he said.

"He was my choice to succeed me, in which choice the executive committee and the whole board concurred. Since his election in 1961, he has shown the qualities of leadership, judgment, forcefulness, and integrity which I was confident he possessed, and I feel that he is fully competent to continue to direct the INA . . . as the chief executive officer."

When the meeting was over, Bradford Smith, Jr., was president and chairman of the board—and chief executive officer.

A new era had begun.

25: 'Against Algerines and Other Barbary Corsairs'

 HAVING GROWN OUT OF A TONTINE (as we have seen in Chapter 3), INA might be said to have started as a life insurance company, although its first insurance policy was a marine cover.

In its 1794 charter the company retained the power to write life insurance, and it did engage in that branch of the business during its early years, most of the life policies being limited to a relatively short term. Almost all of the insureds were sailing men.

Captain John Collet bought a policy on February 11, 1794, insuring him "against Algerines and other Barbary Corsairs in a voyage from Philadelphia to London, in the ship *George Barclay*, himself master, valuing himself at $5,000." For that voyage Collet paid a premium of two per cent, or $100. Like most of the mariners whose lives were insured by INA, Collet survived to sail again.

Not all applicants were accepted. John Holker, who was willing to pay a premium of one and a half per cent for a $24,000 policy covering him from June 6 to September 19,

The Modern Look of a Venerable Giant

Growing faster than the national economy and faster than
the industry as a whole in the quarter century after 1942,
INA by 1967 was the richest multiple-line insurance
company in the nation, with assets of nearly two billion
dollars, and its subsidiary, INA-Life, had almost two and
a quarter billion dollars of life insurance in force. So it
was only natural that its shares should be admitted to
trading on the floor of the New York Stock Exchange.
On March 22, 1965, its ticker symbol, "INA," first went up
on the board of the Exchange, which was founded
in the same year as INA.

INA *Archives*

Under the leadership of Bradford Smith, Jr., INA
adopted automation as quickly as possible, to improve
service and cut costs. Its computer specialists even
developed a special television-like facility (FACING
PAGE, TOP) called AIR for almost instantaneous,
automatic information retrieval. Not one person lost
his job because of automation—or "INAmation," as
the company called it. Eagle Lodge (BOTTOM),
bought by the company during the administration
of Smith's predecessor, John A. Diemand (BELOW),
as a country club for employees and their families,
was in great demand.

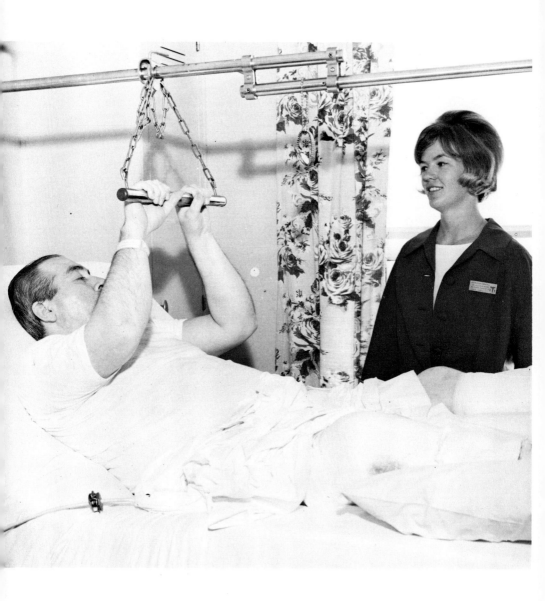

MEND, a rehabilitation program for seriously injured policyholders: Nurse Kathleen Duffly is shown visiting a patient to discuss plans for restoring him to productive activity.

was turned down for some reason that was not recorded. Very wisely, the company also declined to insure Colonel Louis de Tousard's life for $8,000, probably because he was going to spend a year in the West Indies, where the French colonies were being shaken by slave revolts.

One of the early life policies was issued to the magnificently named Bon Albert Briois de Beaumez, "who attained the age of forty-one years in the month of December now last past and is about to sail for India." The $5,000 policy, written at a premium of ten per cent, covered his life "for and during the term and space of eighteen calendar months." It insured him against death from any cause except suicide and "the hand of justice."

Not all of the insured were seamen, nor were they all men of property. The old Revolutionary War leader, Elias Boudinot, who was an INA stockholder, bought small five-year policies on two servants. The second of these policies, issued in 1817, was the last life insurance to be written by the company for more than a century.

As INA's assistant general counsel, William B. Pugh, Jr., commented in 1967 in a humorous and learned Huebner Foundation lecture at the University of Pennsylvania, "In subsequent years the operators of this concern, my present employer, in what must be considered one of the more colossal blunders in the history of American industry, decided there was no future in life insurance."

Although life underwriting got a slow start in the United States, it grew to be one of the most awesome giants in the national economy. By 1931 life insurance in force in this country amounted to $108,900,000,000.

In that year INA's board of directors carefully studied an analysis prepared for it by a firm of actuaries, dealing with the practicality of setting up a life insurance subsidiary, an idea that Benjamin Rush had been mulling over since the previous spring. Because the developing Depression had cast a pall over business, the proposal was dropped in the end, despite the actuaries' optimistic conclusion: "We fully believe that the new company will bring in large financial returns."

(In his private notes on the study, Rush observed that, at the outset, "we would probably have to go into our surplus in the sum of about $350,000 for reserves and cost of putting the business on the books.")

Ten years later, just a few months before Pearl Harbor, the company found itself writing life insurance again, almost by accident, after 124 years. At the request of the Maritime Commission, INA and a number of other companies wrote $5,000 war hazard policies for merchant seamen who were performing an essential service under extremely dangerous conditions. The shipowners paid the premiums on the policies, which provided death and injury benefits.

But that small venture in life underwriting ended with victory, and for more than a decade afterward the only life coverages offered by INA were under the travel and the group accident and sickness policies.

After the war, the introduction of multiple-line under-writing permitted the company to write every kind of insurance except life. State laws still maintained a barrier between the property-liability companies and the life insurers, a separation first required by New York State about 1865.

"One ridiculous aspect [of these laws]," Pugh pointed out in his Huebner Foundation lecture, "is that the two largest present-day stock companies in effect were given 'grandfather rights' in all states, including life, which they have maintained throughout the period even in New York. Every new insurance code solemnly re-enacts these provisions, and it is considered most humorous at code hearings to suggest that either the restriction be removed or the 'grandfather rights' be taken away."

(Under "grandfather rights," individuals or organizations possessing certain legal powers before the passage of a law are permitted to retain those powers, even if the law specifically withholds those powers from other persons or groups.)

Diemand and his associates at INA felt strongly that the company would not be a truly across-the-board insurer until it wrote life insurance too. At a meeting of the board of directors on September 11, 1956, Diemand reported that the executive committee had approved his proposal to incorporate a life insurance subsidiary, to be called the Life Insurance Company of North America.

The board minutes, written by Secretary-Treasurer J. Kenton Eisenbrey, summarized Diemand's arguments:

"The growth of life insurance companies had been tremendous in recent years and . . . there should be an excellent opportunity in this field, taking into consideration the increasing population and the increase in the average amount of life insurance carried per person and per family. . . .

"The surplus of [INA] was the fifth largest in the entire insurance industry, including life companies, and . . . the company, therefore, was in an excellent position financially to invest in a life company. . . .

"The idea of one company or group furnishing every form of insurance would be advantageous and would help an assured to budget his premium payments for all classes of coverage."

Approving the plan, the board allocated $7,000,000 to be used for capital, surplus, and a special reserve fund, a far cry from the modest $350,000 contemplated in 1931. (Over the next seven years, the parent company put $26,000,000 more into the life subsidiary.)

After the subsidiary, informally dubbed INA-Life, was incorporated, a search was conducted for the best man to organize the new operation. For six months Diemand quietly collected the names of likely candidates and systematically screened them.

"I had a dossier of a tremendous number of fellows in the life insurance business," Diemand said, "and I had them arranged in alphabetical order."

The last name on the list, alphabetically, was "Zalinski, Edmund L., C.L.U."

One day Diemand was brooding over the list, as he had before, and the more he read the biographical material on Zalinski the more impressed he became: graduate of Cornell University; Master of Business Administration from Harvard Business School; Ph.D. (*summa cum laude*) from New York University. . . . Bought first life insurance policy in college, began selling insurance while still a student. . . . Went to work 1938 for major life underwriter as special agent, soon became troubleshooter improving rundown branch offices. . . . Named first managing director of industry-supported Life Underwriter Training Council in 1947, original author and instructor of its courses, taught to more than 100,000 agents. . . . In 1949, while still at LUTC, chosen executive vice president, National Association of Life Underwriters, holding both posts until 1951, when he returned to previous life company employer as vice president in charge of sales development. . . . Beginning in 1955, vice president and chairman of agency committee of another life company, one of nation's largest. . . .

At that point Diemand got a telephone call from a Texas insurance executive about proposed legislation in that state. Before hanging up, Diemand asked him if he had a good name to suggest among life insurance men.

"The best guy I know is a fellow by the name of Zalinski," his caller said. "He's up in Boston."

"I know that," Diemand said. "I have all the information on him right here in front of me."

That night Diemand telephoned Zalinski at his home

in Wellesley Hills, where he was giving a dinner party. Zalinski agreed to meet with Diemand and discuss the problems INA would face in setting up a new life company. About four months later, on April 22, 1957, Zalinski became head of INA-Life.

The goal set for him was one that no new life company had ever achieved: to have $1,000,000,000 of insurance in force within ten years.

In fact, the $1,000,000,000 level was reached in 1962, not quite five years after INA-Life began issuing policies. In 1964 the company went over the $1,500,000,000 mark, and two years later, in its ninth year, Bradford Smith, Jr., announced that more than $2,000,000,000 of life insurance was in force, putting INA-Life in the top five per cent of life insurance companies in America.

Those results had been achieved despite the fact that INA-Life did not, for technical reasons, write insurance in New York State until it organized its own subsidiary, INA-Life of New York, on December 28, 1965.

"Although INA-Life is still operating at a deficit," commented Merrill, Lynch, Pierce, Fenner, and Smith, in January 1966, "management has been dramatically successful in developing its young affiliate."

Pointing out that INA-Life's deficit was caused mainly by its rapid growth, the stock brokerage house added that the life company "now appears to be approaching the point of statutory underwriting profits." It predicted that INA-Life would "eventually make significant contributions to the parent's earnings."

It had not been easy, and mistakes had been made along the way, inevitably.

"I think you learn a lot more from your mistakes than you do from your successes," Zalinski said.

The first problem was personnel. A number of men

who had worked with Zalinski previously in other companies joined him at INA-Life, like Rex H. Anderson, Richard S. Cox, Jr., and Leroy G. Steinbeck.

They came from varied backgrounds. For example, Steinbeck, a minister's son, taught English in Ohio schools after college before entering the life insurance business. In 1950 he was invited to head the American Society of Chartered Life Underwriters, a national organization with headquarters in Philadelphia. The society sought to encourage life insurance men to continue their professional training, and so Steinbeck was brought into contact with Zalinski, and the two men worked closely together. On the evening before Zalinski had his first meeting with Diemand, he dined with Steinbeck.

Anderson got into life insurance after working his way through college as a radio announcer. As an insurance man in the field, he wrote a book on how to sell accident and sickness insurance. A life insurance company in New York which was having difficulties with its accident and sickness business asked Anderson to join its home office staff, where Anderson met Zalinski.

In September 1957, there were still fewer than twenty INA-Life employees.

"We have more executives than secretaries right now," Zalinski said at the time.

But in that month the company sold its first policy, under highly ceremonial circumstances.

It was decided that INA-Life's first public activity should be part of a tribute to the American Agency System, which had been started by the parent company 150 years before in Lexington, Kentucky. So Diemand, Smith, Stellwagen, Zalinski, and INA vice president Richard G. Osgood journeyed to Lexington.

There they dedicated a memorial on the grounds of Transylvania College to INA's (and America's) first insurance agent, Thomas Wallace. A local attorney, Stanley Martin Saunier, purchased the first INA-Life policy through Samuel B. Walton, Jr., of the Walton and Nuzum agency. It was believed that the agency was the latest in several generations of agencies that succeeded Wallace's.

The event was a brief respite in a hectic period for Zalinski and his lieutenants. On their return to Philadelphia, they were again confronted with the difficulty of shaping their assistants, men from many different companies and a wide variety of backgrounds, into the INA mold.

"We had a sort of French Foreign Legion around here," Zalinski sighed.

A large number of recruits remained only a short time. Throughout the life insurance business the turnover has always been rather high, but the INA-Life situation was abnormal because of the newness of the company and the need to staff it adequately and quickly.

At first the company sold its policies directly to the public through "career agents" as well as through the established network of independent agents. The "career agent" program proved too expensive; consequently, it was gradually abandoned, which meant that many jobs were eliminated.

Beginning in 1960, Zalinski began what he called "major surgery." It was painful, but it had to be done. In two years nineteen offices were closed, and "fifty judgment-level people" in the field operation were either not replaced or were "terminated." In the home office, the number of executives was cut from fifteen to seven. Fortunately, times were good and jobs plentiful; most of the men who left were snatched up by other companies.

At that time the life company settled down to the approach which was to characterize its sales efforts in later years.

"This program," said Anderson, "is based on training

independent agents, most of whom had been selling only property and liability coverages, to sell life insurance. We showed them why they should be selling life insurance, and helped them to do it."

The system proved itself when life insurance sales increased thirty per cent in 1966.

For the agents who were unused to life-insurance selling, the company had a strong argument.

"Consumer buying habits are changing," Zalinski said. "The buyer wants one-stop service. He wants to go to one man for all his insurance."

To help property-liability agents learn life-insurance selling, INA-Life was ready to send experienced field representatives out to call on selected prospects with the agents. And it was quick to cut red tape that might block a sale.

A San Francisco man wanted a $250,000 policy. Because he traveled a good deal, investigating his medical history was difficult.

"We found that he had had medical treatment in Barcelona," Donald S. Vincent said, "so we telephoned his physician in Spain. We also needed a statement from a clinic in St. Paul, Minnesota, and telephoned them for information. They would not release any information without a signed authorization. Our doctor arranged through one of the press services to have a photo of the authorization sent by wire, and he also made arrangements to have it picked up immediately and delivered to the clinic. The clinic then telephoned us and discussed the case in detail. We were able to issue a standard policy."

Another man was preparing to leave on a trip, and he wanted a $500,000 policy. INA-Life found that the parent company's Bonding Department had a file on him going back to 1935, showing that the company had bonded him for as much as $2,500,000. The policy was approved in two days.

Sometimes applications were rejected for unusual reasons. In June 1966 an application for a $50,000 accident insurance policy on a woman was received. Before issuing the policy, the company looked into the circumstances. Four acquaintances of the woman told INA-Life's investigators that if she were insured for a substantial amount of money, they would not "give a plug nickel for her life." The company turned down the application, and four months later her body, with four gunshot wounds, was found in a burning car. The husband was charged with murder.

The INA tradition of liberal treatment of policyholders was implemented in the life company. On January 13, 1967, a man applied for life insurance and paid the initial premium. Four days later, before the policy had been approved by the company, the man had a heart attack which would have made him uninsurable. Examination of the application showed that he had made a mistake in filling it out. Nevertheless, since he had paid the premium in advance and had been insurable on the day of the application (having no prior history of heart trouble), the company issued the policy.

In Apple Valley, California, a restaurateur named Salvatore Testa was murdered by a bandit in a tavern on August 9, 1961. Testa had applied for a $5,000 ordinary life policy on July 6, paying the premium with his application. At the time of the slaying the application had not yet been approved. Nevertheless, INA-Life determined that Testa was insurable on the day he applied, so it honored the policy.

Fraudulent policy applications and strange claims flowed into Philadelphia. INA vice president James W. Ferriman, later head of the Policyholders Service Division, worked on the life company's claims for a time.

"I swear that in our first couple of years we must have run into every kind of screwball situation," he said.

"One chap left the hospital after an exploratory operation for cancer, which was found to be incurable, went right to our agent's offices, and applied for a life insurance policy below the medical limits, so that there would be no examination.

"Another case involved an insured who took a raft trip down the Colorado River with thirteen other people. The raft hit a rock, and five of the people went into the water. Three of them were fished out immediately, but two were swept downstream. The body of one of those two was found subsequently; but the last body has not been found to this day. And that was the one we insured for $80,000 or $90,000. It was almost certain that he had lost his life. It was very wild country."

Another disappearance involved a city councilman in the Midwest who was leading a civil reform drive, investigating crime and corruption personally. One day his car was found abandoned; the councilman had vanished. INA-Life's investigators began to dig into the case when a claim was presented on his life insurance policy.

"Ultimately we located him in the South," Ferriman said. "He had been beaten, transported South, and thrown out of the car. We found him in a hospital."

Among the most bizarre claims have been several dismemberment injuries that turned out to be intentional.

"It is hard to believe that a man will go out and buy a $250,000 worth of insurance and then cut off a hand or put out an eye," said Alan Waters. "But it happens. Of course, this is very difficult for us to prove because it's so unbelievable. You really have to dig for information."

A Florida man was suspected of having deliberately shot his leg off after buying insurance from several companies, including INA-Life. When they began to probe into the case, INA-Life's claims men found that the man had lied about a kidney problem when applying for his policy, so the company simply rescinded the policy on grounds of misrepresentation. The other insurance companies were less fortunate; feeling that it was doubtful they could persuade a judge and jury that anyone would intentionally maim himself, they settled the claims against them. The self-made cripple collected $134,000.

"Some time later we got a claim from another fellow in Florida," Waters remembered. "His leg had been shot off, too. And then we discovered that he was a next-door neighbor of the first man.

"At that point, as you can imagine, we really got suspicious. In the course of our investigation we found that the first man had set the whole thing up for his neighbor, even to writing the letters to the insurance companies for him. We were able to break that case because our insured had failed when he tried to blow his leg off by himself, so he had hired another man to do the job for him. But he welshed on paying the fellow, so the guy was ready to talk.

"During the investigation, the first crook, the one who had collected and had written the letters for his neighbor, started following his fellow self-made cripple around to see how he was making out. They said it was funny to watch. Here would go our insured (the second crook), and the first fellow would follow him, and our investigator would follow the first man, all of them running around Florida in a line of parade."

And then there was the "Case of the Man Who Sold His Life." He lived in North Carolina, but during a visit to Florida, suspecting that something was wrong with him, he went to a doctor. The doctor discovered that the man had an inoperable brain tumor. He probably would not live more than a year.

So the man went back to North Carolina, contacted some gamblers, and offered to sell them his life. If they would give him a large amount of money to enjoy while he was still alive, he would let them buy $1,500,000 accidental death coverage on him, with them as beneficiaries.

They agreed to the deal. He got a fat wad of bills, and they got a fistful of insurance policies. While the money held out, the tumor victim acted like the last of the big spenders. His last weeks were a frenzied search for pleasure.

When he went broke, it was time to fulfill his side of the deal. He killed himself by driving into a bridge abutment at about ninety miles an hour.

There was a sequel. About the time he died, his beneficiaries were found to have been involved in an automobile insurance frauds ring. The state authorities sought a connection between the death of the tumor victim and the operations of the insurance swindlers.

"They are all in jail now," Waters said.

But INA-Life knew that there would be other cheats to take their place.

26: A Stronghold on the Pacific

THE SUBJECT OF the speech was "The Future of the Medium-Size Property and Casualty Insurance Company," and the speaker standing before the members of the Insurance Brokers Association of California, John T. Gurash, head of the medium-size Pacific Employers Group (PEG), seemed quite optimistic.

Despite all the problems he listed, he predicted that PEG, "as well as other medium-sized property and casualty companies, [would] participate fully" in the "world of golden opportunities" opening before them.

One of the developments he touched on was "the wave of mergers, not only in the insurance industry but in industry generally." Gurash told the San Francisco meeting:

"I seriously doubt that any medium-sized property and casualty company boasting a consistent record of earnings, competent management, and devoid of ownership involvements is an easy subject for merger. That company will be confident of its ability to make its own way in the competitive climate. . . ."

The date was January 28, 1964.

Within a few weeks, Gurash had been approached with two merger offers, and before the year was out, the six insurance companies that comprised PEG, which had the amazing record of showing statutory underwriting profits in all but two of its forty-one years, were taken over by INA.

No one was more amused by the way fate contradicted him than Gurash himself. To a friend he pointed out that his speech, which had been a searching, perceptive analysis of the industry, opened with a typically modest statement: "An assumption that I can predict with any degree of certainty the future of the medium-sized property and casualty insurance company is, of course, presumptuous and leads inevitably to the conclusion I would also be able to walk across the Golden Gate—*on the water.*"

The cloudiness of Gurash's crystal globe was certainly no reflection on his foresight, discernment, or business abilities, as the Pacific chapter of the Society of Chartered Property and Casualty Underwriters made clear later that year by selecting him as the first recipient of its "Insurance Man of the Year" award, established "to give recognition to the person who has made the most outstanding contribution to the insurance industry as well as the general public."

Shortly after the speech, the president of a Seattle insurance company with an outstanding reputation asked Gurash if there was any possibility of acquiring PEG. In the course of the conversation, the caller happened to say, "We are also thinking about going in the title business."

"I think I have a company which you can buy," Gurash replied, and he told the man about a large title insurance company in Los Angeles on whose board he served.

As a result of the conversation, the Seattle company did acquire the title insurance company.

While those negotiations were going on, within a week of the first call, Gurash got a call from Francis F. Owen, INA's

Pacific Coast resident vice president. Owen, whose office was in San Francisco, was an old friend of Gurash.

"John," said Owen, "a few months ago I asked you to let me know if you were ever inclined to sell PEG, and you said you would. And now I hear that you're negotiating with the Seattle outfit."

Gurash assured Owen that the negotiations did not involve PEG, just the title insurance company.

"Good," said Owen. "I'm happy to hear it. But how do you feel about the possibility of INA's taking over PEG?"

"Let me think it over, and then we'll talk about it," Gurash suggested.

The more Gurash thought about it, the better he liked the idea. PEG had two dominant stockholders, the widows of the founders. Both of their estates were in trust. For that reason it would be very difficult to increase the company's capitalization through the sale of another stock issue.

Nevertheless, in spite of its thriving condition, and perhaps because of it, the company needed additional capital if it were to grow. And grow it must, Gurash was certain. As he had said in that speech to the brokers a short time before:

"Growth is a necessary ingredient of any healthy enterprise. It is unlikely that any of us can stand still—to do so invites gradual but steady deterioration and ultimate extinction.

"Generally speaking, companies expand and grow in one of two ways. If it can afford the required time and investment, a company may well choose internal growth, because its business development will be directly fitted to its own needs and in appropriate size and character. On the other hand, the merger route is a legitimate means of growth. The acquisition of existing companies to provide either territorial or product expansion is a rapid means of growth, albeit a hazardous one."

After discussing the merger possibility with Gurash, Owen arranged for him to get together with Bradford Smith,

Jr. The two men hit it off at once, as well they might. Both were reflective men, with a common passion for modern management principles. Both preferred to lead their associates and subordinates by persuasion and encouragement, invoking their authority only as a last resort. Equally dedicated to a level of ethics much higher than one usually encounters, they were deeply conscious of the social responsibilities of business leaders.

Moreover, the two men shared the same attitude toward the insurance industry's need to change and progress with the times, to engage in healthy competition free of unnecessary governmental restrictions, to modernize methods and equipment—and to operate so efficiently as to produce an underwriting profit, instead of merely depending on investment income.

Their companies' philosophies were virtually identical, from fast, fair claims service to independence and freedom to compete. After the SEUA decision in 1944, when the state insurance laws were being enacted, PEG took the lead in California, supported by INA, in persuading the legislature to pass the most liberal law in the country, a statute so sound that more than two decades later legislatures in several other states were considering measures along similar lines.

At that time Victor Montgomery, president of PEG, called on John A. Diemand in Philadelphia. B. Frank King, who later became executive vice president of the California organization, remembered the meeting.

"I was just a young guy," he said. "I was just sitting on the sidelines listening to these two great men talk. Their thinking, as far as freedom from the bureaus and from restrictions on competition was concerned, was identical. They were both rugged individualists.

"During those years of fighting in the industry, Mr. Montgomery was right there, shoulder to shoulder with Mr.

H. Richard Heilman (UPPER RIGHT) became president and "chief underwriting officer" in 1966, the first man in company's history to be so designated. Among other changes as company acquired a new look in the 1960's were programs which drew national attention in the press, like INA's "Care-A-Van" (CENTER AND BOTTOM PHOTOS), a traveling safety show.

Agents and brokers cooperated with
INA in "Friendship" programs,
beginning in 1965, through which
sales of certain types of insurance
resulted in contributions to CARE.
First "Friendship" campaign gave
CARE the equivalent of two million
pounds of food. CARE projects shown
here were among beneficiaries in
underdeveloped countries.

Care

Bradford Smith, Jr. (shown here), the thirteenth chief executive officer of INA. Elected president in 1961, he was elected to the additional posts of chairman of the board and chief executive officer in 1964. An early advocate of automation, Bradford Smith reorganized the company along functional lines, an organizational plan later adopted by other insurance companies. He emphasized "participative management," a concept that established responsibility and encouraged cooperative effort by all executives.

Diemand in his thinking. There were not very many people who supported INA's position in those days. It took a lot of courage. And with a small company it took a lot more courage, because a small company like ours was picked on something awful."

For INA, acquisition of PEG offered two major advantages. First, the Philadelphia company was being hard pressed by its competitors in the field of participating workmen's compensation. (The policyholder has the right to participate in underwriting earnings, if any, under participating policies.) In most states one company cannot issue both participating and non-participating policies for workmen's compensation.

Because INA had concentrated its workmen's compensation efforts on the non-participating type, it was hamstrung in trying to compete with some of its most powerful rivals who were writing the increasingly popular participating policies. On the other hand, PEG, seventy per cent of whose business was workmen's compensation, had been the first stock company in the United States to write participating policies for that coverage through independent agents and brokers. Thus, the business of the two companies was largely complementary, and their merger permitted the companies' agents to sell both types of policies.

The second advantage to INA was that the acquisition gave it a stronghold on the Pacific Coast. Although INA had long had offices and agents on the West Coast, Bradford Smith felt that the company needed a "local identity," a means of establishing "a more intimate connection with the political and economic forces in the region."

"The Pacific Coast is such a rapidly growing area," Smith said, "one of the most dynamic sections of the country, that no national company dare underestimate its importance now and in the future."

[361]

Perils: Named and Unnamed

PEG gave its new parent company a firm footing in California, the nation's third largest state in area, where 19,000,000 people—one of every ten Americans—lived, with more than 1,000 from other states moving there every day to join them. The city of Los Angeles ranked third in the nation in population, and the metropolitan area of which it was a part was second only to New York City. San Francisco was one of the greatest financial centers in the world. Almost a quarter of all prime contracts for military equipment went to California manufacturers; nearly half the nation's budget for civilian space research and development was spent in the state. In value of agricultural production it ranked first in the nation.

And in this immense and growing market, one of the best known and most influential insurance organizations was the Pacific Employers Group, consisting of the Pacific Employers Insurance Company (PEIC—the parent company); the Allied Insurance Company, writing a variety of participating workmen's compensation coverage called "level-dividend" at prices competitive with the direct writers; the Meritplan Insurance Company, providing low-cost auto insurance for carefully selected, preferred risks; the Pacific Employers Life Insurance Company, specializing in credit life and disability coverages; the California Food Industry Company, limiting its participating workmen's compensation protection to large risks in that industry; the Educators Insurance Company of America (in which PEG held a fifty per cent interest), specializing in life and health insurance for that profession; and the Pacific Employers Indemnity Company, writing compensation business in the Southwest.

"In our opinion, the Pacific Employers Group represents a valuable addition to INA's operations," commented the stock brokerage house of Merrill, Lynch, Pierce, Fenner, and Smith.

The history of the group begins with PEIC, but for simplicity's sake we'll call it PEG from the start.

A Stronghold on the Pacific

The story revolves around two men, a boyish prank that had tragic results, and a lot of laundry men.

The men were Victor Montgomery and William R. Kilgore.

Montgomery was a brilliant man, quiet and withdrawn, who loved to think his way through difficult problems. While a student at the University of Nebraska, training for a career as a mining engineer, he worked during his summer vacations in a silver mine in Utah. One day some of the other young fellows in the mine were engaged in horseplay when the brake on an ore car was somehow released. Before Montgomery could get out of the way, the car rolled over one of his legs, severing it. For the rest of his life Montgomery had to use an artificial leg.

The accident was always a taboo subject except for Montgomery's family and Kilgore. Loretta ("Pat") Tibbets, who went to work for PEG as head of its fire insurance department in 1935 and who was a director of INA-PEG in 1967, said that Kilgore believed the accident had a direct impact on the insurance business in later years.

"At the time of Mr. Montgomery's accident," Miss Tibbets pointed out, "there was no such thing as compulsory workmen's compensation, and Mr. Montgomery was left high and dry as far as money went. He made up his mind, so Mr. Kilgore said, that he would see that compensation became compulsory."

Montgomery was about seventeen when the accident occurred. For two years he was in a wheelchair. Knowing that a mining career was no longer possible, he thought that he might become a concert violinist, so he practiced for hours at a time, sitting in his wheelchair.

After he was fitted with the prosthetic device, Montgomery went West to continue his education at the University of California, in Berkeley, where he met the girl he later married. There he decided to go into actuarial work, "because so many of his college credits for mining engineering were in mathematics," according to Mrs. Montgomery.

After graduation, he went to work as an actuary in the state Insurance Department in Sacramento; a brief sketch of the company's history in 1938 said he remained there ten years before he was sent to Los Angeles in 1921 to open an office there for the department. He was deputy insurance commissioner there for two years, until PEG was founded.

One of the insurance companies under Montgomery's supervision was a small mutual owned by the California Laundry Owners Association to write workmen's compensation coverage for its members. The manager of the association was Bill Kilgore.

Kilgore and Montgomery were as different as two men could be. Kilgore was outgoing, exuberant, loud, humorous.

"He never met a stranger," Mrs. Kilgore once remarked.

Traveling in Europe, a Californian once tried to cash a check, but he couldn't find a banker who would honor it. Finally one banker said:

"I've visited your state, but I don't know very many people there."

"I'm a friend of Bill Kilgore," the Californian ventured hopefully.

The banker beamed.

"Oh, I know Mr. Kilgore," he said. "He's a friend of mine. If he's a friend of yours, I guess I can cash your check."

The banker apparently didn't realize that half the state's population consisted of Bill Kilgore's friends, and the rest hadn't bumped into Kilgore yet.

Besides running the laundry owners' association, Kilgore served as its lobbyist at the state capital so successfully that for ten or twelve years he had a private office in the Governor's suite. He remained a power in Sacramento until his death, eight years before INA acquired PEG.

One day John Morris, who was also associated with the

laundry owners' group and active in politics, told Kilgore he ought to go into business for himself.

"What would I do?" Kilgore asked.

"Why don't you go into the insurance business?" Morris suggested.

"I don't know anything about the insurance business," Kilgore protested.

"No, you don't. But there's not a man in California who knows more people or has more friends than you have. And I know a young fellow named Montgomery who has all the know-how. You two would make a wonderful pair."

And so the two got together and organized PEG in 1923.

They did make a perfect team. Kilgore brought in the business and watched out for the company's interests when the legislature was in session, while Montgomery ran the company.

Dissimilar as they were, they nevertheless hit it off superbly. They became such close and lasting friends that when one of them went to buy a car, the other would go along and buy exactly the same model.

In the beginning, they discussed how much money they hoped to make from the insurance company. They decided on $500,000. Less than ten years after the company had opened for business, Montgomery reported to Kilgore that they'd reached their goal.

"We couldn't have done this without the people who work for us," Montgomery said.

"That's right," Kilgore said. "Now let's see to it that they get something."

So they drew up a plan under which employees could buy shares by payroll deduction, with the company putting up part of the money.

"Some of our people got their stock for practically nothing," Miss Tibbets observed, "and were millionaires after INA bought PEG."

They also established one of the earliest profit-sharing plans. At first bonuses were paid every month; later the payments were made semiannually, but the amounts were not reduced. All employees benefited.

"I came to work for this company in September 1935," King said, "and about two months later I got a pay check that was equal to the full month's pay. I thought, 'What in the world is this?' "

By concentrating on one thing, participating workmen's compensation, and doing it well, the company prospered. By 1937 PEG ranked first in casualty writings in California and fourteenth in the nation. Although fire insurance and ocean and inland marine lines were added in the 1930's, they never became a major factor in the company's earnings.

The stature of the company was indicated by the fact that two men associated with PEG resigned to accept appointments as state Insurance Commissioner: F. Britton McConnell, general counsel, vice president, and a director, was Commissioner from 1941 to 1955, and Stafford R. Grady, a director, served in the post from 1960 to 1963.

In 1945 Gurash joined PEG after fifteen years with another insurance company. Organizing Meritplan in 1953 (William H. Erwin headed it in 1967), Gurash became executive vice president of the Pacific Employers Group in 1959 and president the following year, three months before Montgomery's death.

In their latter years, the two founders had continued to make major contributions. To help the industry present its case to the legislature, they organized the Association of California Companies, which eventually included almost all California insurers. The Western Insurance Information Service was organized by Montgomery as the first all-industry public relations organization (direct writers were members, along with stock companies, mutuals, and others), primarily to educate the public on the problems of auto insurance.

A Stronghold on the Pacific

An unusual characteristic of PEG from the beginning was the number of women in executive posts, so many that Montgomery and Kilgore were sometimes needled by men from other companies about running "a petticoat outfit." A 1938 publication listed four women officers.

One PEG operation not found in most insurance companies was its Employers Self-Insurance Service, which was started after the war. Headed by J. Glennon Cahill, Jr., ESIS in 1967 managed twenty-four self-insured accounts. These were large corporations which chose to establish their own insurance funds under state supervision to meet workmen's compensation claims. Although PEG tried to dissuade corporations from engaging in self-insurance, it was willing, if they insisted on self-insurance, to run their funds for them. For a fee which included a commission for the broker, ESIS would provide the client with any or all of four services: claims, safety engineering, statistical reports, and advice.

But the bulk of PEG's income continued to come from participating workmen's compensation, a field that was growing increasingly complicated because of ever more liberal judicial decisions.

The extremes to which these could go was illustrated by a California decision. Ironically, the case involved a defense attorney for a workmen's compensation insurance company (not PEG) who died of cancer. During his last months he filed a claim with the Industrial Accident Commission contending that the tensions of his job compelled him to smoke so heavily that he developed lung cancer. The referee awarded his estate $30,000.

An unexpected asset that INA obtained with its acquisition of PEG was the California company's rehabilitation program, called MEND (for "Medical and Educational Needs of the Disabled"). For years INA had financed rehabilitation of claimants, but this had not been done on an organized, systematic basis.

Because of Montgomery's personal disability, PEG had from its beginning been more active in promoting rehabilitation. But it was not until after Montgomery's death that MEND was established by Gurash as a regular, clearly defined program of rehabilitation.

So impressed by the PEG program was INA that two years after taking over the Pacific Coast organization Bradford Smith, Jr., ordered MEND expanded in scope and extended to all of INA's operations. George Welch was brought to Philadelphia to head the program because of the effective work he had been doing on his own initiative in promoting rehabilitation in the Minneapolis Service Office.

Welch had a personal interest in helping injured persons, for he himself had undergone rehabilitation in an Army hospital in World War II. An infantryman, Welch was wounded by shell fragments in the leg.

His interest in rehabilitation was also stimulated by his wife, who was an Army nurse when they met.

As a claims man in the field, Welch had been troubled, as most insurance men were, by the way all companies handled injury cases.

"Let's say you were injured in an automobile accident," he said. "A claims man would go to see you, and you'd hand him the repair bill for your car and you'd start to talk about your doctor bills and all the money you were losing by not being able to work.

"The claims man would listen and then say, 'Well, wait now, sir. Our insured was convicted of drunken driving and there's no question of his being responsible for the accident. But I can't pay for your car or your medical expenses until you get well.

" 'Then we will negotiate a settlement with you, and we'll ask you to sign a final release for us, and we will pay you fairly.'

"So naturally you would say to the claims man, 'What kind of double talk is this? Your man damaged my car and injured me, and you won't even fix my car so I can get back to work when I recover. And how am I supposed to live in the meantime?'"

Nothing did more damage to the industry's public image, or to its loss ratio, for the enraged victim of the accident immediately telephoned a lawyer and instructed him to get every penny possible out of the insurance company.

Furthermore, without prompt rehabilitation, the man's injuries often became more serious, and he also suffered a psychological letdown that might have contributed to a higher judgment, as well as darkening his own life.

All of that was changed under the MEND program.

"The charge I was given," Welch said, "was to develop the most aggressive rehabilitation program in the industry."

Dr. William J. Erdman II, professor and chairman of the University of Pennsylvania's Department of Physical Medicine and Rehabilitation, agreed to serve as a consultant. A corps of nurses was employed to bring a professional nursing approach to the problems and to serve as a bridge between doctor and patient by helping to explain those details that most doctors simply don't have time to discuss at length.

Most important, the handling of claims was changed. When an INA policyholder was liable and the policy limits were adequate, the company now went to the victim's home. And the conversation might go something like this:

"Sure, we'll pay for your car; here's a check right now. We'll pay the medical and hospital bills as they accumulate. We won't ask you to sign a release. All we ask you to do is to give us credit on the amounts we advance to you against the final settlement, so that if we advance you $2,000, and it turns out that we owe you $8,000, we will pay you $6,000."

At the same time the claims man would give the victim

or his family his business card, a brochure called "At Your Service," a message from Bradford Smith, Jr., expressing sympathy and a desire to help, an envelope for keeping bills and expense records so they wouldn't be misplaced, and a note saying that the case qualified for INA's rehabilitation program.

Welch told of a specific case in Arkansas. A man and his wife were driving to the grocery store with their five children in the car. A motorist insured by INA was on his way to a fishing party with some friends, and he had been drinking. His car crossed the center line and hit the other vehicle head-on.

All seven members of the Arkansas family were confined to the hospital. The wife and children had broken bones and lacerations, but the father was in a coma with brain damage.

The wife and children were soon released from the hospital, and INA's claims man called on them.

"The father was paid by the hour," Welch said, "and when he wasn't working, he didn't get paid. Now, what's the use of talking about rehabilitation of Dad when Mom and the children aren't eating? But that's what our representative found; there was not an ounce of food in the house.

"Then, too, the man was buying a house, so they had mortgage payments to meet. And there were payments to be made on their auto loan, and all sorts of other bills. And no money coming in.

"But in this case our man said, 'Here's an emergency check to be credited on what we owe you, so you can get some food in the house and pay your bills.'

"When the father emerged from the coma and he heard that this big, bad, cold-hearted insurance company had bailed out his wife and kids when he was unconscious and had put food in their mouths, he wasn't inclined to throw our man out of the house or to run to an attorney.

"And he was willing to listen when the INA man told

him, 'You can't speak clearly because of brain damage; you need speech therapy. We're ready to supply this and pay as the bills come due. And after you've reached your maximum recovery and we've got you back to work, we'll sit down with you and figure out what we owe you for pain and suffering and other things. In the meantime, we don't ask you to sign anything.' "

In a report on the MEND program, the *National Underwriter*, a trade journal, said that INA had expanded the rehabilitation concept "to a degree never before experienced in the insurance industry." It described the program as "revolutionary."

On January 13, 1967, *The Wall Street Journal* carried a front page article focused principally on MEND. The newspaper told the story of Robert Burgon, a forty-one year old San Franciscan, who was paralyzed on the left side as a result of an auto accident in 1963.

"Thanks to heavy financial backing from the Insurance Company of North America," said *The Journal*, Burgon was "back in the business he knows best."

"[INA] encouraged Mr. Burgon to make use of his twenty years of experience in the display advertising business," the newspaper went on. "It approved a review by a business consultant of his prospectus for a counseling agency in this field, helped him find and equip an office, provided him with a car specially equipped for him to drive (he is still severely crippled), and advanced initial working capital.

"Mr. Burgon now is running Merchandising Dynamics, a San Francisco agency which helps manufacturers and food processors plan sales promotion and display campaigns. He's doing very well, well enough, in fact, to require no further payments from INA on his insurance policy.

"INA estimates that it would have had to pay Mr. Burgon a total of about $75,000 on his policy if he had been allowed to go on as before without extra help. It had paid him $14,000 before it began rehabilitation efforts and another $33,000 or so to set him up in business, for a total of roughly $47,000. So INA posted a 'profit' of $28,000 by helping him."

In one list of eleven cases Welch estimated that INA had saved more than $500,000 through MEND, and that did not include the mental anguish, the breakup of marriages, and the ruin and waste of lives that had been prevented by restoring people to a self-reliant status, enabling them to live with dignity and self-respect.

MEND promised to go far toward changing the all-too-common public conception of an insurance company as a heartless, impersonal tightwad, searching for legal loopholes in fine print while people suffer.

The program also seemed likely to give insurance men, especially claims adjusters, a sense of pride in being part of a broad campaign to help people. Significantly, when Welch outlined his company's new approach to rehabilitation in an address to the Ontario Insurance Adjusters Association at a meeting in Toronto, he received a standing ovation, the first time such a tribute had been paid in the history of the organization.

27: Shaping Up

WHEN BRADFORD SMITH, JR., took over the reins in 1964, his years of study in management theories and techniques had given him a clear idea of how the company could be reorganized to bring it in tune with the sweeping changes that had occurred in the company, the industry, and the nation.

A portent of things to come had been his closing remarks to a conference of service office managers in 1957. He said then: "Momentum was the key to the '50s. Change is the key to the '60s."

Some of the men listening to him tended to dismiss this as the pep talk to be expected on such occasions. Few of them had any idea how sweeping would be the transformation wrought in the company by Smith, or how many men and women would find their lives profoundly altered by it.

This massive alteration did not come about, obviously, because of a mere whim on Smith's part; it was dictated by sheer necessity. The enormous growth of the company in the prosperous postwar years and the continuing pressure from hard-hitting competitors of a new kind had proved to be more than the traditional organization of the company could cope with. It was like asking a team of horses to pull a truck-trailer at a gallop along a thruway.

One didn't need to be a Wall Street wizard or a statistician to be impressed by the company's development. Between 1945 and 1965 the market value of the company's assets had shot up from $160,999,034 to $1,831,514,000, propelled by investment income and a persistent bull market.

But the company had never forgotten that it was an insurance company, not an investment trust—a distinction which could become critical (had become, for some other companies) if both premium and investment incomes tumbled precipitously during an economic depression. INA's obligation to its stockholders, employees, and even its policyholders (who had to be able to depend on a stable company) was to earn a profit, however modest, on its underwriting. And this it managed to do over the long pull, although there had often been periods of several years when underwriting losses could not be avoided.

The adjective most often applied to INA by its agents and competitors was "aggressive" (along with "reliable" and "fair"). And the postwar growth of the company showed its aggressiveness.

In the two decades after 1945, while the gross national product—the total value of all goods and services used as an index of the country's economic health—increased threefold, the insurance industry as a whole registered a fivefold rise in premium income. But INA's premium income went up *eight and a half times*, a rate more than fifty per cent faster than the industry's.

It was no longer a small, intimate organization in which almost all the employees knew each other. There had been only 3,222 men and women working for the company at the end of the war; twenty years later their number had risen to 10,449.

Shaping Up

The Home Office, by now the "World Headquarters," was bursting at the seams. When INA's eighth home, at 1600 Arch Street, was built in 1925, two of the company's directors objected so vigorously to the "waste" of a sixteen-story building to be occupied only by the company that they resigned in protest. ("We want offices in which George Washington would find himself at home," Benjamin Rush told the architects, but the Father of His Country would have felt distinctly ill at ease in a structure which attempted the impossible task of reconciling Colonial Georgian with twentieth-century skyscraper design.)

For lack of space, many functions of the company had spilled over into the Suburban Station Building, across narrow Cuthbert Street to the south. The two buildings were linked by an underground passage and by a bridge from the fourteenth floor of the Home Office Building.

Some INA operations, including the school, had been moved one block away to a new building on the southwest corner of Sixteenth Street and Kennedy Boulevard.

As the company prepared in 1967 to enter its eighth quarter-century, plans were being studied for accommodating a company which was now, by any standard, part of the relative handful of American corporations which could be called Big Business.

A vast community unto itself, INA had the tendency of all large organizations—business, governmental, or private—to treat individuals impersonally. In turn, this remoteness made it difficult to single out those who were doing the best work so they could be rewarded.

As warm and genuine as it may have been, the relaxed paternalism of the Diemand era was not suited to these new conditions. Only a basic reorganization of the company could help to restore the sense of individuality to employees, by establishing the role of each as a separate entity.

[375]

No longer was it enough for the president's office to be open to everyone in the company; there were too many employees to make that practicable, and their very numbers had made the president, against his own wishes, as remote as a thunderer on Olympus. New ways had to be opened for two-way communication between top management and the lower echelons if the company was to be a cooperative enterprise and not an oligarchy.

An even more pressing factor impelling the company toward different ways of handling its affairs was the rise of the direct writer, foreseen by John A. Diemand in the 1940's. At that time these companies, most of them only ten or twenty years old, were little more than irritating grains of dust in the eyes of the agency companies.

In a sense, agency companies are somewhat like wholesalers. They deal with the public through independent agents, each of whom represents a number of companies, so that the independent agents, to complete the analogy, are like retailers.

On the other hand, the direct writers sell insurance through their own employees or through "exclusive agents," who represent no other companies.

After World War II, the direct writers began to enjoy a "phenomenal rate of growth," as Smith put it in 1958. By 1954 they had made such inroads that insurance commentator Roger Kenney quoted "one of the outstanding leaders in the National Association of Insurance Agents" as warning that "the presently waning agency system . . . faces complete disintegration in many areas of our business."

As the company that established the American Agency System, INA had no intention of allowing that to happen, if it could be avoided. But it was fully aware, as too many agents were not, that only drastic changes, to modernize the industry and make its operations more economical, could enable the agency system to successfully meet the challenge of the direct writers, which still had only about one-fourth of the property-casualty business in 1967.

So change came to INA.

Of course there had been many developments in the company in the 1950's that paved the way.

One involved the tapping of the great reservoir of talented women. As we have seen in the preceding chapter, the insurance industry had been one of the last citadels of masculine exclusiveness on the executive level, and INA was no exception.

But in 1959 Ruth E. Salzmann joined the company as an assistant actuary, and with her election as associate actuary in 1962 she became the company's first woman officer. Before long she was Group actuary for INA-Life, and later she became secretary-Underwriting in the parent company. In 1967 she was joined in the executives' dining room by Mrs. L. Ann Ives, who had risen to head of the Market Research Department.

Although she was unaware of it at the time, Miss Salzmann's arrival caused a tempest in a teapot, as the introduction of women executives in most industries has. Many of the executives, unaccustomed to women in "judgment-level" posts, were aghast at the idea of her lunching in their dining room, but chief actuary L. H. Longley-Cook forced the issue. Before long, many of the men who had been most opposed to opening their sanctum sanctorum to a woman were contentedly sharing a table with her, and somewhat sheepishly making jokes about their earlier reluctance.

A more significant move was made two years earlier with the establishment of what was then called the Rating and Research Department. By the mid-1960's it had evolved into a unit whose function was indicated by the new name, Research and Development (although the department also handled relations with state insurance departments and those rating bureaus to which the company did belong).

Robert K. Syfert, an assistant vice president who came to INA in 1959 from the Ohio Insurance Department, pointed to the commercial package policies as one of the most spectacular results of Research and Development's work. Those policies, in part, explained why INA in 1966 collected nearly one of every ten premium dollars netted by the industry in the Commercial Multiple-Peril line.

In the process of creating new forms of insurance protection, Syfert's staff found themselves becoming experts on all manner of strange things. For the Funeral Directors Package they had to learn, among other things, that one man could handle thirty to forty funerals per year, that the average "funeral home" (a self-contradictory euphemism preferred by the industry) took care of fifty funerals per year, and that funeral directors hated to be called "morticians." The word "undertaker," of course, was interred without ceremony years ago.

An equally, if not more, important step was taken when the company began to adapt its operations to the new concept of automation, which was, for the insurance industry, another INA innovation.

Two men from INA attended a week's seminar in New York on electronic data processing (EDP) systems in March 1952, two years before any American company in any line of business had a computer installation. Three years later an EDP task force was assembled at INA. Among the first recruits was Perros Roebas, who had been engaged in computer work for the Navy. He later became secretary-Research and Systems at INA.

The automation task force was established "before there was any EDP in any insurance company, so we were truly pioneering," said vice president Arthur T. Moyer, who was responsible for overall direction of the operation in the 1960's.

From the beginning, the trend toward automation had the support of Diemand, but Smith was even more enthusiastic, his interest in management practices having drawn him more deeply into study of the potentialities of computers.

As one might expect, there were some skeptics. To prove the usefulness of electronic data processing, the seven-man task force staged a demonstration in New York City for a group of senior officers. The "in-force" calculations of the marine branch were printed out by the computer, which had been programmed by the task force. It was a highly successful experiment.

By November 1960 vice president Thomas E. Walton, Jr., was able to report to an all-industry meeting in Minne-apolis:

"Our expenses are all allocated down to function and line of business within ten days after the close of the month. Our directors' statements, showing the company's overall operation by major class of business, are completed and avail-able for the directors within twelve days after the end of the month. Agency production reports, that used to come out six to eight weeks after the close of a given period, are now avail-able within a couple of weeks."

And that was with the first "generation" of computers. Ten years after the company's EDP operations began, it had already progressed through the second generation of more sophisticated machines and was installing the third generation, still more versatile and efficient. And the computers were being operated twenty-four hours a day, seven days a week, by a programming staff of 125 men and women.

The computer staff was an elite group. Out of every forty prospects interviewed only one was hired for training in a special EDP school operated by INA. The school's high standards were reflected in the fact that one out of four students failed to pass the course.

Instead of using one of the standard computer "languages" designed for all kinds of business, INA developed its own copyrighted language, LOBOC (for "Logical Business Oriented Coding"), especially adapted to the requirements of the insurance industry.

By 1966 the INAmation Services Department, as it was now called, was producing 923 different kinds of reports for management. As though that were not enough, the company's computer staff developed a facility named AIR (for "Automatic Information Retrieval"), which no other corporation had. It consisted of an instrument that looked like a television screen with a keyboard in front of it, on which the request for information was transmitted to the central information storage banks.

"If you have a Champion or Challenger automobile policy," Moyer explained, "we can key in your number, and your name, address, and other facts about you will appear on the screen. By keying in a different query, we can be shown the car or cars that you have insured.

"Best of all, if you send in your check for the premium, but don't give your policy number, we can query the machine for all policyholders with your name, even broken down by types of policy. And the information appears almost instantly on the screen."

Before the end of 1967, the initial part of a computer communications network called the LINK/LOSS System was scheduled to go into effect. The system would connect the company's Philadelphia headquarters with the regional processing offices and claims offices, and, ultimately, with all of the INA service offices on the continent. This network would permit almost immediate reports on any aspect of the business.

The point of all this automation, of course, was to improve efficiency and reduce costs. The first line of business to be computerized was the Champion automobile policy.

"Before computerization," vice president Leroy G. Steinbeck pointed out in 1966, "90,000 Champion policies were handled at an expense ratio of just under thirty-four per cent. Today, 247,000 Champion policies are processed at a ratio of just over twenty-six per cent." (The expense ratio, like the loss ratio, is a percentage of the premium dollar.)

Champion policies were computerized in 1962, with some resistance from agents, who feared that this might be a first step toward INA's becoming a direct writer. It was an unfounded, but understandable, apprehension, for with the direct customer billing which had to be part of an automated system, INA was brought into contact with its policyholders as never before. Previously, only the company's claims men ever dealt directly with the owners of personal insurance policies; now the company would be corresponding directly with the customers.

Nevertheless, not all agents were opposed to this inevitable automation and the resulting direct billing of customers. Early in 1958 a committee of agents had urged the company to computerize whatever functions it could. Seeing the advantages to be gained by agents themselves, the committee said:

"The improving of service can be helped by the cutting of red tape and all activities which prevent the agent from giving full attention to the function of selling and servicing. We believe that in the foreseeable future the insurance industry will undergo major changes in regard to the red tape of agency clerical and administrative work and will free the agent for more time for productive selling and servicing. We believe . . . that costs can probably be cut to keep us competitive by consideration of direct billings and collections."

That went to the heart of the matter. The automation

[381]

of Champion policies did, in fact, prove so useful as a competitive weapon against the direct writers that gradually other INA automobile policies were brought, or scheduled to be handled, under the INAmation system.

Not until 1967, when the company began computerizing its Homeowners policies, did the protests of some agents reach a serious stage, and even then most of the younger, more aggressive agents favored the company's plans. And of those who protested, scarcely any actually withdrew their business from INA, although a few agents got in touch with other insurance companies to see if they would promise not to resort to automation if the agents transferred customers to them from INA.

The chairman of one of the company's major competitors said:

"We told every agent who talked to us that he might as well face the fact that all of us, all insurance companies, were going to be forced by economic pressures to go in for automation. INA just got their system rolling a little earlier than some of the rest of us. But my company will soon be computerizing its personal lines, and so will all the others. The agents have got to start facing realities."

Others felt the same way. In 1964 Roger Kenney republished in *United States Investor* the warning that he had expressed to agents ten years earlier, in which he argued that agents would have to cooperate with company efforts to solve "the whole problem of administrative and acquisition costs."

This, he said, meant "a more receptive attitude, so far as agents are concerned, towards the continuous policy, direct company billing, and payment in advance."

The alternative, he asserted, would be for the agents to "let the mass markets in the automobile and dwelling house lines slip out from under their hands, thereby becoming mere purveyors to the fancy carriage trade—with all that implies in following the corner grocer down the deserted and lonely road to oblivion."

It was a dismal road, and INA and most of its agents were determined to shun it. By the end of 1967 the company hoped to have forty per cent of its personal insurance business computerized. And by then more than 125 of its officers and key personnel would have completed the Computer Concepts course at IBM's facilities in Poughkeepsie or Endicott, New York, part of management's program to open the eyes of its top people to the many unrealized possibilities inherent in automation, such as its helpfulness in decision-making.

Despite the awesome advantages provided by automation, however, the success of the company in the years ahead would still depend on the men and women themselves and on the framework within which they worked.

Bradford Smith had already taken care of that problem.

Over a period of several years he had completely reshaped the company, step by careful step, pausing each time so that the men and women of INA could get used to each gradual shift. The magnitude of the transformation, however, was not lost on outside observers.

"INA's . . . revamping is especially significant when it is considered against the background of its industry," *Dun's Review* commented in December 1964.

"For many segments of the insurance business are probably at least a decade behind the times in their management methods; many companies—even though quite successful—have allowed their structures to mushroom haphazardly. . . . Result: . . . a corporate whole that is often badly 'fractionalized' by organizational overlap, manager duplication, and inefficiency."

By the early 1960's Smith had decided on "where we should be going and how to get there," but he "didn't want to lay it all out at once, because it would fail; you just can't change things that quickly—you have to sell changes gradually."

Somewhere Smith had picked up a phrase, "Total Performance of the Total System," which became the slogan of the reorganization.

It sounded like a statement of the obvious at first, but it meant a great deal more to Smith, and, in time, to the rest of the people in the company. As Smith put it: "I had an idea that we were vastly more powerful than we realized, if we could marshal our strength effectively."

The first move came in the spring of 1964, after more than a year of planning, when a new Special Accounts Department was formed, with Joseph E. Johnson, as secretary, managing it. A company publication described the new unit:

"The 'account approach' will be used in dealing with firms nominated as Special Accounts. [Not only corporations, but universities, dioceses, and other large organizations insured by INA were to be handled as Special Accounts.] Existing insurance of such firms will be analyzed and, where necesssary, a tailor-made program will be specifically fitted to the insured's particular needs.

"All forms of insurance written by INA and INA-Life can be coordinated in the program. Because of its own independent international and aviation facilities, INA is the one American carrier able to underwrite within itself all of an account's insurance needs on a worldwide basis.

"A special account coordinator has been appointed in each service office by the officer manager. The account concept requires that the coordinator be fully informed on the status of all special accounts in his territory on a day-to-day basis so that he can work closely with service office managers, INA producers, and head office personnel and act as a liaison for all the various services entailed."

At a meeting of the newly named service office coordinators, senior vice president Russell H. Petefish, "a tower of strength" to Smith during the entire reorganization, told the men:

"We must be prepared to live in a new world of account handling; inhibitions and traditionalism are *passé*. Agents and brokers are already well advanced in the business of handling an insurance account. We, agents and company alike, must think in terms of account relationship with our insureds. This method of selling and servicing is the only way the company and its producers working together can bring to the risk manager [representing the organizational customer] the total performance of INA's total system."

A different approach was taken by vice president Robert S. Gillespie, who emphasized the new possibilities for providing an organization with tailor-made protection and services through a "single voice" at INA which could speak "for all its facilities and capacities."

"Arranging proper coverage for major accounts," he went on, "calls for as many coverage arrangements as there are risks, and involves a variety of combinations of retrospective and guaranteed-cost insurance, primary and excess-of-loss insurance, small and large deductibles strategically installed, special claims handling and inspection arrangements, special agreements as to coverage terms, and an extremely high degree of individualized service.

"This is what we offer—professional attention to all an insured's needs."

A few weeks later, a Personal Insurance Department was organized, "in keeping with our overall plans to draw together those lines of activity in our company which are naturally associated with each other and thus increase our competitive and underwriting effectiveness," Smith said in a letter to all executives.

"The new facility," he explained, "will ultimately be

responsible for the underwriting and developing of practically all of our personal insurance business, but initially its activities will be confined to our Homeowners, personal inland [marine], and automobile business."

Until his retirement in 1967 the department was headed by vice president Charles A. Sanford. He was succeeded by vice president Edwin H. Marshall.

The next step was one of the most far-reaching of all, appointment of resident managers in the company's service offices. In effect, this transformed each service office into a small home office; the new resident managers found themselves with probably more authority than men in the field for any insurance company had ever before enjoyed, or labored under.

This completed the unification that had just begun with the merger of the Indemnity into INA. Even after that consolidation, the old division between property and casualty men had continued in the field.

"Do you know," said one field man, "it was so bad in many places that if the home office sent a letter by mistake to the casualty manager instead of the property manager, rather than handing it to the guy, who might be at the next desk, he was likely to send it back to Philadelphia, so that it could be sent from there to the property man? And the property men were just as bad."

About 1962 Petefish and Frank G. Harrington, then vice president in charge of the Business Development Department, journeyed to Cleveland to study the functioning of a typical service office.

"We discovered that a service office didn't have one boss—it had many bosses," Harrington recalled. "We found that many people in the head office felt that they had a right to call people in the Cleveland Service Office and ask them to do things, that they had a right to travel there and pre-empt anyone's time. The casualty manager there kept track of the visitors and found that in a three-month period twenty-nine people had gone out there from the head office, taking up the time of the service office men."

Petefish and Harrington also found that the separation of responsibilities was making matters difficult for customers.

"If the customer wanted to buy from us," Harrington pointed out, "he had to buy from different people. Through his agent or broker he dealt with the Fire Department or the Marine Department or the Automobile Department or the Bonding Department—all those varied departments. We felt that our offices should be organized to meet the customers' needs, so that all of his insurance requirements could be handled through one source.

"That meant we must centralize, that we must eliminate overlapping and duplication.

"This would also mean a considerable reduction of expenses. We had a property field man calling on agents, and a casualty field man calling on agents, and they were just following each other around at two-week intervals. Everything was being doubled unnecessarily—secretaries, automobiles, expense accounts, salaries. Unification would end all that."

Cleveland was selected as a pilot project. In January 1964 a resident manager was appointed there. Henceforth, he would be responsible for all the operations of that service office, and everyone in it, whether property, casualty, or marine, whether underwriter, field man, or claims man—everyone would be under his authority.

The experiment worked so well that early in June twenty other service offices were unified with the appointment of resident managers. Two Canadian offices were treated similarly. In November the job was completed with the naming of resident managers for the last eighteen offices.

It was not an altogether painless transition. If the property and casualty managers had been at odds, and one of them was named resident manager, the other was likely to be crushed or resentful.

There were many other problems involving personal relations. But most of the difficulties were resolved satisfactorily.

Soon after the first lot of offices was unified, the Canadian Service Offices became part of the continental network of offices.

In late July Smith sent a telegram to all managers announcing the formation of a new Field Executive Department headed by Harrington. Supplanting the old Business Development Department, the FED was charged with coordinating all field underwriting, administration, and sales in the United States and Canada. Harrington's second-in-command was assistant vice president Charles K. Cox.

In late summer the people of INA—somewhat breathless because of the rapid developments—learned that their company was planning to take over the Pacific Employers Group, adding still another dimension to the company's transformation.

Then came September 29, 1964. Smith addressed a joint session of two staff meeting groups. Reviewing the change that had taken place so far, he told his associates that it was now time for the biggest step of all. The minutes of the meeting summarized Smith's comments:

"He pointed out that it will now be necessary to identify and to realign the company's basic functions in a way that will make the management of each fully responsible and accountable for the results it produces.

"He observed that the traditional division by line of business, which we are using at present in somewhat modified form, has served us well for many years but it is now outmoded. It no longer achieves the results that are needed today and does not take full advantage of the manpower potential available to us.

"Insurance people, he said, are better educated than they have ever been, the business itself is becoming increasingly more complex, and the company has grown so large that professional management must adopt a different approach toward solving the problems of day-to-day operation."

The rationale behind the reorganization along functional lines actually had been expressed best by Smith months earlier, when scarcely anyone in the company knew what he had in mind. Talking to the first group of resident managers, he had said:

"We are not erasing the traditional division in our business. The demands of the modern market are erasing them for us. The world is changing rapidly and we must recognize that a corresponding change in the insurance industry is necessary if we are to survive. More than ever, we must think in broad perspectives, we must realize that there are always opportunities present in change, and that we can and must take maximum advantage of those opportunities. . . .

"We are in an era of profound change. Methods which seemed revolutionary a few years ago are already approaching obsolescence. So we must constantly re-adjust, re-evaluate. Where there is a need, we must move to satisfy it; where there is a challenge, we must meet it with knowledgeable and sensible action."

The basic reorganization along functional lines took place at the end of 1964, but it took many months for all the lines of authority and responsibility to get straightened out.

In the meantime, in 1966, Smith was elected chairman of the board and chief executive officer and H. Richard Heilman, an unassuming, scholarly sort of man widely regarded as one of a handful of brilliant American underwriters, was elected president and "chief underwriting officer," a designation unparalleled in the history of the company. At the same time Edmund L. Zalinski moved up from executive vice president to president of INA-Life.

Perils: Named and Unnamed

By the spring of 1967, the organization chart of the company was a model of simplicity and clarity. At the top was Smith, as chairman, and under him Heilman, as president.

Smith was assisted by senior vice president James M. Crawford, with a sort of roving assignment to act as the chairman's aide. Crawford's special responsibilities were community relations and liaison with underwriting, with special reference to pools and syndicates.

As the chairman's executive officer, Leroy G. Steinbeck was particularly concerned with the evolving shape of the new functional organization.

Two major divisions of the company reported directly to the chairman: PEG, headed by John T. Gurash, and INA-Life, with Zalinski.

Four "line" divisions reported to Smith through Heilman: Underwriting, headed by Charles K. Cox, who had risen in a remarkably short time to senior vice president; Distribution-Risk Selection, senior vice president Frank G. Harrington (this also included the Field Executive Department, advertising and public relations, and other functions); Administration, senior vice president Reginald S. Robins; and Policyholders Service (PSD), vice president James W. Ferriman.

"The Policyholders Service Division," said *Business Week* in a lengthy treatment of the reorganization, "is perhaps the most striking example of what the changes mean."

In this division were brought together all the functions through which INA provided direct services to policyholders, including claims, rehabilitation (the MEND program), recovery, audit, inspection, engineering, and loss prevention.

The nucleus of the PSD idea was the joining of Claim and Loss in 1953. Although some INA people insisted that the company was the first to blend these two, it was not. But it was one of the earliest, and fourteen years later many other insurers were just beginning to think about combining them.

(Actually, the two words mean the same thing; traditionally, casualty people gave the name "claim" to what fire and marine insurance men called a "loss.")

By bringing all of the policyholder services together in one division, INA was able to prevent duplication and overlapping. Previously, one man from the company might be on the premises of an insured corporation, making a premium audit, while another was there engaged in safety engineering, a third settling a claim, and a fourth investigating the possibility of salvaging some damaged goods.

"We were falling all over each other before PSD was organized," said one veteran claims man; "the way the fellows in a lot of the other companies are still doing."

One of the best things about PSD was that it enabled the company to focus, as never before, on loss prevention. This had long been an INA ideal. Thirty years earlier *Fortune* had said:

"[Benjamin] Rush would like to make [INA] primarily a preventive company. . . . He makes no pretense that he would like to see his premium income diminish, but what he now pays out in losses he would rather pay out in preventive measures. In other words, in the literal sense of the phrase, he would like to insure *against* fire."

In fact, INA had often cut its rates to policyholders that took effective loss-prevention steps suggested by the company.

One of the most striking demonstrations of INA's effectiveness in loss prevention was the work of INA's James H. Reck with officials of the Port of New York Authority and the contractors who built a third tube for the Lincoln Tunnel under the Hudson River. In 1952 INA agreed to provide workmen's compensation and employer's liability insurance for the tunneling project on a retrospective rating basis, and Reck began working closely with the Authority officials, engineers, and the "sand hogs" boring through the soft silt of the river bed.

The engineering feat was completed five years later, with not a single fatality and with very few accidents, a safety record unmatched in tunnel construction history, thanks to Reck's constant supervision, suggestions, and assistance.

The safety record also returned $1,306,506 to the insureds under the retrospective rating policy.

The reorganization of INA along functional lines did not end with the formation of PSD and the other major divisions at the end of 1964. The following year all Group insurance written by INA was moved into the Life subsidiary, where Group business was brought together in a single department.

About the same time a Commercial Insurance Department, paralleling the Personal Insurance Department, was set up, with vice president Robert S. Gillespie as chief. These two departments were assigned to the Underwriting Division, as was the Transportation Department (including marine and aviation), with vice president Francis A. Lewis at its head.

More important, perhaps, than the new framework which had been erected to give the company a modern base of operations was the new spirit of the company and its people. They were on the move again, as they had been so often in the past, but with a different feeling now.

The day after he became chief executive officer, Smith had told his executives: "We are departing from the old authoritarian concept of management based on strict obedience, because it tends to limit horizons and to obscure objectives."

His own philosophy he called "participative management," an awkward but descriptive label. This did not mean management by committees. Basically, it required each executive to know every facet of his own job and his subordinates', and to understand the "objectives, duties, and responsibilities of his boss's job."

"By helping his senior reach his targets," Smith said, "he earns reciprocal help with his own growth and development. And to the extent that he aids the development of his subordinates, he earns their invaluable assistance in the improvement of his own job performance."

"The New Art of Free-Form Management" it was called by *Dun's Review*, in an article linking the spirit of INA's reorganization with that of several other major companies, none of them in the insurance field.

But the reaction most gratifying to Smith must have been the spate of announcements, about a year after he reshaped INA, that a half-dozen or more insurance companies, including several of the largest, were planning to reorganize along functional lines too.

28: 'The Revolution Is Not Over'

AS INA CELEBRATED ITS 175th anniversary in 1967, "perils, named and unnamed," to borrow an ancient phrase from some insurance policies, threw a shadow over the entire industry. Some observers, like Alexander Picone of the *Journal of Commerce*, went so far as to call it a crisis. Although that word had become commonplace by the latter half of the twentieth century, which had been dubbed "The Age of Crises" by some, it nevertheless could be applied without overstatement to insurance.

There were many facets to the predicament in which the industry found itself.

For more than a quarter of a century, inflation had been affecting the national economy. This had struck a double blow against insurance companies. First, it had prevented them from sharing in the national prosperity; from 1960 to 1965 for example, while property-casualty premiums rose thirty-five per cent, losses soared sixty per cent. The problem posed by inflation was explained by Edwin H. Marshall:

"In its simplest possible terms, in our business a five per cent inflation means that if an insurance company . . . writes exactly the same risks in 1966 that it wrote in 1965, and those risks suffer exactly the same loss occurrences each year, the loss ratio will be five per cent higher in 1966 than in 1965. So without any change in the risk or its loss occurrences, losing risks will become worse, marginal risks will become losers, and profitable risks will produce reduced profit."

The result was shown in a study by the First Manhattan Company of 1965 results of all property-casualty insurance companies: they were able to pay dividends only by dipping into surplus for $25,000,000, a plight to which INA, fortunately, was not reduced. But it could draw only on its investment income to show a profit.

And even this was threatened. Two state insurance commissioners decided that investment income must be considered in rate-making; five other commissioners were weighing the question; and about a dozen state legislatures were considering inclusion of such a requirement in the state insurance laws, although only the exemption of investment income from the rate-making process had enabled many insurance companies to survive periods of severe financial distress in the economy, like the Depression of the 1930's.

Little wonder that many of the biggest property-casualty insurance companies were undergoing legal and organizational changes designed to put them as subsidiaries under holding companies. This enabled such companies to circumvent state laws which prohibited insurance companies from engaging in non-insurance activities. Thus, they could seek in diversification the profits denied them by the continuing plight of the insurance market.

At the same time a great many companies were taking other steps, necessary for their survival but harmful to the public, to counter what Bradford Smith, Jr., called "the destructive consequences of this profitless prosperity." He listed some of the industry's actions:

"Markets are drying up to the distress of the insurance-buying public, agents, and public officials alike. Worse yet, there have been wholesale cancellations of business, withdrawal of facilities in large geographical areas, and other restrictive underwriting practices."

Adding to the general distress was the fact that the lines of insurance most affected included some which had special importance because of the social changes taking place in American society. We have already seen (in Chapter 20) the effects of the shrinking insurance market on owners of automobiles. But this also involved the problem of providing adequate insurance protection for property in the blighted areas of our great cities.

The distress of our urban centers has been examined at length in many studies, and there is no room, or need, to go into details about it here. The results of rapid urbanization, with the influx of great numbers of unskilled farm workers, could be seen in every large city, as H. Richard Heilman pointed out—"physical deterioration, absentee ownership, and sharply increased incidence of crime."

As the Negro ghettoes and other low-income districts in the cities sank into an ever more appalling blight, insurance company losses on such areas rose to such a level that some companies stopped writing insurance there and many others became highly selective in their underwriting.

This problem grew much more acute in 1964, when riots in two New York City ghettoes, Harlem and Bedford-Stuyvesant, resulted in considerable property damage. But that was only the beginning. In 1966 and 1967 similar riots—with terrible bloodshed, loss of lives, burning of buildings, and looting of stores swept the nation: Los Angeles, Chicago, Cleveland, Boston, Tampa, Cincinnati, Detroit, Milwaukee, Newark —the list seemed endless. By August 4, 1967, *Time* estimated that the damage throughout the country so far that summer, with the calming effect of cold weather still far off, had already

[396]

exceeded $1,000,000,000. Much of it represented losses to the property-casualty insurance companies.

Although the insurance industry previously had put together two different voluntary plans to provide insurance protection in slum areas, an "Urban Areas" plan in Boston in 1960 and the "Watts Pool" after the riot in that section of Los Angeles in 1965, it was obvious that the problem had reached such proportions that a totally new approach would have to be found.

"The plight of great masses of our people in our cities may well have the most far-reaching effect on our business," INA's 1965 annual report said.

The Governor's Commission that investigated the Watts riots had delineated the paradox of modern American society in its report:

"Of what shall it avail our nation if we can place a man on the moon but cannot cure the sickness in our cities?"

That commission had also observed that "maintenance of law and order is a prerequisite to the enjoyment of freedom in our society"—to which the company added, "It is likewise a prerequisite to the maintenance of an insurance industry to serve the public interest."

Complicating all attempts to cope with these proliferating dilemmas was the widening breach in understanding between the public and the insurance industry.

In 1961, less than half (forty-six per cent, to be precise) of a sample of Americans with college educations thought that insurance companies were very interested in safety and health matters, according to a study by the Opinion Research Corporation for the Insurance Information Institute.

Bad as that finding was, it worsened: within three years the percentage of those who thought well of the industry dropped to thirty-seven.

Strangely, the same study showed that the percentage

of those who thought the insurance industry was highly competitive dropped from fifty-four to forty-nine in the same three-year period, although competition, as we have seen, had never been as ardent and widespread as it was in the 1960's.

Obviously, the public was very ill informed about the insurance business. It was angry, understandably, about constantly rising automobile insurance rates; in the first three months of 1967 more than 6,000 insurance measures, most of them dealing with auto policies, had been introduced into forty-seven state legislatures. Wherever there were large cities, charges were broadcast that insurance companies were refusing to write policies on ghetto properties because of prejudice —again an understandable, though mistaken, suspicion.

Many of the problems of the insurance companies could be traced to state insurance laws which required the prior approval of the insurance commissioner before a rate could become effective. The initial argument for this had been that it would guarantee the solvency of the insurance companies and keep rates down. Just the reverse was true: Texas, with the most stringent rating law, had almost as many insolvencies as all the other states combined. And California, where most lines of insurance were not covered by prior-approval requirements, enjoyed rates as low as, or lower than, other, comparable states, as a result of free competition.

After a two-year investigation, the Senate Antitrust and Monopoly Subcommittee reported in 1961 that it "was most impressed by the kind of rate regulation adopted by California for fire and casualty."

The same group commented that the evidence it had examined "suggests that the American insurance industry might well be the victim of over-regulation."

Instead of being required by law to study and approve rates before they could be put into effect, the Senate subcommittee said, "the major burden of the commissioner's duty should be the safeguarding of company solvency."

Another argument against the prior-approval laws was the additional expense, reflected in premiums, caused by the cumbersome legal process.

Moreover, the state departments were simply not equipped to do an adequate job of prior examination. In one year, for example, Pennsylvania's Insurance Department reported it had examined 37,972 rate filings, policies, riders, and related forms submitted by 1,100 insurance companies, but the entire staff of the department's regulatory bureau consisted of only eight professional and technical employees and five secretaries, all under the supervision of the bureau chief.

Another difficulty was that the average tenure of a state insurance commissioner was only two and one-half years, hardly time enough to learn about the industry.

Because almost every witness before the Senate subcommittee urged that regulation of the insurance industry be left in the hands of the states, which was INA's position too, the Senate report made a similar recommendation. But in the course of its scathing denunciation of state regulation, the report warned: "The response of a long-suffering public and an impatient Congress . . . may lead to legislation aimed at faulty regulation by the states."

Despite the clear warning, the quality and nature of insurance regulation by the states did not improve during the half-dozen years that followed the report. Social problems related to insurance were increasingly aggravated.

There appeared to be sharp and puzzling differences in attitudes toward insurance on the state and federal levels.

Most state officials, in the opinion of insurers, took an opportunistic, even demagogic, approach to regulation. Sensing a chance to make political capital by trading on the widespread public misunderstanding of insurance, such officials threatened and often attempted to force underwriters to accept or retain risks or lines of business which had cost the insurers heavy losses. Punitive and repressive measures were proposed in a number of states, and clearly unworkable schemes were advanced—for example, an assigned-risk plan for insuring city property in blighted areas. In effect, businessmen were being compelled to lose money without hope of recovering or even stemming their losses.

This contrasted sharply with the more objective, restrained, and moderate sentiment displayed toward the industry by Congressmen and other federal officials—somewhat to the chagrin of the leading men in the insurance business, who had always advocated state control instead of federal. By training, and often by nature, men of a truly conservative mind, they had been used to grumbling disdainfully about "those bureaucrats" in Washington. But now they found that Senators and Representatives tended to be more responsible and thoughtful in considering insurance problems than did their counterparts on the state level. And the same was true of officials in the various governmental departments.

To those who thought it better for the country that insurance regulation remain in the hands of the states, there were a number of straws in the wind that seemed to point to a growing possibility that the federal government might take over from the states in the not-too-distant future.

In the Senate a bill was introduced in 1967 providing for a Federal Motor Vehicle Guarantee Fund, to protect the public by guarding against company insolvencies.

As we saw (in Chapter 22), the Administration, with the approval of the insurance industry, introduced a bill that would make industry and government partners of sorts in Wave Wash and Flood damage insurance. During the summer riots of that same year, 1967, a similar arrangement was proposed in the Senate to provide insurance protection for the owners of business establishments in the ghettoes.

That spring Bradford Smith, Jr., observing that "the federal government has noticeably increased its interest in insurance problems," said: "There is considerable evidence that the time left for . . . reform at the state level may be running out."

Whatever changes the future might bring, no matter how dark business or political conditions might be for a time, there seemed little question that INA would endure and, in the long run, prosper.

For INA, so conservative in some respects, had always welcomed change and bent with it.

Changeless and yet forever changing, the company had always recognized that change lay at the heart of the miracle that is America. As Dr. Benjamin Rush observed in 1783: "The American war is over, but this is far from being the case with the American Revolution."

For the Insurance Company of North America, the great American revolution would never end.

Author's Note

NO BOOK ABOUT an organization as old, as large, and as busy as the Insurance Company of North America can hope to include all the men and women who played significant roles in its history, and this work is no exception.

The writer is keenly aware that many persons whose contributions were important have been passed over with little or no mention in these pages because of lack of space and literary considerations.

Out of the past, many names come to mind, among them Philip H. Cooney, whose investment skill meant so much to the company's strength; Calvin S. Roberts, who helped to keep the company's network of field offices working together during and immediately after World War II; Thomas E. Walton, Jr., whose untimely passing ended a promising career; Clarence Palmer, who as INA's first advertising manager set up the Archives Department and the historical collection; and many others.

Some of the important men in the company at the time this book was written do not appear in these pages. For example, the New York office is one of the company's major operations, but little space has been given to it in this work, and its two resident vice presidents—Edward Q. Field and Thomas M. Torrey—have gone unmentioned, although each might well have received a chapter. And the same is true of the resident vice president for Philadelphia, John W. Hess, and of some of the men in top management posts in the world headquarters—vice president-controller William J. Robinson, vice president Charles J. Hare, vice president William P. Arnold, Jr., vice president S. Davidson Herron, Jr., vice president John B. Wyatt, and vice president Frederick J. Hislop.

The author has had complete freedom in the preparation and the writing of this book, and for this Bradford Smith, Jr., must be thanked. He saw to it that any material desired by the writer was made available to him, no matter how confidential, and he imposed no bars on its use. Perhaps more important, however, was the example he set for other officers and employees by discussing every aspect of the company's history—or that part which was known to him—with utmost candor.

The same frankness was exhibited by almost all of the scores of other men and women with whom the writer talked, those presently on the staff as well as a number of retired people. Incidentally, many members of the company's Quarter Century Club were helpful by providing suggestions.

Most of those insurance men outside the company who were interviewed wished to remain anonymous because of the controversial nature of much of this story. While respecting their wishes, the author wishes to express his gratitude for their cooperation, which was not withheld by a single person.

Others who were helpful in the preparation of this work included Dr. Harry J. Loman, president emeritus of the American Institute for Property and Liability Underwriters and the Insurance Institute of America, and professor emeritus of insurance at the University of Pennsylvania; W. E. Taylor; and Mrs. V. I. G. Petersen.

None of those named bears any responsibility for the facts, or the interpretations placed on them, in this book. The writer alone is responsible for what appears in these pages.

Space does not permit listing of all of the company personnel who joined in gathering documentation, but a few must be singled out for their outstanding assistance, among them Acis Jenkinson III, head of the Education Department; Mrs. George Anne Daly, chief archivist; Mrs. Adelaide S. Herman, chief librarian; Mrs. L. Ann Ives, head of the Marketing Research Department; and Miss Jean Smith of the Public Relations Department.

The large number of interviews imposed a heavy burden on Mrs. Hazel S. McCourt, head of the Transcription Department, and her assistants, especially Mrs. Georgiana Chilton.

Finally, special thanks must be given to those who worked most closely with the author in research, preparation of manuscript, and details of publication: Mrs. Patricia King, Mrs. Patricia Cloyd, and Robert DeP. Brown—a patient, good-humored group whose spirit helped to make the writing of this book a pleasure.

Sources

A large part of the material in this book has come from the personal recollections and files of the men and women who took part in the events chronicled here. The author also had access to many company records and publications, including:

The Board of Directors Minute Books (confidential).

Annual reports.

INA World, a monthly house organ.

INA Fieldman, a monthly periodical for agents.

Memoranda, speeches, notes, and minutes retained by the company's Archives Department.

Training manuals covering almost every phase of insurance in detail, prepared by the company's Education Department for use in its own classes.

Some useful information about the company also was found in its application to the New York Stock Exchange for listing. The application, designated "A–22286," was dated February 18, 1965.

Although the general press—newspapers and magazines—has been a source of some material, the trade press, as one might expect, produced much more. The pages of the following publications were particularly helpful:

Annals of the Society of Chartered Property and Casualty Underwriters.

Best's Insurance News.

The Insurance Buyer.

Insurance Counsel Journal.

Insurance Law Journal.

International Insurance Monitor.

Journal of American Insurance.

The Journal of Commerce.

Journal of Insurance.

Journal of the American Association of University Teachers of Insurance.

The National Underwriter.

Proceedings of the Casualty Actuarial Society.

Proceedings of the National Convention of Insurance Commissioners.

The Spectator.

United States Investor (Roger Kenney's articles in this periodical over the years are invaluable for insurance research).

United States Review.

The Weekly Underwriter.

In the pages of those newspapers and magazines are to be found the week-to-week, and sometimes day-to-day, developments with which this book is concerned. Space does not permit listing each of the thousands of news items and longer articles that appeared in the insurance press during the tumultuous years of INA's struggle for independence.

The books, pamphlets, monographs, speeches, and statements which proved useful are the following source materials.

Bibliography

ALLEN, FREDERICK LEWIS. *Since Yesterday*. New York: Harper, 1940.

————. *The Big Change*. New York: Harper, 1952.

BALTZELL, E. DIGBY. *Philadelphia Gentlemen*. Glencoe, Illinois: The Free Press, 1958.

BEEBE, LUCIUS, AND CHARLES CLEGG. *San Francisco's Golden Era*. Berkeley: Howell-North, 1960.

BERGE, WENDELL. "Insurance in a System of Free Enterprise." Address before the New England Associations of Insurance Agents, 1946. (Mimeographed.)

BERGSON, HERBERT A. "Regulation Versus Competition." Address before the National Association of Independent Insurers, 1956.

Best's Fire and Casualty Aggregates and Averages. New York: Alfred M. Best Company, Inc. Published annually.

Best's Insurance Reports. New York: Alfred M. Best Company, Inc. Published annually.

BITTAN, DAVID. "Life Insurance: North America Cooks Up a $1 Billion Recipe," *Philadelphia*, September 1957.

BLANCHARD, RALPH H. "Insularity in Insurance," *Proceedings of the Casualty Actuarial Society*, Vol. XXVIII (1941–2).

BOSWORTH, ALLAN R. *America's Concentration Camps*. New York: Norton, 1967.

BROOK, HERBERT C. "Public Interest and the Commissioners'-All Industry Laws," *Law and Contemporary Problems*, Vol. XV (Autumn 1950).

BROOKS, JOHN. *The Great Leap*. New York: Harper and Row, 1966.

Bureau of the Census, U.S. Department of Commerce. *Statistical Abstract of the United States*. Washington: Government Printing Office. Published annually.

Bureau of the Census, U.S. Department of Commerce. *Historical Statistics of the United States from Colonial Times to 1957*. Washington: Government Printing Office, 1960.

BURT, NATHANIEL. *The Perennial Philadelphians*. Boston: Little, Brown, 1963.

BURT, STRUTHERS. *Philadelphia: Holy Experiment*. Garden City, New York: Doubleday, Doran, 1945.

BUTTERFIELD, ROGER. *The American Past*. New York: Simon and Schuster, 1957.

CLARK, THOMAS D. *Frontier America*. New York: Scribner's, 1959.

COCHRAN, THOMAS C., AND WILLIAM MILLER. *The Age of Enterprise*. New York: Harper, 1961.

DAUM, ROBERT W., WITH DARN B. CLOSE. "International Insurance—the Practical Side," *International Insurance Monitor*, January-February, 1965.

Bibliography

DAVIDS, LEWIS E. *Dictionary of Insurance*. Paterson, New Jersey: Littlefield, Adams, 1959.

DE CONDE, ALEXANDER. *The Quasi-War*. New York: Scribner's, 1966.

DENENBERG, HERBERT S., ET AL. *Risk and Insurance*. Englewood Cliffs, New Jersey: Prentice-Hall, 1964.

DIEMAND, JOHN A. *Where Do We Go from Here?* Philadelphia: Insurance Company of North America, 1960.

————. *Growth Industry?* Philadelphia: Insurance Company of North America, 1957.

————. "Developments in Comprehensive Property-Casualty Insurance (Multiple Line Underwriting)." Address before annual meeting of American Association of University Teachers of Insurance, 1946. (Mimeographed.)

DINEEN, ROBERT E. "The Battle of the Bureaus." Address before the 68th annual convention of the New York State Association of Agents, 1950. (Mimeographed.)

DIRLAM, JOEL B., AND IRWIN M. STELZER. "The Insurance Industry: A Case Study in the Workability of Regulated Competition," *University of Pennsylvania Law Review*, Vol. 107, No. 2 (December 1958).

EHRENZWEIG, ALBERT A. *"Full-Aid" Insurance for the Traffic Victim*. Berkeley: University of California Press, 1954.

————. *Negligence Without Fault*. Berkeley and Los Angeles: University of California Press, 1951.

ELY, ROBERT B. III. "Governmental Regulation of Insurance Marketing Practices," *Insurance Law Journal*, No. 374, March 1954.

ELY, ROBERT B. III. "Bleak House, U.S.A." Unpublished manuscript; n.d.

EPES, W. PERRY. "Independence in Property Insurance Since Public Law 15." Address before the National Association of Independent Insurers, 1959.

"Extraordinary Service," *United States Review*, February 2, 1963.

FARNUM, HENRY W. *The Role of the Marine Insurance Industry in Foreign Trade*. Philadelphia: Insurance Company of North America, 1964.

FITZGERALD, ANTHONY W. "A New 'Philadelphia Story'—150 Years Old," *The Weekly Underwriter*, October 16, 1954.

Florida Automobile Liability Insurance Study and Conclusions; and Highway Accident Prevention Study and Recommendations. Florida Action Committee for Traffic Studies, 1966.

FRANK, WOLFGANG (translated by R. O. B. Long). *The Sea Wolves: The Story of German U-Boats at War*. New York: Rinehart, 1955.

GILLESPIE, ROBERT S. *Casualty Insurance for Major Risks*. Philadelphia: Insurance Company of North America, 1964.

————. *Nuclear Energy Liability Insurance*. Philadelphia: Insurance Company of North America, 1958.

Bibliography

GREEN, LEON. *Traffic Victims.* Evanston: Northwestern University Press, 1958.

GREENE, EVARTS BOUTELL. *The Revolutionary Generation: 1763–1790.* New York: Macmillan, 1956.

GREENE, MARK R. *Risk and Insurance.* Cincinnati: South-Western Publishing Company, 1962.

HARRINGTON, FRANK G. *The Next Decade.* Philadelphia: Insurance Company of North America, 1966.

HARRISS, C. LOWELL. *The American Economy.* Homewood, Illinois: Irwin, 1962.

HEILMAN, H. RICHARD. "The Problem of Fire Insurance Coverage in Blighted Areas." Statement to the Pennsylvania Legislature, June 13, 1966. (Mimeographed.)

————. "The Outlook for Hard-to-Place Risks," *Underwriters Review,* April 1966.

————. *Property Insurance Against Nuclear Hazards.* Philadelphia: Insurance Company of North America, 1958.

HENSLEY, ROY J. *Competition, Regulation, and the Public Interest in Nonlife Insurance.* Berkeley and Los Angeles: University of California Press, 1962.

HUNT, FREDERIC J., JR. "Homeowners—the First Decade," *Proceedings of the Casualty Actuarial Society,* Vol. 49 (1962).

"INA's Billion Dollar Baby," *Philadelphia,* August 1962.

"INA's New Corporate Symbol: Designed to Win a Growing Market," *Philadelphia,* April 1959.

"INA's Reinsurance Business at New Record," *International Insurance Monitor,* Vol. XVI, No. 4, April 1962.

"INA Ties Itself into a Package," *Business Week,* January 9, 1965.

Inside INA. Philadelphia: Insurance Company of North America, 1967. (Also published in two earlier editions.)

Installment Premium Endorsement: A Case Study of Reasonable Competition and State Regulation in the Fire Insurance Market. Philadelphia: Insurance Company of North America, 1951. (Mimeographed.)

"Insurance and Government: Rate Regulation Revisited," *Insurance Series,* Vol. II, No. 4. Madison, Wisconsin: University of Wisconsin, 1960.

Insurance Costs and Controls: A Reappraisal. New York: American Management Association, 1958.

Insurance Executives Association and Association of Casualty and Surety Executives. *Summary of Proposals for Multiple Line Underwriting, Problems Involved, and Conclusions.* New York: Insurance Executives Association, 1944.

Bibliography

Insurance Facts. New York: Insurance Information Institute. Published annually.

JAMES, MARQUIS. *Biography of a Business: 1792–1942.* Indianapolis: Bobbs-Merrill, 1942.

JOHNSON, JOSEPH E. *Observations on Excess Liability Insurance for Gas Utilities.* Philadelphia: Insurance Company of North America, 1959.

KARTMAN, BEN, AND LEONARD BROWN (eds.). *Disaster!* New York: Berkley Books, 1948.

KATZ, C. S. "INA's 'New' Claims Men Wear Many Prestige-Building Hats," *The National Underwriter,* April 15, 1966.

KEETON, ROBERT E., AND JEFFREY O'CONNELL. *After Cars Crash.* Homewood, Illinois: Dow Jones-Irwin, 1967.

KULP, C. A. *Casualty Insurance.* New York: Ronald Press, 1956.

LAWRENCE, STEPHEN R. "The INA-Care Friendship Program: The Sales Campaign Built Around Public Relations," *Public Relations Journal,* February 1966.

LEMMON, VESTAL. "Report of the General Manager." Address before the 13th annual meeting of the National Association of Independent Insurers, 1957. (Mimeographed.)

LEUCHTENBURG, WILLIAM E. *Franklin D. Roosevelt and the New Deal, 1932–1940.* New York: Harper and Row, 1963.

LEWIS, FRANCIS A. "An Appreciation of Marine Insurance." Address before the Pittsburgh Insurance Buyers Conference, April 24, 1962. (Mimeographed.)

LEWIS, OSCAR. *San Francisco: Mission to Metropolis.* Berkeley: Howell-North, 1966.

LONG, JOHN D., AND DAVIS W. GREGG (eds.). *Property and Liability Insurance Handbook.* Homewood, Illinois: Irwin, 1965.

LONGLEY-COOK, L. H. *The Dwelling Problem.* Philadelphia: Insurance Company of North America, 1965.

———. *The Future of Inadequate Rates and The Twenty Years Following SEUA.* Philadelphia: Insurance Company of North America, 1965.

———. "Package Policies: A Report on the First Decade," *Insurance,* January 19, 1963.

MACINTYRE, DONALD. *The Battle of the Atlantic.* New York: Macmillan, 1961.

MAGEE, JOHN H., AND DAVID L. BICKELHAUPT. *General Insurance.* Homewood, Illinois: Irwin, 1964.

MARSHALL, EDWIN H. *New Trends In A & S Insurance for Business Concerns.* Philadelphia: Insurance Company of North America, 1961.

Bibliography

MICHELBACHER, G. F. *Multiple-Line Insurance.* New York: McGraw-Hill, 1957.

MONTGOMERY, WILLIAM M. "Steps Toward a Modernized Organizational Concept," *The Spectator,* December 1964.

MOWBRAY, ALBERT H., AND RALPH H. BLANCHARD. *Insurance: Its Theory and Practice in the United States.* New York :McGraw-Hill, 1961.

NETTELS, CURTIS P. *The Emergence of a National Economy: 1775–1815.* New York: Holt, Rinehart and Winston, 1962.

NEW YORK LEGISLATURE. *Report of the Joint Legislative Committee on Insurance Rates and Regulation.* 1963.

NORTH, DOUGLASS C. *The Economic Growth of the United States: 1790–1860.* Englewood Cliffs, New Jersey: Prentice-Hall, 1961.

"One Hundred and Sixty Years Young," *Newsweek,* April 13, 1953.

Outline of History of Acquisition Cost Adjustments. Philadelphia: Insurance Company of North America, 1949. (Mimeographed.)

Pennsylvania Rate Deviation Case. Philadelphia: Insurance Company of North America, 1949. (Mimeographed.)

PHILLIPS, JOHN C. *North America's Experience with Government Regulation.* Philadelphia: Insurance Company of North America, 1952. (Mimeographed.)

———. "The Courtroom Influence," *Journal of Insurance Information,* July–August 1965.

———. *Report on the Installment Premium Endorsement.* Philadelphia: Insurance Company of North America, 1950. (Mimeographed.)

Proceedings: Meeting of the Committee on Interpretation of Underwriting Powers. Chicago: National Association of Insurance Commissioners, March 20–21, 1953.

PUGH, WILLIAM B., JR. *Hearings and Court Proceedings, 1945–1959.* Philadelphia: Insurance Company of North America, 1959. (Mimeographed.)

———. "Multiple Line Regulation." Huebner Foundation Lecture, University of Pennsylvania, 1967. (Mimeographed.)

———. "Rate Regulation in the Fire and Casualty Industry." Lecture delivered to a graduate seminar at the Wharton School of Business and Finance, University of Pennsylvania, November 20, 1962. (Mimeographed.)

REDDIG, WILLIAM M. *Tom's Town: Kansas City and the Pendergast Legend.* Philadelphia: Lippincott, 1947.

ROBBINS, SIDNEY M., AND NESTOR E. TERLECKJ. *Money Metropolis.* Cambridge, Massachusetts: Harvard University Press, 1960.

ROEBAS, PETER, AND WILLIAM G. SMELTZER. *LOBOC: Logical Business Oriented Coding.* Philadelphia: Insurance Company of North America, 1962.

Bibliography

RUSH, BENJAMIN. "The Duty of the Insurance Organization to the Public." Address before the Insurance Society of New York, 1926.

SEDERBERG, ARELO. "California's 'Free' Insurance Law Works," *Miami (Florida) Herald*, January 29, 1967.

Selected Speeches of Executive Management, 1939–1950. Philadelphia: Insurance Company of North America, 1951. (Mimeographed.)

SMITH, BRADFORD, JR. "The Case of the Isolated Executive," *Dun's Review*, January 1967.

————. *Change—Are You with It?* Philadelphia: Insurance Company of North America, 1966.

————. *Toward a Solution of the Automobile Insurance Problem.* Philadelphia: Insurance Company of North America, 1966.

————. "A New Approach to Flood Insurance," *Underwriters Review*, June 1965.

————. "The Outlook for Multiple Line Insurance." Address before the annual convention of the Financial Analysts Federation, May 19, 1965. (Mimeographed.)

————. "The INA Friendship Program." Address delivered at Carnegie International Institute, New York City, March 22, 1965. (Mimeographed.)

————. "The Future of Insurance." Address before the Harvard Business School Club of Philadelphia, February 17, 1965. (Mimeographed.)

————. "Three Important Principles of Management at INA." Policy statement, November 1964. (Mimeographed.)

————. *A Call for Competitive Freedom.* Philadelphia: Insurance Company of North America, 1961.

————. *This Is Your Business.* Philadelphia: Insurance Company of North America, 1961.

————. *Policyholder Interest—the Key to Success.* Philadelphia: Insurance Company of North America, 1960.

————. *Review of Fire and Casualty Insurance Rating Laws.* Philadelphia: Insurance Company of North America, 1960.

————. *Current Developments in Insurance Rate Regulations.* Philadelphia: Insurance Company of North America, 1959.

————. *An Underwriter's Comments on Deductibles and All-Risk Physical Damage Insurance.* Philadelphia: Insurance Company of North America, 1958.

————. *What's Ahead for the Insurance Producer.* Philadelphia: Insurance Company of North America, 1958.

————. *The Future of the Premium Dollar.* Philadelphia: Insurance Company of North America, 1956.

[411]

Bibliography

————. "Events Leading Up to the NYFIRO Affair." Memorandum, 1955. (Mimeographed.)

————. "The Inland Marine Definition Today." Address before New Jersey chapter, Society of Chartered Property and Casualty Underwriters, October 15, 1953. (Mimeographed.)

SNYDER, LOUIS L., AND RICHARD B. MORRIS (eds.). *A Treasury of Great Reporting.* New York: Simon and Schuster, 1949.

STELLWAGEN, HERBERT P. *A Condition—Not a Theory.* Philadelphia: Insurance Company of North America, 1958.

————. *Confessions of an Underwriter.* Philadelphia: Insurance Company of North America, 1958.

"Stressing the Package," *Business Week,* June 6, 1964.

TAYLOR, W. E. "Growing Pains of the American Reinsurance Market," *International Insurance Monitor,* Vol. XVI, No. 4, April 1962.

"The $124,000,000 NA Companies," *Fortune,* February 1937.

"The Underwriters: When the Supreme Court Said Insurance Was Commerce, Their World Turned Upside Down," *Fortune,* Vol. XLII (July 1950).

TODD, A. L. *A Spark Lighted In Portland: The Story of the National Board of Fire Underwriters.* New York: McGraw-Hill, 1965.

U.S. Senate, Committee on Banking and Commerce. *Insurance and Other Programs for Financial Assistance to Flood Victims.* 89th Congress, second session, 1966.

U.S. Senate, Subcommittee on Antitrust and Monopoly of the Committee on the Judiciary. *Hearings: The Insurance Industry.* 85th Congress, second session, and 86th Congress, first session, 1958–1960.

U.S. Senate, Subcommittee on Antitrust and Monopoly of the Committee on the Judiciary. *Report: The Insurance Industry.* Report No. 1834. 86th Congress, second session, August 10, 1960.

WANDEL, WILLIAM HAMLIN. *The Control of Competition in Fire Insurance.* Lancaster, Pennsylvania: privately printed, 1935.

WATTENBERG, BEN J., in collaboration with Richard M. Scammon. *This U.S.A.,* Garden City, New York: Doubleday, 1965.

WEINER, JACK B. "The New Art of Free-Form Management," *Dun's Review,* December 1964.

WELCH, GEORGE T. Rehabilitation: Control of Extent, Duration of Disability," *Insurance,* January 28, 1967.

WHITNEY, SIMON N. *Antitrust Policies.* (Two volumes.) New York: Twentieth Century Fund, 1958.

WINTER, WILLIAM D. *Marine Insurance.* New York: McGraw-Hill, 1952.

ZWONICEK, CHARLES. "The Development of Marine Insurance During and After World War II," *International Insurance Monitor,* September 1963.

Index

Abbott, H. Paul, 227–230
Accident and health insurance, 122, 216–8, 286, 346, 356
Accountants, 325, 331–2
Actuaries, 241–3, 282–4, 345–6
Adams, John, 23, 84
Adams, John Quincy, 26, 83
Administration Division, 390
Aero Insurance Underwriters, 246–7
Aeronautics, U.S. Bureau of, 243
Agents, 7, 55–7, 105–6, 108–10, 114–6, 137, 147–9, 150, 153–5, 165, 229, 252–9, 260, 269, 270–2, 279, 299, 308, 332, 376–7, 379, 381–3
AIR (Automatic Information Retrieval), 380
Air Commerce Act, 243
Airlines, See Aviation Insurance
Air pollution, 328
Ak-Sar-Ben, 174
Alabama, 27
Alice in Wonderland, 262–3
Allen, Frederick Lewis, 202
Alliance Insurance Company, 73, 75–6, 81, 97, 337–8
Allied Insurance Company, See Pacific Employers Group
All-Industry Committee, 143–4, 259, 277
Amazonas, Las, 237
American Agency System, 7, 55–6, 177, 299, 350–1, 376–7
American Airlines, 244
American Bar Assn., 288
American Cargo War Risk Reinsurance Exchange, 205–6, 221–2
American Foreign Insurance Assn., 183
American Gas Assn., 330
American Hull Insurance Syndicate, 329
American Institute of Architects, 334
American Institute of Marine Underwriters, 205
American Insurance Assn., 266
American Management Assn., 147
American Medical Assn., 330
American Society of Chartered Life Underwriters, 350
American Society of Composers, Authors, and Publishers, 101
American Surety Company of New York, 155

"American system," 155–6, 268, 346
American Trial Lawyers Assn., 326–7
America's Concentration Camps, 211
Anderson, Rex H., 350–2
Andrea Doria, 4
Annals of the Society of Chartered Property and Casualty Underwriters, 159
"Anti-compact" laws, See Monopoly
Antimenes of Rhodes, 34
Antitrust, See Monopoly
Antitrust Policies, 254
Apple Valley, California, 353
Architects, 325, 332
Arendt, Hannah, 291
Argentina, 319
Arizona, 199, 276, 279
Arkansas, 166
Armstrong, John, Jr., 320
Army Air Transport Command, 3, 217
Arnold, Thurman, 136, 139, 151
Arson, 54
Art Collections, 9
Arthur, Charles, 226
Arthur, Chester A., 29
Asbury Park, New Jersey, 100, 322
Ashkota Society, 174
Assn. of California Companies, 366
Assn. of Casualty and Surety Companies, 280
Assn. of Casualty and Surety Executives, 142, 158
Assn. of Fire Underwriters (Baltimore), 169
Associations, 103–16, 149, 150, 160–72, 173–4, 252–66, 267–80
Athenia, 205
Atlantic City, New Jersey, 322
Atlantic Mutual Insurance Company, 51, 155
Atomic Bomb, 1–3, 209, 217
Energy, See Nuclear Power
Australia, 199, 205, 237
Austria, 92, 201
Authoritarianism, 392
Automation, 378–83
Automobile Insurance, 9, 112, 155–6, 215–6, 263, 290–303, 336, 380–2, 386, 396, 398, 400
Aviation Insurance, 3, 5, 155, 217–8, 241–51, 309, 319–20, 392
"Azteca, La," 235–7

[413]

Index

Index

Index

Index

Index

Index

London, 34–5, 235, 237
London Coffee House (Philadelphia), 37
London, Jack, 74
Longley-Cook, L. H., 241–3, 282–3, 377
Los Angeles, 187, 243, 311, 329, 358, 362, 364, 396
Loss prevention, 116, 390–2
Louisiana, 28, 299
Louisville, Kentucky, 55
Louvre, 11
Lucas, G. Brinton, 125, 170, 317
Lusitania, 93
Lutine Bell, 317

McCarran-Ferguson Act, See Public Law 15
McConnell, F. Britton, 366
McConnell, Matthew, 11, 40, 42
McHugh, Donald P., 272
McIlvain, Dave, 225
McKittrick, Roy, 135–6
McMaster, John B., 59
Macao, 187, 196–7
Macintyre, Donald, 220
Macon, Georgia, 334
Madison, James, 10, 60
Maiming, 354–5
Maine, 27
Malpractice, 325, 330–2
Manhattan District, 1–2, 217
Mansfield, Burton, 156
Manufacturers' Output policies, 262–3, 268
Maplecrest, Ohio, 307
Marine, inland, See Inland Marine
Marine insurance, 4, 5, 7, 8, 17–9, 20–9, 30–2, 34–7, 43–5, 49, 51, 53, 62–9, 84–9, 90–3, 94, 96–9, 100, 112, 115, 125, 130–1, 155, 157, 218–9, 220–2, 235, 316–9, 320–2, 329, 392
Maritime Commission, U.S., 346
Market Research Dept., 377
Marshall, Edwin H., 122, 217–8, 248–9, 309, 386, 394–5
Maryland, 26, 168–9, 337
Maryland Rating Bureau, 168–9, 171–2
Massachusetts, 7, 26, 27, 62, 155
Mayer, Manfred H., 318
Meakim, Phil, 225
Medical costs, 297
Medical Economics, 330–1
Medicine, 4

MEND (Medical and Educational Needs of the Disabled), 367–9, 370–2, 390
Merchant Marine, See Marine Insurance
Merion Cricket Club, 203
Meritplan Insurance Company, See Pacific Employers Group
Merit rating—See "Safe Driver" Plan
Merrill, Lynch, Pierce, Fenner, and Smith, 349, 362
Mexico, 199, 235–7
Miami, Florida, 299
Middle Department Assn. of Fire Underwriters, 167–8
Middle East, 3
Mifflin, Thomas, 50
Miller, William, 96, 104
Mills, H. C., 208, 235
Milwaukee, 396
Minneapolis, 368
"Miss America" Pageant, 9
Mississippi, 165
Missouri, 108, 110, 134–6
Moncton, 235
Monopoly, 12, 13, 82, 103–9, 110–6, 134–9, 140–5, 146–9, 150–9, 160–1, 267–9, 270–9, 280
Monopoly, Senate investigation of, See Senate Subcommittee on Antitrust and Monopoly
Montgomery, Victor, 360, 363–8
Monticello, 10
Montoswald, 90–1
Montreal, 235, 248, 288
Moore, Thomas L., 42
Morley, Christopher, 83
Morris, John, 364–5
Morrison, Robert A., 247, 250–1
Morro Castle, 99, 100
Morse, Jedediah, 47
Môrtefontaine, Convention of, 24–5, 29, 30
Mortgage Impairment Insurance, 286
Motion picture industry, 100
Mount Vernon, 10
Mowbray, Albert H., 111
Moyer, Arthur T., 378–9, 380
Moylan, Jasper, 40, 42, 44–5
Multi-Peril Insurance Conference, 265
Multiple line insurance, 4, 114–5, 149, 152–3, 155–9, 160, 261–6, 267–8, 311–2, 335, 378
Multiple-location coverage, 261

Index

Index

Index

Index

Index